Arthur Gilman, Alfred John Church

Carthage or the Empire of Africa

Third Edition

Arthur Gilman, Alfred John Church

Carthage or the Empire of Africa
Third Edition

ISBN/EAN: 9783337063252

Printed in Europe, USA, Canada, Australia, Japan

Cover: Foto ©ninafisch / pixelio.de

More available books at **www.hansebooks.com**

CARTHAGE

OR

THE EMPIRE OF AFRICA

BY

ALFRED J. CHURCH, M.A.

PROFESSOR OF LATIN IN UNIVERSITY COLLEGE, LONDON, AUTHOR OF "STORIES FROM HOMER," ETC., ETC.

WITH THE *COLLABORATION* OF
ARTHUR GILMAN, M.A.

THIRD EDITION.

London
T. FISHER UNWIN
26 PATERNOSTER SQUARE
NEW YORK: G. P. PUTNAM'S SONS
MDCCCLXXXVII

Entered at Stationers' Hall
By T. FISHER UNWIN.

Copyright by G. P. Putnam's Sons, 1886
(For the United States of America).

PREFACE.

IT is difficult to tell the story of Carthage, because one has to tell it without sympathy, and from the standpoint of her enemies. It is a great advantage, on the other hand, that the materials are of a manageable amount, and that a fairly complete narrative may be given within a moderate compass.

I have made it a rule to go to the original authorities. At the same time I have to express my obligations to several modern works, to the geographical treatises of Heeren, the histories of Grote, Arnold and Mommsen, Mr. Bosworth Smith's admirable "Carthage and the Carthaginians," and the learned and exhaustive "History of Art in Phœnicia and its Dependencies," by Messieurs Georges Perrot and Charles Chipiez, as translated and edited by Mr. Walter Armstrong. To this last I am indebted for most of the illustrations of this book.

I have had much help also from Mr. W. W. Capes' edition of " Livy " xxi., xxii.

PREFACE.

I have not thought it necessary to discuss the critical questions which have been raised about the Duilian column (p. 135). The inscription, as it at present exists, may be supposed to bear a general, though not a faithful, resemblance to the original.

A. C.

HADLEY GREEN,
    May 27, 1886.

PROVINCIAE CARTHAGINIENSIBUS SUBDITAE

LONDON: T. FISHER UNWIN, 26, PATERNOSTER SQUARE, E.C.

CHRONOLOGICAL TABLE.

	B.C.
Carthage founded by Dido	850
The Campaigns of Malchus	550
The Battle of Alalia	536
First Treaty with Rome	509
First Battle of Himera	480
Second Treaty with Rome	440
Hannibal invades Sicily	410
Third Treaty with Rome	405
Capture of Agrigentum	406
Treaty between Carthage and Dionysius	405
Renewal of the War	397
Siege of Syracuse by Himilco	396
Return of Himilco to Africa	396
Mago invades Sicily	393
Treaty of Peace with Dionysius	392
Renewal of the War	383
Dionysius attacks Carthage	368
Death of Dionysius	367
The Conspiracy of Hanno	340
The Battle of Crimessus	339
Death of Timoleon	337
Agathocles defeated at Himera	310
He transfers the War to Africa	310
He returns to Sicily	307
Pyrrhus invades Sicily	278
He leaves Sicily	276
Beginning of First Punic War	264
Defeat of the Carthaginian Fleet by Duilius at Mylæ	260
Victory of Regulus at Ecnomus	256

CHRONOLOGICAL TABLE.

	B.C.
Landing of Regulus in Africa	256
Defeat of Regulus by Xantippus	255
The Siege of Lilybœum begun	249
Defeat of the Roman Fleet under Claudius at Drepanum	249
Hamilcar Barca comes into Sicily	247
Death of Hannibal	247
Defeat of Carthaginian Fleet by Catulus at Ægusa	241
Conclusion of First Punic War	241
War of the Mercenaries	241–236
Hamilcar Barca invades Spain	236
Death of Hamilcar	229
Assassination of Hasdrubal	221
Capture of Saguntum by Hannibal and Commencement of Second Punic War	218
Battles of Ticinus and Trebia	218
Battle of Trasumennus	217
Battle of Cannæ	216
Hannibal winters in Capua	215
Roman Conquest of Syracuse	212
Hannibal takes Tarentum	212
Defeat and Death of the Scipios in Spain	211
Hannibal marches on Rome—Fall of Capua	211
Publius Scipio goes to Spain	210
He captures New Carthage	209
Death of Marcellus	208
Hasdrubal enters Italy	207
His defeat at Metaurus	207
Scipio sails to Africa	204
Hannibal returns to Carthage	203
Defeat at Zama	202
End of Second Punic War	201
Death of Hannibal	183
Roman Embassy at Carthage	174
The Third Punic War begins	149
Fall of Carthage	146

CONTENTS.

PART I.
LEGEND AND EARLY HISTORY.

I.

	PAGE
THE LEGEND OF DIDO	3–8

The building of Carthage, 5—Dido and Æneas, 7.

II.

THE GROWTH OF CARTHAGE 9–18

The Tyrian traders, 11—Malchus and Mago, 13—Treaties with Rome, 15—Carthaginian possessions, 17.

PART II.
CARTHAGE AND GREECE.

I.

HAMILCAR AND HANNIBAL . . . 21–34

Hamilcar's army, 25—The fate of Hamilcar, 27—Hannibal before Selinus, 29—Attack on Himera, 31—Hannibal's vengeance, 33.

II.

CARTHAGE AND DIONYSIUS (406-405) . . 35-45

Siege of Agrigentum, 37—Execution of the generals, 39—Agrigentum evacuated, 41—Gela abandoned, 43—The plague at Carthage, 45.

III.

CARTHAGE AND DIONYSIUS (397) . . . 46-63

Siege of Motya, 47—Motya assaulted, 49—Himilco's advance, 51—Battle of Catana, 53—Siege of Syracuse, 55—Plague in Himilco's camp, 57—Himilco's escape, 59—Carthage saved, 63.

IV.

THE LAST STRUGGLE WITH DIONYSIUS . . 64-69

Mago defeated, 65—Defeat of Dionysius, 67—The end of the war, 69.

V.

CARTHAGE AND TIMOLEON 70-74

Timoleon declares war against Carthage, 71—Battle of the Crimessus, 73.

VI.

CARTHAGE AND AGATHOCLES 75-91

Agathocles in extremities, 77—Agathocles invades Africa, 81—Revolt of Bomilcar, 85—Pyrrhus, 89—Pyrrhus leaves Sicily, 91.

PART III.

THE INTERNAL HISTORY OF CARTHAGE.

I.

CARTHAGINIAN DISCOVERERS 95-101

Along the African Coast, 97—Gorillas, 99—A strange tale, 101.

II.

The Constitution and Religion of Carthage 102–114

Magistrates of Carthage, 103—Estates of the realm in Carthage, 105—Justice and religion, 109—Carthaginian Deities, 113.

III.

The Revenue and Trade of Carthage . 115–125

Carthaginian Mines, 117—Trade, 119—Ivory and precious stones, 121—Art and literature, 123—Wealth and luxury, 125.

PART IV.

CARTHAGE AND ROME.

I.

The War in Sicily and on the Sea . . 129–140

The Romans gain Messana, 131—Capture of Agrigentum, 133—Battle of Mylæ, 137—Battle of Ecnomus, 139.

II.

The Invasion of Africa 141–151

Defeat of Hamilcar, 143—Xantippus, 145—Defeat of Regulus, 147—Horace on Regulus, 149—Revenge for Regulus, 151.

III.

In Sicily Again 152–165

Roman Losses at sea, 153—Roman disasters, 157—The Romans gain Eryx, 159—Hasdrubal's successes, 161—Battle of Ægates Island, 163—Conclusion of War, 165.

CONTENTS.

IV.

CARTHAGE AND HER MERCENARIES . . 166–177

Revolt of the mercenaries, 167 — Siege of Utica, 171 — Massacre of prisoners, 175 — End of war with mercenaries, 177.

V.

CARTHAGE AND SPAIN 178–184

Hamilcar in Spain, 179 — Hannibal, 181 — Siege of Saguntum, 183.

VI.

FROM THE EBRO TO ITALY 185–194

Passage of the Rhone, 187 — Route over the Alps, 189 — Rocks split with vinegar, 193.

VII.

THE FIRST CAMPAIGN IN ITALY . . . 195–205

Scipio retires to the Trebia, 199 — Sempronius eager to fight, 201 — The Carthaginians victorious, 205.

VIII.

TRASUMENNUS 206–211

Lake Trasumennus, 207 — Slaughter of the Romans, 209 — Hannibal's policy, 211.

IX.

FABIUS AND HIS TACTICS . . . 212–217

Hannibal a master of stratagem, 213 — Fabius and Minucius, 215 — Varro and Paullus in command, 217.

CONTENTS.

X.

CANNÆ 218–224

Hannibal's army, 219—The struggle, 221—Will he march on Rome? 223.

XI.

AFTER CANNÆ 225–231

Mago at Carthage, 227—Hannibal's prospects, 229—Tarentum gained, 231.

XII.

THE TURN OF THE TIDE 232–244

Attempted relief of Capua, 233—Capua lost to Hannibal, 235—Carthage loses Sicily, 237—Roman successes in Spain, 239—Death of the Scipios, 241—Capture of New Carthage, 243.

XIII.

THE LAST CHANCE OF VICTORY . . . 245–252

The death of Marcellus, 247—Nero's great march, 249—Ode from Horace, 251.

XIV.

THE LAST STRUGGLE 253–264

Scipio and Syphax, 257—Hannibal recalled, 259—Zama, 261—Terms of peace, 263.

XV.

HANNIBAL IN EXILE 265–271

Hannibal with Antiochus, 267—Hannibal in Bithynia, 269—Character of Hannibal, 271.

XVI.

THE BEGINNING OF THE END . . . 272–279

Cato's hostility to Carthage, 273—Africanus the Younger, 275—Expedition against Carthage, 277—War declared, 279.

XVII.

THE SIEGE AND FALL OF CARTHAGE . . 280–301

The walls of Carthage, 281—The Romans lose their ally Masinissa, 285—Scipio in command, 289—Attack on the Megara, 293—Engagements between the fleets, 295—Fighting in the city, 297—Successors of Carthage, 301.

INDEX 303

LIST OF ILLUSTRATIONS.

	PAGE
CROSSING THE ALPS	*Frontispiece*
CARTHAGINIAN STELE FROM SULCI (SARDINIA)	16
PLAN AND SECTION OF A CARTHAGINIAN TOMB AT MALTA	17
PHŒNICIAN SARCOPHAGUS FOUND AT SOLUNTE (SICILY)	23
ONE OF THE TOWERS OF ERYX	36
CARTHAGINIAN PLATTER-SILVER	40
THE WALL OF MOTYA	48
VOTIVE BAS-RELIEF TO PERSEPHONE	61
AFRICAN AQUEDUCT	79
RURAL CISTERNS	83
PLAN OF THE RUINS OF UTICA	87
VOTIVE STELE FROM CARTHAGE (HIPPOPOTAMUS)	98
VOTIVE STELE TO TANIT	107
A STELE TO TANIT	110
VOTIVE STELE TO TANIT FROM CARTHAGE	111
VOTIVE STELES FROM CARTHAGE	113
CARTHAGINIAN COIN	115
CARTHAGINIAN COIN (ELECTRUM)	116

LIST OF ILLUSTRATIONS.

	PAGE
CARTHAGINIAN COIN (SILVER)	116
VOTIVE STELE FROM CARTHAGE	121
WRITING-CASE	123
VOTIVE STELE (BULL)	124
DUILIAN COLUMN	135
RESERVOIRS OF CARTHAGE	142
CROSS SECTION OF CISTERN WALL. (FROM DAUX)	143
STELE AT LILYBÆUM	155
COIN: THE TEMPLE AND RAMPARTS OF ERYX	159
PHŒNICIAN WALL AT ERYX	161
POSTERN IN THE WALL OF ERYX	162
PLAN OF HARBOUR AT UTICA	169
MAP OF PENINSULA OF CARTHAGE	173
CROSSING THE ALPS	191
ITALIA SEPTENTRIONALIS	197
TREBIA	203
ITALIA MERIDIONALIS	255
THE TRIPLE WALL OF THAPSUS	281
THE GREAT WALL AT THAPSUS	283
PORT OF CARTHAGE (FROM SARCOPHAGI)	287
THE HARBOURS OF CARTHAGE (ACCORDING TO BEULÉ)	290
HARBOURS OF CARTHAGE (ACCORDING TO DAUX)	291
ARRANGEMENTS OF THE BERTHS (ACCORDING TO BEULÉ)	293
PLAN OF WALL AT BYRSA	293
AFRICAN COLISEUM	299

PART I.

LEGEND AND EARLY HISTORY.

    I.—The Legend of Dido.
    II.—The Growth of Carthage.

Unfortunately we know very little about the history of this period; and that little is difficult to assign to any particular time. Our chief authorities are Justin, a writer of uncertain date, who wrote an epitome of an earlier work composed by one Trogus Pompeius (B.C. 85–15?); and Polybius, who gives us the text of the treaties made between Carthage and Rome. Of Polybius we shall have something to say hereafter.

THE STORY OF CARTHAGE.

I.

THE LEGEND OF DIDO.

"MALGERNUS, King of Tyre, died, leaving behind him a son, Pygmalion, and a daughter, Elissa or Dido, a maiden of singular beauty. Pygmalion, though he was yet but a boy, the Tyrians made their king. Elissa married Acerbas, whom some also call Sichæus, her mother's brother, and priest of Hercules. Among the Tyrians the priest of Hercules was counted next in honour to the king. Acerbas had great wealth, which he was at much pains to hide, so that, fearing the king, he put it away, not in his dwelling, but in the earth. Nevertheless the thing became commonly known. Thereupon King Pygmalion, being filled with covetousness, and heeding not the laws of man, and having no respect to natural affection, slew Acerbas, though he was brother to his mother and husband to his sister. Elissa for many days turned away her face from her brother, but at last, putting on a cheerful countenance, feigned to be reconciled to him. And this she did, not because she hated him the less, but because she thought to fly from the country, in which counsel she had for abettors many nobles of the city, who also were greatly displeased at the king. With this purpose she spake to Pygmalion, saying, 'I have had enough of sorrow. Let me come and dwell in thy house, that I be no more reminded of my troubles.' This the king heard with great joy, thinking that with his sister there would also come into his hands all the treasures of Acerbas. But when he sent his servants to bring his sister's possessions to his palace she won them over to herself, so that they became partakers of her flight. Having thus put all her riches upon shipboard, and taking with her also such of the citizens as favoured her, she set sail, first duly performing sacrifice to Hercules. And first she voyaged to Cyprus, where the priest of Jupiter, being warned of the gods, offered himself as a sharer of her enterprize on this condition, that he and his posterity should hold the high priesthood for ever in the city which she should found. From Cyprus also she carried off a company of maidens, that they might be wives for her people. Now when Pygmalion knew that his sister had fled he was very wroth, and would have pursued after her and slain her. Nevertheless, being overcome by the entreaties of his mother, and yet more by fear of vengeance from the gods, he let her go; for the prophets prophesied, 'It will go ill with thee, if thou hinder the founding of that which shall be the most fortunate city in the whole world.'

"After these things Queen Elissa came to Africa, and finding that the people of those parts were well affected to strangers, and had a special liking for buying and selling, she made a covenant with them,

THE BUILDING OF CARTHAGE.   5

buying a piece of land, so much as could be covered with the hide of an ox, that she might thereon refresh her companions, who were now greatly wearied with their voyage. This hide she cut into small strips that she might thus enclose a larger piece. And afterwards the place was called Byrsa, which is, being interpreted, the Hide.

"To this place came many of the people of the land, bringing merchandize for sale; and in no great space of time there grew up a notable town. The people of Utica also, which city had been before founded by the men of Tyre, sent ambassadors, claiming kindred with these new comers, and bidding them fix their abode in the same place where they themselves dwelt. But the barbarous people were not willing that they should depart from among them. Therefore, by common consent of all, there was built a fair city, to which the builders gave the name of Carthage; and it was agreed between Elissa and the people of the land that she should pay for the ground on which the said city was founded a certain tribute by the year. In the first place where they were minded to lay the foundations of the city there was found the head of an ox. Of this the soothsayers gave this interpretation, saying, 'This signifieth a fruitful land, but one that is full of labour, and a city that shall ever be a servant to others.' Therefore the city was moved to another place, where, when they began to dig foundations again, there was found the head of a horse. Thereupon the prophets prophesied again: 'This shall be a powerful nation, great in war, and this foundation augureth of victory.'

"After these things, the city greatly flourishing and the beauty of Queen Elissa (for she was very fair) being spread abroad, Iarbas, King of the Moors, sent for the chief men of Carthage to come to him; and when they were come he said, 'Go back to the Queen, and say that I demand her hand in marriage; and if she be not willing, then I will make war upon her and her city.' These men, fearing to tell the matter plainly to the Queen, conceived a crafty device. 'King Iarbas,' said they, 'desireth to find some one who shall teach his people a more gentle manner of life; but who shall be found that will leave his own kinsfolk and go to a barbarous people that are as the beasts of the field?' The Queen reproved them, saying, 'No man should refuse to endure hardness of life if it be for his country's sake; nay, he must give to it his very life, if need be.' Then said the messengers, 'Thou art judged out of thine own mouth, O Queen. What therefore thou counsellest to others do thyself, if thou wouldst serve thy country.' By this subtlety she was entrapped, which when she had perceived, first she called with much lamentations and many tears on the name of her husband Acerbas, and then affirmed that she was ready to do that which the will of the gods had laid upon her. 'But first,' she said, 'give me the space of three months that I may lament my former estate.' This being granted to her, she built, in the furthest part of the city, a great pyre, whereupon she might offer sacrifices to the dead, and appease the shade of Acerbas before that she took to herself another husband. Upon this pyre, having first offered many sheep and oxen, she herself mounted, having a sword in her hand. Then looking upon the people that was gathered about the pyre, she said, 'Ye bid me go to my husband. See then, for I go.' Thereupon she drave the sword into her heart, and so fell dead."

Such was the legend of the founding of Carthage as Virgil found it when he was writing his great poem, the *Æneid*. He took it, and boldly shaped it to suit his own purposes. This is how he tells it.

"Æneas, saved by the gods from the ruin of Troy to be the founder of Rome, comes after many wanderings to the island of Sicily, and thence sets sails for Italy, the land which has been promised to him. But Juno, who cannot forget her wrath against the sons of Troy, raises a great storm, which falls upon his fleet and scatters it, sinking some of the ships, and driving the rest upon the shore of Africa, near to the place where Elissa, who is also called Dido, had newly founded her city of Carthage. By her he and his companions are hospitably received. But this is not enough for Venus, his mother. 'For,' says she to herself, 'haply the mind of the Queen and her people will change concerning my son, and they will deal unfriendly with him and the men of Troy.' Thereupon she devises this device. She causes her son Cupid, or Love, to take upon him the shape of Ascanius, the young son of Æneas; but Ascanius himself she carries to her own bower in Cyprus, and there lulls him to sleep. Meanwhile Æneas is entertained by the Queen at a great banquet, and tells the story of the fall of Troy and of his wanderings; and as he tells it, the false

Ascanius sits in the Queen's lap, and breathes into her heart the spirit of love. After this comes Juno to Venus, and says to her: 'Why should there be enmity between me and thee? I love Carthage, and thou lovest the men of Troy. Let us make an agreement that these two may join together in one city; and to this end let Dido take Æneas for her husband.' To this Venus gave her assent; and so it was contrived.

"But the thing pleased not Jupiter that Æneas should so forget the greatness to which he was called. Therefore he called Mercury, that was his messenger, and said to him: 'Go to the Trojan chief where he now lingers at Carthage, forgetting the city which he must build in Italy, and tell him that he must make ready to depart.' So Mercury bore the message to Æneas; and Æneas knew that the will of the gods was that he should depart, and bade his companions forthwith make ready the ships. This they did; and when the time came, though it was sorely against his will, Æneas departed, knowing that he could not resist the will of the gods. And when Dido saw that he was gone, she bade them build a great pyre of wood, and mounting upon it, slew herself with the very sword which Æneas had left in her chamber."

II.

THE GROWTH OF CARTHAGE.

I HAVE said that it was a bold change by which Virgil sought to shape the legend of Elissa or Dido to suit the purpose of his own poem. Bold indeed it was, for he brings together in the Queen of Carthage and the Hero of Troy, persons who must have been separated from each other in time by more than two hundred years. Ascanius, he tells us himself in the Æneid, was to found Alba, and at Alba the kingdom should remain for three hundred years, till the priestess of Vesta should bear a son to Mars, who should found the great city of Rome. There must therefore have been more than three hundred years between the coming of Æneas into Italy and the founding of Rome. But, on the other hand, it was commonly agreed that Carthage was not a hundred years older than Rome. If we are to follow Justin, from whom I have taken the legend told in the first chapter, its foundation may be put in the year 850; but it must not be supposed that this date is as certain as that of the Declaration of American Independence, or that of the Battle of Waterloo.

The legend tells us that the first founders of Carthage came from Tyre. Very likely this is true; it is certain that they belonged to the nation of which Tyre was the chief city, the Phœnicians. This people dwelt in the little strip of land (not much larger than the American State of New Hampshire, or about twice the size of the English county of Yorkshire) which is called Palestine, and which occupies the south-eastern corner of the Mediterranean coast. The inland tribes of this people, who are known to us in the Bible history under the name of Canaanites, were subdued and nearly destroyed by the Hebrews, when, after their escape from slavery in Egypt, they invaded the country about fourteen hundred years before Christ. But many of the dwellers of the coast remained unsubdued. In the south were the Philistines with their five cities, almost always at war with their Hebrew neighbours, sometimes almost conquering them,[1] and sometimes, as in the days of David and Solomon, paying tribute. In the north, again, were the great cities of Tyre and Sidon. Between these and the Hebrews there seems to have been commonly friendship. They were a nation of seamen and traders, and they had to import the food[2] which they did not wish, or perhaps were not able, to grow for themselves. For this food they paid either with the produce of their own artists and handicrafts-

---

[1] Thus we read (1 Samuel xiii.) that the Israelites were obliged to go down to the Philistines to sharpen their tools, and that only the king and the king's son possessed sword and spear.

[2] Thus we find Solomon paying Hiram, king of Tyre, for the help that he had given in the building of the Temple with wine and oil. And more than a thousand years after, the men of Tyre are unwilling to remain at enmity with King Herod, because their country is "nourished from the king's country."

men, with timber cut in the cedar forest of Lebanon, or work in bronze and iron, or rich purple dyes, or with merchandize which they had themselves imported. As traders, indeed, they travelled very far, and while seeking new markets in which to buy and sell, they made great discoveries. They went as far south, some say, as the Cape of Good Hope, certainly as far as Sierra Leone; and as far north as Britain, from which they fetched tin, and probably copper. But I shall have more to say of this hereafter. It was, however, chiefly the coasts of the Mediterranean that they were accustomed to visit; and along these it was that they established their trading posts. It is the story of the most famous of these posts that I have now to tell.

The word Carthage—in Latin *Carthago*, and in Greek *Karchēdon*—contains in another form, changed to suit European tongues, the word Kirjath, a name familiar to us in the Bible in the compounds Kirjath-Arba and Kirjath-Jearim.¹ Kirjath means "Town," and the name by which Carthage was known to its own inhabitants was Kirjath-Hadeschath, or the "New Town"—*new*, to distinguish it either from the old town of Tyre, from which its settlers had come forth, or from the older settlement of Utica, older by nearly

---

¹ These resemblances of Carthaginian and Hebrew names are very interesting, and show us how close was the kindred between the Jews and the Canaanite or Phœnician tribes, enemies to each other though they mostly were. The chief magistrates of the city, for instance, had the title of *Shophetim*, the Hebrew word for "judges," which the Romans changed into *Suffetes*. One of the Hamilcars again, of whom I shall have to speak hereafter, bore the surname of *Barca*, and Barca is the same as the Hebrew *Barak*, or "lightning."

three hundred years, which lay about fifteen miles to the north-west.

The "New Town" was built in a little bay of the great natural harbour, the finest and most commodious that is to be found along the whole of the north coast of Africa, which is now called the Bay of Tunis.[1] The site was very happily chosen. A river, the Bagradas (now the Mejerda) was near.[2] The land was well watered and fertile, rich with corn and wine and oil. It is a proof of its natural advantages that within two centuries of its total destruction, Carthage became the third city of the Empire, and that its modern successor is one of the largest and most prosperous of all the purely Mahometan cities of the world.

Of the city's early history we know very little; indeed, it may be said, nothing. More than two centuries are an absolute blank. We hear nothing for certain of Carthage and its doings, though we may guess that it was busy trading, and sometimes fighting with its neighbours and with the inhabitants of the African coast, of Sicily, and of Spain. Then about the middle of the sixth century B.C. (but the date is quite uncertain) we hear of a certain king or chief who bore the name of Malchus.[3] Malchus made war against the African tribes in the neighbourhood of the city, and subdued many of them. From

---

[1] The present city of that name occupies a site a little to the south-east of the ancient Carthage. There was a Tunis or Tunes in classical times, but it was always a small town.

[2] Its actual mouth was at Utica.

[3] Note again the Hebrew names. The high priest's servant whose ear Peter cut off at Gethsemane "was named Malchus."

Africa he crossed over into Sicily, and conquered a part, doubtless the western part, of the island. From Sicily, again, he went on to Sardinia. There he was beaten in a great battle. The Carthaginians, who were always cruel and often unjust to their defeated generals, condemned him to banishment. Malchus refused to obey, and led his army against his native city. The magistrates sent out his son Carthalo to intercede with him, but in vain; Carthalo was seized by his father, and actually crucified in sight of the city walls. After a while the city was compelled to surrender; but Malchus was content with putting to death ten of his chief opponents. Those whom he spared not long afterwards brought him to trial, and condemned him to death.

After Malchus came Mago, who still further increased the military power of the city. His reign or chief magistracy—Carthage once had kings, but it is not easy to say when the title was abolished; indeed it is sometimes given to the chief magistrate down to a late period of her history—may be said to cover the latter part of the sixth century B.C. And now for the first time, the State takes a definite place in history. The inhabitants of Phocæa, one of the Greek colonies on the western coast of Asia Minor, had fled from their native city rather than submit to the rule of the Persians, binding themselves by an oath never to return till a lump of iron which they threw into the harbour should rise to the top of the water. But before they had been long gone, home-sickness proved stronger than their oath, and more than half of them returned. The remainder pursued their journey with their wives and children, and settled at Alalia in Corsica, a place which had been already colonized by Greeks. There they took to the trade of piracy, a more respectable employment, it must be remembered, then than now. After five years the Carthaginians and the Etruscans, Rome's neighbours on the north, and then an independent and a powerful nation, combined against them. A great sea-battle followed. The Phocæans had the sixty ships in which they had migrated from their native town; their enemies had double the number, half coming from Carthage, half from the sea-ports on the Etrurian coast. The victory fell to the Greeks; but it was a victory which was as bad as a defeat; for they lost forty out of their sixty ships, and they were compelled to leave their new settlement and to seek refuge elsewhere. This battle is supposed to have happened in the year 536 B.C.

Twenty-seven years later we hear of Carthage again. Polybius[1] tells us that he had himself seen in Rome copies of the three treaties which had been made between that State and Carthage. The oldest of the three, written, he says, in language so antiquated that even the learned could scarcely understand it, was concluded in the year 509, the next after that in which the kings had been driven out from Rome. The provisions of this treaty are interesting. "The Romans and their allies shall not sail beyond the Fair Promontory." The "Fair Promontory" was to the north of Carthage. Polybius thinks that the Romans were forbidden by this

---

[1] See the account of him in the Introduction to Part iv.

article of the treaty to sail southwards to the country of the Little Syrtis (now the Gulf of Cabos), then one of the richest in the world, and for that reason called the *Markets*. It seems more probable that "beyond the Fair Promontory" meant *westward* of it, and that it was specially intended to protect the Carthaginian markets in Spain. "Merchants selling goods in Sardinia and Africa shall pay no customs, but only the usual fees to the scribe and crier." The Carthaginians, it seems, were, so far, "free traders." "If any of the Romans land in that part of Sicily which belongs to the Carthaginians, they shall suffer no wrong or violence in anything." Finally, Carthaginians bind themselves not to injure any Latin city, whether it was subject to Rome or not. Some years later—how many we cannot tell—we hear of another treaty made between the same parties. The conditions are now much less favourable to Rome. Two other limits besides the Fair Promontory (unfortunately we do not know what places are meant by them) are imposed on the Roman traders. These, too, are now forbidden to trade either in Sardinia or Africa. They must not even visit these countries except to get provisions or to refit their ships. In Sicily and at Carthage they were allowed to trade. The Carthaginians claim the power to take prisoners and booty out of any Latin city not subject to Rome. The city itself, however, they must yield up. In other words, they were not to get a footing in Italy. It is clear that in the interval the power of Carthage had increased and that of Rome had decreased. The latter city did indeed suffer many losses during the first hundred years after the driving out of the kings. So much we may see even from the flattering accounts of the Roman historians.

We can thus get some idea of the power and dominions of Carthage. It has power over much of the coast of Africa, though it still continues to pay a ground rent for the soil on which its capital was

CARTHAGINIAN STELE FROM SULCI (SARDINIA).

built. We hear, indeed, of this payment having been refused in the days of Hasdrubal and Hamilcar, sons and successors of Mago, of the African tribes making war for the purpose of enforcing it, and compelling the Carthaginians to renew it. Sardinia it claims as entirely its own. This island is said to have been conquered by the Hasdrubal and Hamilcar mentioned above, Hasdrubal dying of his wounds in the course of the war. Of Sicily it has a part, of which I shall say more hereafter. Malta probably belongs to it.

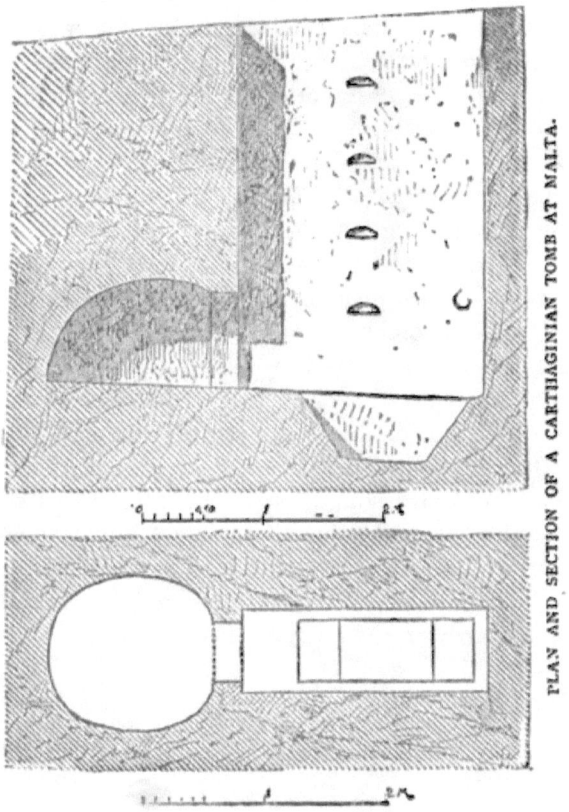

PLAN AND SECTION OF A CARTHAGINIAN TOMB AT MALTA.

Of Spain, which was afterwards to form an important portion of the Empire, for the present we hear nothing.

While Carthage was thus busy extending and strengthening its dominions, it narrowly escaped a great danger from what was then the most powerful empire in the world. In the year 525 Cambyses, the second king of Persia, conquered Egypt, a task which he seems to have accomplished with great ease. He then looked about for other countries into which he might carry his arms. The great cities of Cyrene and Barca, lying about five hundred miles to the west of the mouths of the Nile, submitted to him. He thought that he might push his conquests still further in the same direction and make Carthage itself a tributary. But a distance of two thousand miles and more was too much for his army, and the conquest would have to be made by his fleet. Here he met with an obstacle which he could not overcome. The fleet consisted for the most part of Phœnician ships, and the Phœnicians refused to take part in the expedition. "We are bound," said they, "to the Carthaginians by solemn oaths. They are, too, our children; and it would be wicked in us to make war against them." The Great King was obliged to be content with this answer and to give up his scheme.

PART II.

CARTHAGE AND GREECE.

I.—Hamilcar and Hannibal.
II.—Carthage and Dionysius (406–405).
III.—Carthage and Dionysius (397).
IV.—The Last Struggle with Dionysius.
V.—Carthage and Timoleon.
VI.—Carthage, Agathocles and Pyrrhus.

Here our chief authority is Diodorus Siculus, a Greek writer who "flourished" about the beginning of our era. He was a native of Sicily, and in his Universal History, or "Historical Library," as he seems to have called it himself, wrote an account of the world from the earliest time down to his own day. With this work he took much pains, travelling over many of the countries of which he intended to write the history, and collecting the works of authors who had treated the same subjects before him. Much of his History is lost, but the ten books from the eleventh to the twentieth have been recovered. As he was naturally very much interested in the affairs of his own island, he seems to have taken special pains with this part of his work, which includes the one hundred and seventy-five years from the beginning of the second Persian war (480) down to the year 305. He had before him the best authorities, as, for instance, Timæus, who wrote the History of Sicily from the earliest times down to 264 (he himself died in 256, at the age of ninety-six); but he had not much judgment in using his materials. Still, his book is of very great value for this portion of our story. Fragments, too, of the lost books that followed the twentieth have been preserved. Justin also tells us something about this time, so that, on the whole, we have plenty of authorities.

I.

HAMILCAR AND HANNIBAL.

SICILY would naturally be the place in which Carthage would first seek to establish a foreign dominion. At its nearest point it was not more than fifty miles distant; its soil was fertile, its climate temperate; it was rich in several valuable articles of commerce. We have seen that, in the treaty which was made with Rome about the end of the sixth century B.C., the Carthaginians claimed part of the island as their own. It is probable that this part was then less than it had been. For more than two hundred years the Greeks had been spreading their settlements over the country; and the Greeks were the great rivals of the Phœnicians. If they were not as keen traders—and trade was certainly held in less estimation in Athens, and even in Corinth, than it was in Tyre and Carthage—they were as bold and skilful as sailors, and far more ready than their rivals to fight for what they had got or for what they wanted. The earliest Greek colony in Sicily was Naxos, on the east coast, founded by settlers from Eubœa in 735. Other Greek cities sought room for their surplus population in the same field; and some of the colonies founded fresh settlements of their own. The latest of them was Agrigentum on the south coast, which owed its origin to Gela, itself a colony of Cretans and Rhodians. As the Greeks thus spread westward the Carthaginians retired before them, till their dominions were probably reduced to little more than a few trading ports on the western coast of the island. As long, indeed, as they could trade with the new comers they seemed to be satisfied. They kept up, for the most part, friendly relations with their rivals, allowing even the right of intermarriage to some at least of their cities.

But in point of fact they were only waiting their opportunity, and the opportunity came when the Persians invaded Greece for the second time. Some historians tell us that it was agreed by the two powers that a combined effort should be made, that, while Persia was attacking the mother-country of Greece, Carthage should attack its important colonies in Sicily. Others insist that there is no proof of any such agreement having been made. It is not easy to see what proof we could expect to find. But there is nothing, I think, improbable about it. The Phœnician admirals in the service of the Great King who had refused to obey Cambyses when he ordered them to sail against their kinsmen in Carthage, may very well have managed a matter of this kind. Anyhow it is clear that Carthage knew that the opportunity had come, and eagerly seized it. One of the family of Mago, Hamilcar by name, was appointed commander-in-chief. He set sail from Carthage with a force which, when it had been joined by auxiliaries gathered from Sicily and elsewhere, amounted, it is said, to three hundred thousand men. There would have been even

PHŒNICIAN SARCOPHAGUS FOUND AT SOLUNTE (SICILY).

more had not the squadron which conveyed the chariots and the cavalry been lost in a storm. The number is probably exaggerated—the numbers in ancient history are seldom trustworthy—but we may take as genuine the list of the nations from which the army was recruited. The land-force consisted, we hear, of Phœnicians, Libyans, Sardinians, Corsicans, Iberians, Ligyes, and Helisyki. The first four names need little explanation. The Phœnicians were native Carthaginians and men of kindred race from the mother-country of Phœnicia, from Cyprus, and from other settlements on the Mediterranean shore. Sardinia, we know from its mention in the treaty of 509, belonged to Carthage; Corsica had probably been since acquired. The Iberians were Spaniards, over whose country Carthage was gaining some influence. The Ligyes were the Ligurians from the northwest of the Italian peninsula;[1] the Helisyki may have been Volscians, neighbours of Rome on the south-east and for some time its most formidable enemies.

Hamilcar reached Panormus (now *Palermo*) in safety with the main body of his fleet. "The war is over," he is reported to have said, thinking that only the chances of the sea could have saved Sicily from such an army as his. At Panormus he gave his army three days' rest, and repaired his ships. Then he marched on Himera. There he dragged his ships on shore, and made a deep ditch and a rampart of wood to protect them. His forces he divided between two camps. The crews of his fleet occupied one, his soldiers the

---

[1] The modern Piedmont.

other. The two covered the whole of the west side of the city. A force from the city which encountered his advance guard was driven in, and Theron, the tyrant of Agrigentum, who had been appointed to take command of the garrison by Gelon of Syracuse, the most powerful monarch in the island, sent off in hot haste for help to his chief. Gelon had everything ready, and marched at once with an army far greater than any other Greek state could then have raised, fifty thousand infantry and five thousand horse. After thoroughly fortifying the camp which he had pitched near the city, he sent out his cavalry to attack the foraging parties of the Carthaginians. These suffered a signal defeat; and the people of Himera now grew so confident that they actually threw open the gateways which, in their determination to make a desperate resistance, they had at first bricked up.

The conclusive battle was not long delayed, and Gelon is said to have won it by the help of a curious stratagem. His scouts had intercepted a letter from the people of Selinus to Hamilcar, in which there was a promise that they would send on a day named a force of cavalry to his assistance. Gelon instructed some of his own horsemen to play the part of the cavalry of Selinus. They were to make their way into the naval camp of the Carthaginians, and then to turn against their supposed allies. A signal was agreed upon which they were to show when they were ready to act. Gelon's scouts were posted on the hills to watch for it, and to communicate it to the main body of his army in the plain. The fight was long and bloody; it lasted from sunrise to sunset, but the Carthaginians had lost heart, and the Greeks were confident of victory. No quarter was given, and by night, one hundred and fifty thousand men (it must surely be an impossible number!) had fallen. The rest fled to the hills, and were there compelled by want of water to surrender to the people of Agrigentum. Of the fate of Hamilcar nothing was ever certainly known. Some said that he had been slain by the pretended allies from Selinus; others that, being busy with a great sacrifice at which the fire was piled high to consume the victims whole, and seeing that the fortune of the day was going against him, he threw himself into the flames and disappeared. His body was never found, but the Greeks erected a monument to his memory on the field of battle; and the Carthaginians, though never accustomed to be even commonly just to their beaten generals, paid him, after his death, honours which it became a custom to renew year by year. The rest of the story is curiously tragic. Twenty ships had been kept by Hamilcar to be used as might be wanted, when the rest of the fleet was drawn up. These and these only escaped out of the three thousand vessels of war and commerce, which Hasdrubal had brought with him. But even these did not get safe home. They were overtaken by a storm, and one little boat carried to Carthage the dismal news that their great army had perished.[1] The city was over-

---

[1] Note how a similar story is told of the return of Xerxes from Greece, after his defeat in the Persian War. According to Herodotus (on excellent authority, as he was born in 484, *i.e.* four years before the war) Xerxes returned by land with a considerable part of his army; nevertheless the Roman poet Juvenal writes—

whelmed with dismay and grief. An embassy was at once sent to Gelon to beg for peace. Peace was granted, but on hard conditions. Carthage was to pay a ransom of two thousand talents, to build two chapels in memory of the event, and, one writer tells us, to abolish the hideous practice of human sacrifices. If this last condition was ever agreed to, it was certainly not kept.

It has been said, and one would like to believe, that the great battle of Himera, by which the Greek colonies in Sicily were relieved from the pressing fear of Carthage, was fought on the very same day on which the Persians were defeated at Salamis.

Carthage could not have been long in recovering from this loss, for we find her able soon afterwards to dictate a treaty to Rome, but she did not meddle with Sicilian affairs for many years. But in 410 a Sicilian town, Egesta, invited her aid against their neighbours of Selinus.[1] Both towns were near the Carthaginian settlements; and it was possible that these might suffer, if Selinus, which was said to be the aggressor, were allowed to become too powerful. But probably the desire to avenge the defeat of seventy years before was the chief reason why Carthage promised the help that was asked. It so happened, too, that Hannibal, grandson of the Hamil-

"Through shoals of dead, o'er billows red with gore,
A single ship the beaten monarch bore."

But then Juvenal wished to point the moral of "the vanity of human wishes."

[1] Curiously enough it was a quarrel between these same two towns that had been the immediate cause of the disastrous expedition of Athens against Syracuse.

car who had perished at Himera, was the senior of the two first magistrates of the city. He had been brought up in exile—for Gisco, his father, had been banished after the defeat of Himera—and at this very city of Selinus. "He was by nature," says the historian, "a hater of the Greeks," and he did all he could to persuade his countrymen to undertake the war.

After some negotiations which came to nothing, Hannibal sent a force of 5,000 Africans and 800 Italian mercenaries to Sicily. The army of Selinus, which was busy plundering the territory of their enemies, was surprised, and lost a thousand men and all the booty which it had collected. Selinus now sent to Syracuse to beg for help, and Egesta, on her part, made a fresh appeal to Carthage. This appeal was answered in a way that took the Sicilians by surprise. Hannibal had collected a great force of Spaniards and Africans. This he carried to Sicily in a fleet of as many as 1,500 transports, escorted by sixty ships of war. It numbered, according to the smallest estimate, 100,000 men, and was furnished with an abundance of all the engines used for sieges. The general lost no time. Without a day's delay he marched upon Selinus, invested it, and at once began the assault. Six towers of wood were brought up against the walls; battering-rams headed with iron were driven against them, while a multitude of archers and slingers showered arrows and stones upon their defenders. The fortifications had been allowed, during a long period of peace, to fall out of repair; and the Italian mercenaries were not long in forcing their way in. These were driven out again with great loss, and for a time the assault was suspended. The besieged sent their swiftest horsemen to beg for instant help from Syracuse, Gela, and Agrigentum. It was promised, but while it was being prepared Hannibal was pressing his attack with the utmost fury. A great part of the wall was thrown down by the battering-rams; but the people of Selinus still fought with the courage of despair. For nine days and nights the struggle went on, every street, almost every house, being fiercely contested. At last the numbers of the barbarians overpowered resistance. Between two and three thousand of the armed men escaped; about twice as many of both sexes were made prisoners; the rest were massacred. As many as sixteen thousand bodies are said to have been counted.

At the very time when Selinus was taken, the advance guard of the Syracusan army reached Agrigentum. They tried to make terms with the conquerors. An embassy was sent to Hannibal, begging him to ransom the prisoners and respect the temples of the gods. Hannibal replied, "The men of Selinus have not been able to keep their freedom, and must make trial of slavery. As for the gods, they have left Selinus, being wroth with its inhabitants." To a second embassy, headed by a citizen who had always been on friendly terms with Carthage, he made a gentler answer. The survivors might return, dwell in their city and till their lands, paying tribute to Carthage. The walls were razed to the ground, and according to some accounts, the whole city was destroyed. To this day the ruins of the temples show the marks of the crowbars by which the columns were overthrown.

But Selinus was not the real object of Hannibal's expedition. That was to be found elsewhere, at Himera, where, seventy years before, his grandfather had perished. To Himera, accordingly (it lay on the opposite, *i.e.* the north coast, of the island) he marched without delay. Forty thousand troops he posted at some distance from the city, probably to deal with any relieving force from the other Greek cities. With the rest of his army, now increased by twenty thousand auxiliaries from the native Sicilians, he surrounded the walls.

He did not intend, however, to wait for the slow operation of a blockade, but attacked the town as fiercely as he had attacked Selinus. The walls were battered and undermined, and more than one breach was made in them. At first he was repulsed. The people of Himera fought with all the courage of their race, and they had the help of four thousand soldiers from Syracuse and elsewhere. The Carthaginians were driven back, and the breaches repaired. This success emboldened them to attack the besiegers. Leaving a sufficient force to guard the walls, they sallied forth, and fell on the hostile lines. Taken by surprise, the Carthaginians gave way. Their very numbers were against them, for they were too closely thronged to be able to act, and suffered almost more, says the historian, from each other than from the enemy. The assailants, who numbered about ten thousand, were roused to do their best by the thought of their helpless kinsfolk, women and children and old men, who were watching them from the walls. At first it seemed as if Himera was to be another Marathon. As many as six thousand of the besiegers (to take the smallest and most reasonable computation) were slain. But the pursuit was pushed too far. Hannibal brought down his army of reserve from the hills on which it had been posted, and fell upon the victorious Greeks. A fierce fight ensued, but the people of Himera and their allies were overpowered. The main body of them retreated into the city, but three thousand were unwilling or unable to leave the field, and, after performing prodigies of valour, perished where they stood.

At this crisis came twenty-five Syracusan ships of war, which had been taking part in the war then being carried on between Athens and Sparta. At first the besieged were full of hope. It was rumoured that, besides the ships, the Syracusans were coming to their help with a levy *en masse*. But then came a most disquieting report. Hannibal was filling, it was said, his own ships with the picked troops of his army, and intended to fall upon Syracuse when that city should be stripped of its able-bodied men. The Syracusan commander dared not stay at Himera in the face of this alarm. The ships of war must, he said, sail home at once. But they would take as many of the helpless population of Himera as they could hold. The offer was accepted; for dreadful as it was thus to leave their homes, it was the only hope of escape that the poor creatures had. The ships were filled till they could hold no more. Then the

Syracusan general marched out of the town in such haste, we are told, that he did not even stop to bury his own dead. Many of the inhabitants who could not be received on board the ships accompanied him on his march, preferring this to waiting for the return of the fleet; for this was to come back and carry off the rest of the population.

It was well for them that they did so. The next day the Carthaginians renewed the assault. The besieged were sadly reduced in numbers and weary, for after the battle of the day before they had spent the night in arms upon the walls. Still they held out. All that day the battle was kept up. On the morrow the ships came back, but at the very moment of their coming in sight a great part of the wall was broken down by the battering-rams, and the Spaniards in Hannibal's army rushed in. A general massacre followed, and was continued till Hannibal issued strict orders that all that remained were to be taken alive. It was no feeling of mercy that prompted these orders. The women and children were divided among the conquerors; the men were taken to the spot where Hamilcar had been last seen alive, and there to the number of three thousand cruelly slaughtered, an expiatory sacrifice to the spirit of the dead. Himera itself was utterly destroyed. The walls and houses were razed to the ground; the temples were first plundered and then burnt.

The rest of the Greek cities in Sicily must have trembled lest the fate which had fallen on Selinus and Himera should overtake themselves. But for the time, at least, their fears were relieved. Hannibal had done what he came to do, had avenged the defeat of Himera, the death of his grandfather, and his father's exile, and he was satisfied. He sent the native Sicilians who had joined him to their homes, dismissed many of his mercenaries, and, after leaving sufficient force to hold the territory which he had occupied, carried the rest of his army to Carthage. He brought with him much spoil and many trophies, and his countrymen received him with the highest honours. He had won in a few weeks' time victories that surpassed all that had ever been gained by Carthage before.

II.

CARTHAGE AND DIONYSIUS (406–405).

HANNIBAL'S success in Sicily had encouraged the Carthaginians to hope that the whole island might yet be theirs. They resolved on making another expedition, and appointed Hannibal to the chief command. At first he declined the office, pleading his advanced age, but consented to act when Himilco son of Hanno, a kinsman of his own, was joined with him in the command. The two generals sent envoys to treat with the chiefs in Spain and the Balearic Islands; they went themselves to enlist troops among the African tribes and in the various Phœnician settlements along the coast. Mercenaries were also hired from other countries, and especially from Italy. The Italians in Hannibal's former army, thinking themselves badly treated by the general, had taken service with Syracuse, and were, as their late general knew, a very formidable force. At last in 406—four years, *i.e.*, after the first expedition—the invading force set sail. They numbered, on the lowest calculation, 120,000; one writer puts them down at nearly three times as many. They were carried across in more than a thousand transports; and these again were convoyed by a fleet of one hundred and twenty ships of war. The Greeks, taught by experience, were resolved not to be behindhand this time with their preparations for resistance. Forty Carthaginian ships had been sent on in advance to Sicily. Against these the Syracusans sent a squadron of equal strength. The two fleets met near the famous promontory

ONE OF THE TOWERS OF ERYX.

of Eryx. After a long struggle the Greeks were victorious, and sank fifteen of the enemy's ships, the rest retiring to the African coast. Hannibal, hearing of the reverse, sailed out with fifty fresh ships. Before this new force the Syracuse squadron retired. It was now evident that the invasion could not be prevented

All that remained was to make the best possible preparations for resisting it. Syracuse sent embassies begging for help to the Greeks in Italy and to Sparta, as well as to all the communities of the same race in the island. The city which felt itself most in danger was Agrigentum, the richest and most populous place in the island after Syracuse, and, indeed, scarcely inferior to that. The Agrigentines lost no time in preparing for defence. They engaged Dexippus, a Spartan, who was then at Gela with a body of 1,500 soldiers, and they also hired the Campanian mercenaries, eight hundred in number, who in the former invasion had served under Hannibal. It was in May, 406, when the great Carthaginian host appeared before their walls. Hannibal began by offering conditions of peace. He proposed an active alliance; if this did not please the Agrigentines, it would be enough if they would be friendly to Carthage, but take neither side in the war which she was preparing to wage. The Agrigentines, unwilling to desert the cause of their countrymen, refused both offers. Then the siege began. The town had a very strong position, which had been carefully improved. It was built on a range of hills, rising in some places to the height of more than a thousand feet. On the slope of these hills a wall had been built, or, in some places, hewn out of the solid rock. Only one place was practicable for an assault. Against this the Carthaginian generals brought up their engines, especially two towers, from which they attacked the defending force upon the walls. The fighting lasted throughout the day without any result; at night the besieged sallied forth and burnt the enemy's engines. Hannibal then determined to use the stones of the tombs—which, as usual, were outside the walls—to build mounds from which he might renew the attack. The most splendid of these tombs was the sepulchre of Theron, who had reigned in Agrigentum some eighty years before, and had borne a part in repelling the first Carthaginian invasion. While the men were busy in pulling it down it was struck with lightning. A religious panic followed. The sentinels declared that they were haunted by the spectres of the dead whose graves had been violated. A pestilence broke out in the camp. Great numbers died, and among them Hannibal himself, and the prophets declared that the gods were thus sharing their wrath at the impiety which had been committed. Himilco ordered that no more tombs should be pulled down. As an expiation of what had been done, he sacrificed a child to Saturn or Moloch, and threw a number of animals into the sea as an offering to Neptune. Meantime he pressed on the siege, damming up one of the rivers by which three sides of the town were surrounded. While he was thus engaged the relieving force arrived; it comprised auxiliaries from Magna Græcia[1] and from most of the Greek cities in the island. The general's name was Daphnæus, and he had with him thirty thousand infantry and five thousand cavalry. A squadron of thirty ships of war sailed along the coast, keeping pace with the army. Himilco sent against them his Spanish and Italian troops. A battle was

---

[1] The name commonly given to the collection of Greek colonies in Southern Italy. See "The Story of Rome," page 39.

fought on the western bank of the Himera, and was obstinately contested. In the end the Greeks were victorious, routing the enemy with the loss of six thousand men. The whole force indeed might, it was thought, have been destroyed but for the caution of Daphnæus. Remembering how the men of Himera had been attacked and slaughtered in just such a moment of victory, he held back his men from pursuit. The same fear that Himilco, who of course had vast forces in reserve, might take them at a disadvantage, kept the Agrigentine generals from sallying forth upon the fugitives as they hurried past the walls. When the relieving force had entered the city, there was naturally much talk among the soldiers about the events of the day. Some loudly accused the generals of cowardice; others even declared that they had been bribed. The populace rushed to the market-place and held a public assembly, before which the Agrigentine generals were put upon their trial. Menes of Camarina, one of the leaders of the relieving force, was the chief accuser. The furious people would not listen to any defence from the accused. Four out of the five were seized and stoned to death; the fifth was pardoned on account of his youth.

At first Daphnæus thought of attacking the Carthaginian camp; but the place was too strongly fortified, and he contented himself with scouring the roads with his cavalry and cutting off the supplies. The distress soon became very great; many died of starvation, and the mercenaries crowded round Himilco's tent, clamouring for their rations, and declaring that unless they were satisfied they would take service with the enemy. The general had just heard that the Syracusans were taking a convoy of

CARTHAGINIAN PLATTER-SILVER.

provisions by sea to Agrigentum. His only hope of relief was in getting hold of this. He entreated the mutineers to wait for a few days, giving them meanwhile as pledges the costly drinking-cups and plate of the

Carthaginian officers. The Syracusan fleet had no expectation of being attacked, as Himilco had never attempted to claim command of the sea. They were taken by surprise and completely defeated. Eight of the ships of war were sunk, the others chased to the shore, and the whole of the convoy captured. This event changed the whole aspect of affairs. It was Agrigentum that was now in distress. Before long the Italian mercenaries in the city departed. They alleged that their time of service had expired; but it was said that Dexippus, their commander, had been bribed by the besiegers to tell them that there was no food in the city, and that they would find more profitable service elsewhere. That there was no food was too true; for when the generals came to examine the stores, they found that there was nothing to be done but at once to abandon the city.

That very night the plan was carried out. Guarded by the troops from the pursuit of the Carthaginians, the whole population of Agrigentum, with the exception of some who could not and others who would not leave their homes, crowded the road that led eastward to Gela. At dawn Himilco entered the city. It was one of the richest cities in Greece, and from its foundation three hundred years before it had never had an enemy within its walls. The houses were full of pictures and statues, of rich furniture, of gold and silver plate. The treasuries of the temple were rich with the offerings of many generations of worshippers. Himilco spared nothing. Everything that was valuable, sacred property as well as profane, was carried off.[1] The richest citizen of Agrigentum, unwilling to leave his native country, had taken refuge in the shrine of Athené. When he found that its sacredness would not protect him, he set it on fire and perished in the ruins. Himilco, who took the city just about mid-winter (*i.e.*, eight months after his first landing in the island), occupied it till the spring of the following year. When he was ready to take the field again, he levelled the houses to the ground and defaced the temples. This done he marched against Gela, ravaged the country, which indeed there was no attempt to defend, and then assailed the city. Gela was for the time left to its own resources; it was neither so well placed nor so strongly fortified as Agrigentum. Still it held out bravely, the women, who had refused to be sent away to a place of safety, being conspicuous by their courage.

Meanwhile Dionysius, the Syracusan commander,[2] had collected a relieving force numbering, to take

---

[1] The most precious possession—indeed, the only one mentioned by name—seems to have been the famous "Bull" of the tyrant Phalaris, which dated back to about a century and a half before. The Bull had been made by Perillus, a native worker in brass, as an instrument of torture (victims were enclosed in it and roasted alive). The artist is said to have been the first who suffered in it. This may be a fable; and, indeed, the story is told of more than one inventor of instruments of cruelty, as, for instance, of Dr. Guillotine, contriver of the machine which bears his name. But the existence of Phalaris and his cruelty, and his use of this particular engine of torture, seem to be historical facts, for they are alluded to by Pindar, who was not much later in point of time. We shall hear of the Bull again.

[2] This was the famous tyrant, the first of the name. He had taken advantage of the discredit brought on his rivals by the Carthaginian victories to establish himself in supreme power at Syracuse.

the lowest estimate, thirty thousand infantry and a thousand cavalry, and accompanied by fifty decked vessels. With this he marched to the help of Gela, and pitching his camp between the Carthaginians and the sea, endeavoured to cut off their supplies. After twenty days' skirmishing, in which little good was effected, he determined to make an attempt upon the camp. The assault was to be delivered simultaneously from three places—from the sea, from the western side of the city, and from that part of the wall which was especially threatened by the siege engines. The sea-front of the camp was the weakest; and here the attack, which was not expected, was successful for a time, and, but for the failure of the other movements, would probably have decided the day. The division that was to operate on the west was too late, for by the time it came into action the fight at the sea-front was over. That which was told off to attack the siege-works, and was commanded by Dionysius himself, never came into action at all.

Nothing now remained but to leave Gela to the same fate which had overtaken Agrigentum and Himera—to abandon it to the fury of the enemy. This was done the same night, Himilco having been put off his guard by a request from Dionysius that he would grant a truce the following day for the burial of the dead. All that had strength for the journey left the city. Camarina was evacuated in the same way. Both cities were plundered and destroyed.

It now seemed as if the whole of Sicily were within

the grasp of Carthage. The only first-rate town that remained to be conquered was Syracuse. We are inclined to ask, "Why did not Himilco march upon Syracuse after the fall of Gela and Camarina?" just as we shall be inclined to ask hereafter, "Why did not Hannibal march upon Rome after Cannæ?" Doubtless he remembered that, a few years before, the most powerful expedition ever sent forth by a Greek state had been destroyed before the walls of this same city. It must have been difficult, too, to feed and pay so vast an army. But probably his strongest reason was the second breaking out of the plague. It had raged in his camp through the summer of the year before; and now that the hot weather had returned it probably [1] broke out again. Anyhow we know that when he returned to Carthage he had lost half his army by sickness. Whatever the cause, he sent unasked to Syracuse envoys to treat for peace. Dionysius was only too glad to listen, and a treaty was concluded on these terms:—

1. Carthage was to keep her old settlements, and those of the Sicanian tribes.

2. Selinus, Agrigentum, Himera, Gela, and Camarina, might be reoccupied by such of their old inhabitants as survived. But they were to be unwalled, and were to pay tribute to Carthage.

3. Leontini, Messana, and the Sikel tribes, were to be independent.

4. Syracuse was to be under the rule of Dionysius.

[1] I say "probably" because the fact is not expressly stated by the historian (Diodorus Siculus), though it is strongly implied.

5. Prisoners and ships taken by either party were to be restored.

Successful as the campaign had been it ended in disaster to Carthage. The army carried back the plague with it. Carthage and the neighbouring districts caught the infection, and multitudes perished.

III.

CARTHAGE AND DIONYSIUS (397).

WE have seen that the rule of Dionysius in Syracuse was one of the articles of the treaty of 405. Such foreign support, of course, did not tend to make him popular, and as soon as he felt himself strong enough, he threw it off. In 397 he called an assembly of the Syracusans, whom he was then doing his best to conciliate, and proposed war against Carthage. "Just now," he said, "Carthage is weakened by the plague; but she has designs against us which she will carry out on the first opportunity. We had better deal with her before she has recovered her strength." The people greatly approved the proposal; all the more because Dionysius allowed them to plunder the property of Carthaginian citizens who where residing in Syracuse, and the ships of Carthaginian merchants that happened to be in harbour. News of what had been done spread over the island, and produced something like a massacre. Carthage had used her victory cruelly, and her misdeeds were now remembered against her. Carthaginian rule was oppressive, especially in the amount of tribute which was exacted; and Carthaginian habits and ways of life seem to have been particularly offensive to the taste of the Greeks. The result was a rising in the Greek cities which had been made tributary by the last treaty. Most of the Carthaginian residents perished. The example of the Greeks was soon followed by the native Sicilians, and in a very few days the dominions of Carthage in the island were reduced to her strongholds on the western coast.

All this happened before war had been formally declared. This declaration Dionysius did not omit to make. He sent envoys to Carthage with a message: if she would restore freedom to the Greek cities of Sicily she might have peace; otherwise she must prepare for war. For war Carthage was but ill prepared. The losses of the last campaign, and of the pestilence which had brought it to an end, had been terrible. Still it was impossible to accept the condition which had been offered, and the government prepared to resist. Of money, at least, they had an unfailing supply, and with money they could always purchase men. Some members of the council were at once sent off with large sums to hire mercenaries in Europe.

Dionysius, probably without waiting for the return of his envoys, marched to the west of the island. His object of attack was Motya, the chief harbour and arsenal of Carthage in Sicily. He was joined on his way by the whole force of all the Greek cities, and his army numbered eighty thousand infantry and upwards of three thousand cavalry, while he had a fleet of two hundred ships co-operating with him. Motya was strongly situated on an island divided from the mainland by a channel six furlongs broad. This channel was ordinarily crossed by a mole. But the mole could be removed in time of necessity, and this was at once done. Dionysius, after reconnoitring the place in company with his engineers, set about a siege. The harbour and all the shore were blockaded, and the channel, or at least part of the channel, was filled up, so that the engines might be brought up to the walls of the city. On the other hand, Himilco, who had been put in command of the Carthaginian force, was

THE WALL OF MOTYA.

not idle. He sent ten ships from Carthage to Syracuse itself, and destroyed much of the shipping in the harbour. He then made a more formidable attack on the besieging force at Motya. Taking command in person of a squadron of a hundred ships he crossed by night from Carthage to Selinus, and sailing thence along the coast appeared at daybreak off Motya, sank or burnt the blockading squadron, and made his way into the harbour. The Greek ships were drawn up on land, and Dionysius did not venture to launch them. The harbour was too narrow for him to use his numbers with advantage. But he constructed a road of planks across a neck of land which divided the harbour from the sea, and made his men drag his ships along this. When Himilco endeavoured to interrupt the work he was driven off with showers of missiles from the Syracusan force on land, and by the arrows discharged by the catapults. Catapults were a new invention at the time, and probably caused something of the consternation which is felt by savages at the first sight of firearms. Himilco, whose fleet was only half as strong as that opposed to him, did not venture to give battle, but returned to Carthage.

The attempt at relief having thus failed, Dionysius pushed the siege vigorously. The walls were battered with the rams, while the catapults, with a constant discharge of arrows, drove the garrison from the walls. Towers were wheeled up against the fortifications. They had six stories, each of them filled with men, and were as high as the houses of the town. The people of Motya, on the other hand, defended themselves vigorously. They raised great masts with yard-arms, from which men, protected from the missiles of the besiegers by breastworks, threw ignited torches and bundles of flax steeped in pitch on the engines that were being used against the walls. Some of these were set on fire, and the assailants had to turn their attention to extinguishing the flames. Still the attack went on, and before long the rams made a breach in the wall. A fierce battle followed. The Greeks burned to avenge the cruelties that had been done to their countrymen; the Phœnicians, who could hope for no mercy, and who had no way of escape open to them either by sea or land, resisted with the courage of despair. When they had to give up the walls, they made barriers across the streets, and defended every house as if it had been a fort. The Greeks brought their siege-towers into the streets, and from them made their way into the upper stories of the houses. Still the people of Motya did not lose courage, but fought with a resolution which reminds us of the Jews when they defended Jerusalem against the Romans under Titus. The Greeks suffered heavily in this street fighting. Their opponents were utterly reckless of their lives, and they knew the place where they were fighting. At last a stratagem succeeded where force had failed. For several days the Greeks had retired from the conflict as evening approached, the signal for retreat being given by a trumpet, and the people of the town came to regard this as the regular course of things. But one night Dionysius sent a picked force to renew the attack after dark. This detachment established themselves in some of the houses before the besieged were aware of what had happened; the rest of the army poured across the channel now filled up, and Motya was taken. One of the horrible massacres which make these wars so terrible followed. Dionysius tried in vain to stop it, not so much from any feeling of mercy, as because prisoners might be sold for slaves, and would bring in considerable sums of money. The soldiers paying no heed to his orders, he made proclamation that such of the inhabitants as still survived should take shelter in the temples. This was effectual. The soldiers then began to plunder. This Dionysius did not attempt to hinder. Wishing to encourage his men for the campaign which lay before them, he gave up to them all the booty in the town. To the leader of the party which had surprised the town he made a present of about £400, and was liberal in his gifts to all who had distinguished themselves.

Carthage meanwhile had been preparing a formidable force with which to re-establish her dominion in Sicily. It amounted to one hundred thousand men, taking again, as being the most probable, the smallest estimate. Thirty thousand more joined it after it had landed in Sicily. Himilco was appointed to the command. Aware that Dionysius had his spies in Carthage, he gave to the captain of each transport sealed orders directing them to sail to Panormus. They were attacked on their way by a Syracusan squadron, which sank fifty of their number, and with them five thousand men and two hundred chariots. Himilco then came out with his war-ships, and the Syracusans retired. The Carthaginian general marched along the coast to Motya, and recovered it without any difficulty. Dionysius did not venture to attack him, but retired to Syracuse.

Himilco now conceived a very bold scheme, nothing less than to make his way to Messana, in the extreme north-east of the island. It had an admirable harbour, capable of holding all his ships, which numbered more than six hundred. It was near the mainland of Italy, from which he hoped to draw fresh forces, and it commanded the approach from

Greece. He marched along the north coast, his fleet accompanying him, and pitched his camp at Pelorum, the extreme north-eastern point of Sicily, which was about twelve miles from the city. The Messanians were struck with terror. Their walls were out of repair; they had no allies at hand, and part of their own military force was absent at Syracuse. The first thing was to send away the women and children and the most precious of their possessions. Then they prepared for defence. Some were encouraged by remembering an old oracle, "The sons of Carthage shall bear water in the streets of Messana," which they took to mean that there should be Carthaginian slaves in their city. They sent a military force to the spot where Himilco was encamped, with instructions to resist any attempt to occupy the country. Himilco at once sent a squadron of two hundred ships to attack the town, which would now, he reckoned, be almost stripped of defenders. An opportune north wind carried the ships rapidly to their destination—more rapidly than the Messanian soldiers could follow them. Himilco's hopes were fulfilled. His ships landed the troops which they carried. These made their way into the city through the spaces in the walls, and the place was captured almost without a struggle. Some of the Messanians fell in a vain attempt at resistance; many took refuge in the neighbouring forts; two hundred and more had recourse to the desperate expedient of swimming the strait between their city and Italy. Fifty succeeded in the attempt. Himilco, after trying in vain to capture the forts, marched on Syracuse.

His first object was the city of Catana, which lay on the southern slopes of Mount Ætna. His original plan was to march his army along the coast, with the fleet keeping pace with it. But this plan could not be carried out. A severe eruption of Ætna took place at the very time of his march, and the stream of lava which poured down the eastern or seaward slopes of the mountain made it necessary for him to make a circuitous march round the western side.

Dionysius at once took advantage of this division of the Carthaginian forces, resolving to attack the fleet while it was unsupported by the neighbourhood of the army. He marched with his own army along the sea-coast nearly as far as Catana, while Leptines, the Syracusan admiral, sailed alongside with the fleet. Mago, who was in command of the Carthaginian ships, felt at first no little dismay at the sight of the combined force which was coming to meet him. He had, however, no alternative but to fight; and indeed his fleet was a very powerful one, numbering, along with the transport ships, which were furnished with brazen beaks for purposes of attack, as many as five hundred ships. The Syracusan admiral, who probably bore the character of being too adventurous, had been strictly ordered by Dionysius to keep his fleet in close order, and on no account to break the line. It was only thus that he could hope to hold his own against the superior numbers of the enemy. These orders he disregarded. Picking out thirty of his fastest sailers, he advanced far ahead of the rest of the fleet, and boldly attacked the Carthaginians. At first he was successful, sinking many of his antagonists But the numbers which were brought up against him were overwhelming. It became more and more difficult to manœuvre; at close quarters, when it was possible for the enemy to board, one ship, however skilfully commanded, was not much better than another. Before long Leptines was glad to escape to the open sea with such of the ships as were left to him. The rest of his fleet, who had thus lost the leadership of their admiral, and who came on in disorder, made but little resistance to the enemy. More than a hundred ships were taken or destroyed. Nor was the near neighbourhood of the army on shore of much service to those who tried to escape from the wrecks. The Carthaginians had manned a number of boats which intercepted the fugitives, and slaughtered them in the water before the eyes and within the hearing of their countrymen. More than twenty thousand men are said to have been lost by the Greeks in this battle.

Dionysius was strongly urged to meet Himilco at once before the news of the disaster to the fleet had become known through Sicily. At first he was inclined to follow the advice. But more cautious counsels prevailed, and he retreated on Syracuse. This was probably a mistake. Not only did he disgust many of his allies, but he lost an opportunity of inflicting a great blow on the enemy. Immediately after the battle bad weather came on, and the Carthaginian fleet could not keep the sea. Had the Greek army still occupied their position on the shore they might have inflicted immense damage on their opponents. As it was, Himilco came up with his army in time to assist his fleet. His own ships, and those which had been captured from the Greeks, were drawn up on the shore and repaired. The men had some days given them for rest and refreshment; and he then marched on to Syracuse. Before starting for this last stage he sent envoys to the little town of Ætna, where the Italian mercenaries of Dionysius were strongly posted, inviting these troops to change side and take service with himself. They were strongly inclined to do so, but could not. They had given hostages to their master, and their best troops were actually serving in his army. They were thus compelled to refuse the offer, and Himilco was obliged to leave them in his rear.

On arriving at Syracuse his first step was to make a great demonstration of force. He sailed into the Great Harbour with all his fleet. There were more than two hundred ships of war, which he had adorned with the spoils of those captured off Catana, and nearly two thousand others of all kinds and sizes. The harbour, though measuring more than a mile and a half one way and two miles and a half the other, was absolutely crowded with them. The army is said to have numbered three hundred thousand; but this is doubtless an exaggeration. Altogether the display of force was overwhelming, and the Syracusans did not venture to show themselves outside either their harbour or their walls.

The Carthaginian general prepared to blockade the city, building three forts, which he stored with wine and other provisions. His merchants were sent at the same time to Sardinia and Africa to fetch new supplies. Dionysius, on the other hand, sent to Greece and Southern Italy in the hope of collecting a force of volunteers and mercenaries.

The tide of success now began to turn against Carthage. One of Himilco's corn-ships was approaching his camp when five of the Syracusan ships sallied forth from the Inner Harbour and captured it. The Carthaginians sent out a squadron of forty ships to drive off the assailants. On this the Syracusans manned their whole fleet, attacked the hostile squadron, sinking twenty-four out of the forty, and capturing the admiral's ship. They then paraded their force in front of the Carthaginian position, and challenged the invaders to a general engagement. The challenge was not accepted.

And now, for the third time, pestilence, the old ally of the Greeks, appeared to help them. Himilco had shown himself as careless of the religious feelings, not only of his foes, but also of his friends, as his predecessors had done. He had broken down the tombs outside the city to get materials for his forts, and he had robbed such temples as, being without the line of fortifications, had fallen into his hands. One specially rich and famous shrine had been thus treated, that of Demeter and Persephone.[1] It was to this impiety that the disasters were generally attributed; but the natural causes at work were sufficient to account for them. An enormous force was crowded together. It was the most unhealthy season of the year; and the heat of the summer, that was now coming to an

[1] Ceres and Proserpine.

end, had been unusually great. The plague that now broke out in the army seems, from the description that the historian gives of it, to have been much of the same type as the disease now known by that name. It began with swellings, and ended, after a most painful illness of five or six days, almost invariably in death. The danger or the fear of infection prevented due attention to the sick, or even the burial of the dead. We are told that as many as one hundred and fifty thousand corpses at one time lay rotting on the ground. The marvel is, if this or anything like this be true, not that so many died, but that so many survived.

The Syracusans did not fail to take advantage of the distress of the invaders. Dionysius planned a simultaneous attack by sea and land. Leptines, with a Spartan officer, was put in command of a squadron of eighty ships, and Dionysius himself directed the movements of the troops. He marched out of the city at night, and delivered an unexpected attack about daybreak on the landward side of the Carthaginian camp. At first he suffered a reverse; but this he had fully planned, for it enabled him to get rid of a body of disaffected mercenaries. Put in tne front, and deserted by the troops which should have supported them, they were cut to pieces by the Carthaginians. But when Dionysius advanced in force, these, in their turn, were driven back, and one of the forts was captured. Meanwhile the Syracusan ships attacked on the other side. The Carthaginian ships were but ill manned, a great part of their crews having doubtless perished in the plague. Anyhow they suffered a crushing defeat, and the army, weak itself, and distracted by the assailants on the other side, could give them no very effectual help. Many of the ships were deserted. To these the Greeks set fire. The flames spread from vessel to vessel till nearly the whole of the fleet, both war-ships and merchantmen, was in a blaze. They even spread to the camp, which itself was, at least in part, consumed. In short, the victory of the Syracusans was complete, and Dionysius encamped that night near the temple of Zeus, in which Himilco had lately had his headquarters.

Reduced to these straits, the Carthaginian general resolved to open communications with Dionysius personally, and without the knowledge of the people of Syracuse. He offered three hundred talents if he would allow him to remove to Africa what was left of his army. Dionysius replied that it would be quite impossible to conduct so extensive an operation as the removal of the whole of the army without exciting the suspicion of the people. But Himilco himself and the Carthaginian officers would be allowed to escape. He was not anxious to push the Carthaginians to extremities. Their friendship might be useful to him on some future occasion, for his own power was not very firmly established, and he had more than one proof of late that there was a strong party at work in Syracuse to overthrow it. Himilco accepted these terms. It was arranged that he and the other native Carthaginians should depart secretly on the fourth night following, and Dionysius led back his army to the city. The money was duly sent, and at the time appointed, Himilco, with his officers and friends, and such of his troops as belonged to Carthage, embarked. They filled, it is said, forty ships of war. Their escape did not pass unnoticed. News of what was going on was taken to Dionysius. As he seemed to be tardy in his movements, the Corinthian ships that were in harbour acted for themselves, pursued the fugitives, and captured some of the worst sailers in the squadron.

The army that was thus shamefully abandoned by its general fared, perhaps, better than might have been expected. The native Sikels at once left the camp, and thus anticipating the attack of the Syracusans, reached their homes for the most part in safety. The Spaniards offered such a bold front to their enemies, that Dionysius was glad to take them into his own service. The rest of the army surrendered, and were sold as slaves.

Himilco did not long escape the punishment which was due to his treachery and cowardice. All Carthage was plunged into mourning by the terrible disaster which had happened. Every house, every temple, was closed; all rites of worship were stopped, and private business was suspended. The city crowded to meet the ships which were bringing back Himilco and his followers, and inquired the fate of friends and relatives. When the whole truth was known, a cry of wailing went up from the crowd. The general himself landed from his ship clad in the meanest garb. Stretching his hands to the sky, he bewailed aloud the disasters which had fallen on himself and on his country. The only consolation which he could offer was that he had been conquered not by the enemy, but by the will of heaven. At the same time he publicly confessed his own impiety, and took the blame of what had happened on himself. After visiting every temple in the city with this confession on his lips, he went to his own house, blocked up his doors, and, refusing admission even to his own children, starved himself to death.

The misfortunes of Carthage were not yet at an end. She had seemed to be on the point of subduing all Sicily, and indeed only one, city remained to be taken; and within a few months she had to fight for her own existence. Her African allies and subjects, with whom she seems to have been exceedingly unpopular, rose by one consent against her. An army numbering one hundred and twenty thousand was soon raised. They made their headquarters at Tunes, and for a while, so superior was their strength, kept the Carthaginians within their walls. For a time the city was in despair. Besides the visible dangers that threatened, the people dreaded the anger of heaven. Their general had grievously insulted the gods of Greece. He had made a dwelling-house of one temple at Syracuse, and had robbed another. The government at once set itself to calm these fears. The offended gods, especially Demeter and Persephone, who had never before been worshipped in Carthage, were propitiated by sacrifices in Greek fashion, which the handsomest youths of Greek race that could be found were appointed to perform. This done, they applied themselves to the business of defending the city. And indeed the danger was soon over. The

VOTIVE BAS-RELIEF TO PERSEPHONE.

hosts that threatened them were nothing more than irregular levies, who could not agree among themselves, and who had no leaders worthy of the name. Provisions soon failed them, for they had no ships, whereas the Carthaginians had command of the sea, and could import as much food as they wanted from Sardinia. Nor was it only in this way that their vast wealth served them. They used it also to buy off some of their most formidable enemies. In the course of a few months the great Libyan army broke up, and Carthage was safe.

IV.

THE LAST STRUGGLE WITH DIONYSIUS.

THE power of Carthage was now limited to a small region in the western part of the island. But she was not content to remain within these borders; and she seized the first opportunity of seeking to extend them. Dionysius had set himself to reduce the native tribes—always hostile to the Greeks, and always ready to swell the forces of an invader. The Sikels (there were two tribes of the natives, Sikels and Sikanians) had established a new settlement at Tauromenium. Dionysius did his utmost to capture this place, but was repulsed with much loss, and was himself wounded. Some of the Greek cities now threw off their allegiance; and the Sikels generally rose against him. The general in command of the Carthaginian districts—Mago by name—who had been doing his best to make himself popular among subjects and neighbours, at once took the field, and ventured to march as far eastward as Messana. Dionysius encountered him on his way back, and after a fierce battle defeated him, Mago losing as many as 8000 in the struggle. Carthage, however, was now beginning to recover her strength; and was resolved to make another effort to regain, at least, part of the island. She drew from her usual recruiting grounds —Africa, Sardinia, and Italy—a force of 80,000 men, and sent it into Sicily, with Mago again in command. Mago marched through the country of the native tribes, calling them all to take up arms against Dionysius, but failed with one at least of the most powerful chiefs. Receiving this check he halted. Meanwhile, Dionysius had collected a force of 20,000; with this he marched against the invaders, and making common cause with the Sikel chiefs, soon reduced them to extremities. The battle which Mago wished to force on him, and which some of his own followers desired, he declined. The Carthaginians, encamped as they were in their enemies' country, found their supplies fall short, and were obliged to sue for peace. It was granted; but one of the conditions was that the Sikels, valuable allies in past time to Carthage, should now be subjects of Syracuse. So far the war ended in a distinct loss to the Phœnician power.

The next war seems to have been provoked by Dionysius. His position at Syracuse was now firmly established, and his power had steadily increased. He was now desirous to consolidate it by finally expelling his remaining rivals from the island. The dependencies of Carthage were, as usual, disaffected. Dionysius listened to their complaints, encouraged them to revolt, and received them into alliance with himself. Carthage sent embassies to complain of these proceedings, and receiving no redress, resolved upon war. Foreseeing that it would be a formidable undertaking, they made more than ordinary preparations. Besides hiring, as usual, a large force of mercenaries, they also raised a body of troops of their own citizens, a most uncommon circumstance, and indicating their sense that it was a critical time to which they had come. The war seems to have been carried on—why and how we do not very clearly know—both in Italy and Sicily. Of the operations in Italy we know little or nothing. In Sicily two great battles were fought. The first was at Cabala. In this Dionysius inflicted a severe defeat on his opponents, killing, it is said, more than 10,000, and taking as many as 5,000 prisoners. The survivors were compelled to take refuge on a height where there was no supply of water. Mago, the general, had fallen in the engagement. The Carthaginians began negotiations for peace. Dionysius replied that he would grant it only on these conditions, that they should evacuate all the towns in Sicily, and should pay an indemnity for the expenses of the war. The terms seemed harsh beyond endurance; but it was necessary to temporize. The generals in command replied that they were not competent to make so important a treaty on their own authority, especially as the surrender of Carthaginian towns was concerned. They must refer the matter to the authorities at home, and they begged for a few days' truce. This Dionysius readily granted. Meanwhile the Carthaginians prepared for resistance. They gave a magnificent funeral to the remains of Mago, and appointed his son, a mere youth in years but singularly able and brave, to take the command. Every hour of the time was spent in drilling the troops and making them ready to renew the war. When the truce expired, they marched out of their camp and offered battle to Dionysius. The engagement took place at Cronium, and ended in disaster to the Greeks. Dionysius commanded one wing, and his brother Leptines, of whom we have heard as admiral of the Syracusan fleet more than once before, led the other. Dionysius, who had the best troops of the army under him, was for a time successful; Leptines was defeated and slain. When his death became known throughout the army there was a general panic. The Carthaginians gave no quarter, and by the time that the darkness put an end to the pursuit, 14,000 Greeks, it is said, had perished. The Carthaginians, however, did not pursue their victory, but retired to Panormus. Anxious to secure what they could before fortune turned against them, they sent an embassy to Syracuse offering peace. Dionysius was glad to accept their terms. These were, that a thousand talents should be paid by way of indemnity, and that Carthage should have, besides their own towns, Selinus and its territory, and all that had belonged to Agrigentum west of the Halycus.

This treaty was kept for fifteen years. Then Dionysius saw another opportunity of attacking his old enemy. Carthage was again suffering from the evils which seem to have troubled her over and over again —pestilence, and revolt among her African subjects.[1]

[1] Eleven years before we hear a story of how the Carthaginians sent an expedition to Italy; and how, after it had been brought to a successful end, a terrible plague broke out at home, so terrible that Carthage was likely to lose her dominions, both Africa and Sardinia revolting

On the ground that the Carthaginians had trespassed beyond their boundaries, he marched into their territory with an army of 38,000 infantry and 3,000 horse. Selinus, Entellus, and Eryx, either were conquered or capitulated; and he then laid siege to Lilybæum, a flourishing port near the promontory of that name. At first he pressed the siege with vigour, but found that the place was too strongly garrisoned to be soon taken. Then came news that the docks at Carthage had been burnt. Thinking that all the enemy's fleet must have perished, he sent many of his own ships home, keeping a squadron of 130 at Eryx. The Carthaginians, who seem not to have suffered so much as had been thought, manned two hundred ships and sent them to Sicily. The Greek admiral was taken by surprise, and lost more than half his squadron. As winter was now approaching a truce was concluded. Before the time for another campaign had come, Dionysius was dead.[1]

against her. "At this time," says the historian Diodorus, "there fell on the Carthaginians many troubles by the ordering of the gods, strange terrors and unceasing panic fears, making men think that the enemy had entered into the city, so that they leapt armed out of their houses, and fell upon one another, slaying some and wounding some."

[1] He died, it was said, from the effects of a banquet which he had given to celebrate the success of one of his tragedies in a competition at Athens. An oracle had told him that he should die when he got the better of them that were better than he. He had understood this to mean the Carthaginians, and, says the historian, somewhat absurdly, had always been careful not to push too far his victories over them. But the real meaning of the prophecy was quite different. He was a bad poet, and yet, by the verdict of flattering judges, was judged to be better than poets who were really better than he. When his tragedy was successful, the oracle was fulfilled, and he died.

The war was not finished by his death, but nothing more of much consequence seems to have happened About a year afterwards peace was concluded, and for the next twenty years the " story of Carthage " is almost a blank.

V.

CARTHAGE AND TIMOLEON.

I SAID in my last chapter that for twenty years and more after the death of Dionysius the story of Carthage is "almost a blank." We know, however, so much about her as to be sure that she was gaining strength in Sicily. The condition of the Greek cities in that island was going from bad to worse. Most of them had fallen into the hands of tyrants, and these tyrants were always intriguing or fighting against each other. Carthage all the while was steadily watching her opportunities and extending her power. In 344 she had become so dangerous that some Syracusan citizens, who had been banished by the younger Dionysius, son of the tyrant of that name of whom so much was said in the last chapter, resolved to call in the aid of Corinth. Corinth was the mother-city of Syracuse,[1] and the tie between the two had always been close. The Corinthians listened to their request, and, as it happened, had at hand just the man who was wanted. Timoleon was one of the best and noblest of their citizens; but he was the most unhappy. He had had a terrible duty put upon him. A brother whom he had loved had tried to make

[1] The founder and first colonists of Syracuse had come from Corinth.

himself tyrant in Corinth, and Timoleon had ordered him to be put to death, or, as some say, had killed him with his own hand. After this dreadful act done to save his country, he had shut himself up in his house. When the Syracusan envoys came with their request, he was glad to go, and his countrymen were glad to send him.

It was but a small force that Timoleon could get together for his enterprise—ten ships of war, and seven hundred mercenaries. The Carthaginians sent a squadron to intercept him. This he contrived to escape, and landed in Sicily. The tale of his wonderful achievements does not belong to my story. It must be enough to say that he gained possession of Syracuse, though one of his opponents had actually introduced the Carthaginians into that city; that he gave it free government, and that he did the same service to other Sicilian towns. To gain means for these enterprises he is said to have plundered the Carthaginian territory. However this may be, we may be sure that Carthage would not look upon these proceedings with favour. War was declared before long, and the Carthaginians exerted themselves to the utmost to meet their new enemy. They collected an army of 70,000 (it may be noticed that the numbers become smaller and more credible as we go on), well furnished with the artillery of the time, and supplied with abundance of provisions. As usual, this army consisted for the most part of mercenaries, but it contained also a numerous force—one historian puts it at ten thousand—of native Carthaginians. The fleet transported it safely to Lilybæum, and it at once commenced its march eastward. Timoleon had but a small force with which to meet this great host. In Syracuse he could not raise more than three thousand; of mercenary troops, after he had sent away a thousand laggards and cowards, he had about as many more. But he boldly marched out with his six thousand, and found the enemy encamped on the river Crimessus.

It was nearly midsummer, and the heat of the sun had drawn up from the low ground near the river a thick fog. The Greeks could see nothing of the enemy's camp, but they could hear the confused hum of many voices rising up from it. As the sun grew stronger, the mist began to lift from the valley, though it still lingered on the hills; and as it cleared away the river could be seen, and the great Carthaginian army in the very act of crossing it, with the four-horse chariots in front, and after them a solid body of infantry, ten thousand in number, splendidly armed and bearing white shields. These were the native Carthaginians, and their march was orderly and slow. After them came the mixed crowd of hired troops, disorderly and unruly, struggling who should first cross the river. Timoleon saw his opportunity, while the army of the enemy was still divided, some being actually in the river, and some on the further shore. The native Carthaginians were just struggling up the bank and forming themselves in line, when the Greek cavalry fell upon them. At first charge after charge was made in vain. The chariots of the enemy were driven furiously backwards and forwards in front of the army, and the Greek horsemen had to do their very best to prevent their own lines being broken by them; on the lines of the enemy they could make no impression. Timoleon, who had about him a small force of Syracusans and picked mercenaries, came up to the help of his cavalry. They were no longer, he said, to attack the front line of the enemy—that with that he would himself engage—but were to fall upon the flanks. Putting his men into as compact a body as possible, something, we may guess, like the phalanx with which the Macedonians won so many victories, he charged the enemy. But even he for a time could do nothing. The iron breastplates, the helmets of brass, the great shields which covered almost the whole of the body, resisted the Greek spears. At this moment fortune, or, as the Greeks would have said, Zeus the cloud-compeller, helped him. Suddenly a storm, with loud peals of thunder and vivid flashes of lightning, burst from the hills. The mist, which had been hanging about the heights, came down again upon the plain, and brought with it a tempest of rain and wind and hail. The Greeks only felt them behind; the Carthaginians had them dashing in their faces; the rain and hail and lightning blinded them; the thunder would not allow them to hear the words of command. Then the ground grew slippery beneath their feet; and the heavy armour became a hindrance rather than a protection. They could hardly move from place to place; they found it difficult to stand; when once they had fallen it was impossible to rise. Then came a new trouble. The river, partly swollen by the rain, partly, it is said, dammed back by the multitude of troops that were crossing it, overflowed its banks, and the heavy-armed Carthaginians stumbled and rolled about in the water. First the front line was cut to pieces; then the whole vanguard was broken; finally the army gave way. Many were cut down in the plain, many drowned in the river, and yet more intercepted by the light troops as they were attempting to reach the hills. Ten thousand lay dead upon the field, and of these no less than three thousand were Carthaginian citizens. The city had never suffered such a loss before. It was not now Africans or Spaniards, but her own children for whom she had to mourn.

Even after this crushing defeat the war was not at an end. The Greeks were, as usual, divided among themselves; and the enemies of Timoleon invited Carthage to continue the war, and promised their own help. Another battle was fought, and with the same result. Then Carthage asked for peace. It was granted on the condition that she should keep herself to the western side of the Halycus, and that she should not pretend to interfere with the government of the Sicilian cities.

VI.

CARTHAGE AND AGATHOCLES.

TIMOLEON died in 337; for twenty years and more there was peace in Sicily; then the Greeks fell out among themselves. Carthage was called in to help one of the parties. Timoleon had restored Syracuse to freedom; but it had fallen again into the hands of a tyrant, Agathocles. Thousands of the citizens had been banished by the usurper; and these, under the leadership of a certain Deinocrates, made a treaty with Carthage. In 309 a powerful expedition set sail for Sicily. There was a contingent of native Carthaginians numbering two thousand, among whom were some of the noblest-born of the citizens, African and Italian mercenaries, and a thousand slingers from the Balearic Islands. Its start was unlucky. A great storm sank sixty of the ships of war, and more than two hundred transports, and the rest of the fleet reached Sicily in a sadly battered condition. It was easy, however, to find recruits in the island, and Hamilcar, who was in command, had soon under him an army of 40,000 infantry and 5,000 horse. Agathocles met him at a place famous in the history of Sicilian wars, the river Himera. The battle that followed began well for the Greeks. Some troops which Agathocles had put in ambush near the river fell upon a Carthaginian detachment as it was crossing the stream, laden with plunder, and drove them in confusion to their camp. Their commander thought it a good opportunity for a general attack. At first everything went well; the Greek army assaulted the Carthaginian camp, and at one time seemed likely to take it. Then the fortune of the day changed. The Balearic slingers were brought into action, and killed and wounded many of the assailants. These still kept up the attack, but at this moment appeared a fresh squadron from Africa, and took them in the rear. The defenders of the camp took fresh courage; the attack was finally repulsed, and soon changed into a rout. Five miles of level ground lay between the two camps; the Carthaginian cavalry could act on this with freedom, and they made dreadful havoc among the fugitives. Another cause, and this a strange one, increased the Greek loss. The battle was fought in the heat of summer and at midday. Many of the fugitives had made for the river rather than for their camp, and they reached it in a state of raging thirst. The water was salt, or at least strongly brackish, but they drank greedily of it, and with fatal results. Many unwounded corpses were found upon the banks. The total loss of the Greeks was seven thousand, that of the Carthaginians not more than five hundred. Agathocles shut himself up in Gela, hoping thus to divert Hamilcar's attention from Syracuse, where the people would then gain time to gather in their harvests. The Carthaginian general began the siege, but seeing that he had little chance of taking the place, soon changed his plan. His first step was to win over the other Greek cities by kind treatment and liberal offers. Many of them joined him; their own danger was imminent, and they hated Agathocles.

Reduced to the last extremity, for nearly all Sicily, with the exception of Syracuse, was lost to him, this extraordinary man conceived one of the boldest devices which history records. He determined to transfer the war to Carthage itself. That city, he knew, was not prepared for an attack, and its African subjects were always ill-affected, and he believed, and rightly believed, that it could be best attacked. This scheme he kept a profound secret. The measures that he took for carrying it out were most skilful, and, it must be added, most unprincipled. He began by choosing the force which he was to take with him most carefully. The greater part of it was cavalry. Horses he had no means of transporting to Africa, but he hoped to find them there, and the men were ordered to furnish themselves with bridles and saddles. He had to guard against a revolution in Syracuse during his absence; and he was careful to take hostage for good behaviour from all the most powerful families in the city; putting one brother, for instance, in the garrison, and enlisting another in his own army. Then he wanted money. He gave notice that any citizen who might be unwilling or unable to endure the hardships of a siege was at liberty to depart. The offer was accepted by numbers of the rich. They had the means of living elsewhere, and they hated the rule of the tyrant. They were accordingly permitted to depart, and to take their property with them. But Agathocles sent some of his mercenaries after them. The unhappy men were robbed and murdered, and the tyrant found himself amply provided with means.

He then embarked his force, which filled sixty ships of war. The first necessity was to avoid the blockading squadron, which was much stronger than his own. Just at the right time a fleet of corn-ships appeared off the harbour. The Carthaginians left their post to pursue them, and Agathocles took the opportunity to get out of the harbour. For a time the Carthaginian admiral expected an attack, thinking that the Syracusan fleet had come out to fight for the corn-ships; then seeing that it was sailing in the other direction, he gave chase. The result was a double success to Agathocles. The corn-ships got safely into harbour, and relieved the city, which was already beginning to suffer from scarcity; and the squadron, which had got a considerable start, escaped. The escape, indeed, was a narrow one. The race lasted for five days and nights. On the morning of the sixth day the Carthaginian fleet unexpectedly appeared close at hand. Both sides strained every nerve; but the Greeks won the race. They reached the land first, but the foremost of the Carthaginian ships were close upon them. In the skirmish that followed these were too weak to act with any effect, and Agathocles not only landed in safety, but was able to fortify a camp, close to which he beached his ships.

But he had in his mind a yet bolder stroke. He burnt his ships. Forced thus to give up all hope of

AFRICAN AQUEDUCT.

AGATHOCLES INVADES AFRICA.

escape, the army must now conquer or perish. At first they were in despair; but Agathocles did not give them much time to think about their situation. He led them to attack a district in which the wealthiest citizens of Carthage had their farms and country houses. It was a region of rich pastures, of oliveyards and vineyards, and the Sicilians were astonished at the plenty which they saw. Two towns fell easily into their hands, and their despair was soon changed into confidence. At Carthage there was the utmost dismay. It was commonly believed that the whole force in Sicily had perished, for no one could suppose that Agathocles could have ventured to leave Syracuse in danger and attack Africa. Some were for treating for peace; others advised delay till the truth could be found out. When news of what had really happened arrived, they were, of course, greatly encouraged, and prepared to attack the invaders.

In the first battle that took place, it is interesting to see the list of combatants on either side. Agathocles, besides his own Syracusans, had Samnites, Etruscans, and Celts (probably Gauls) in his army. The whole amounted to about eleven thousand, but many of them were insufficiently armed. There was no little discouragement among them,[1] and the result seemed doubtful. The day, indeed, might have gone in favour of Carthage but for

[1] A strange story is told of the device by which Agathocles endeavoured to give confidence to his men. He had a number of tame owls which he let loose in the court. The birds settled on the shields and helmets of the soldiers. The owl was the sacred bird of Athené (Minerva), and the soldiers looked upon this incident as a proof of the goddess' favour.

the misfortune of the death of one of her generals, and the treachery of another. The two Suffetes of the year were Hanno and Bomilcar. Hanno was in command of the Sacred Band of native Carthaginians. Eager to break the opposing line, where Agathocles himself was in command, he exposed himself too rashly, and was killed. Bomilcar had designs of making himself a tyrant in Carthage, and felt that the defeat of the invaders would not help him in his object. He seems even to have had a treacherous understanding with the enemy. To his own officers he pretended that the death of his colleague made it necessary to retreat. The Carthaginian mercenaries soon took to flight; the Sacred Host held its ground for a long time, but was at last compelled to retreat. The camp fell into the hands of the Greeks.

Agathocles continued his successes, and carried the war almost up to the walls of Carthage. Meanwhile things had been going well with him at Syracuse. Hamilcar had made a night attack upon the city, had failed, and had been taken prisoner. His head was cut off, and sent to Agathocles in Africa. Carthage suffered defeat after defeat in a series of battles, which it would be tedious to relate. At last the people found out one cause, at least, of their ill-fortune. Bomilcar had all along been playing the part of a traitor. He now thought that the time was come for seizing the prize of absolute power which he had always had in view. He ordered a review of the troops in the city, When it had been held, he dismissed all that were not pledged to support him.

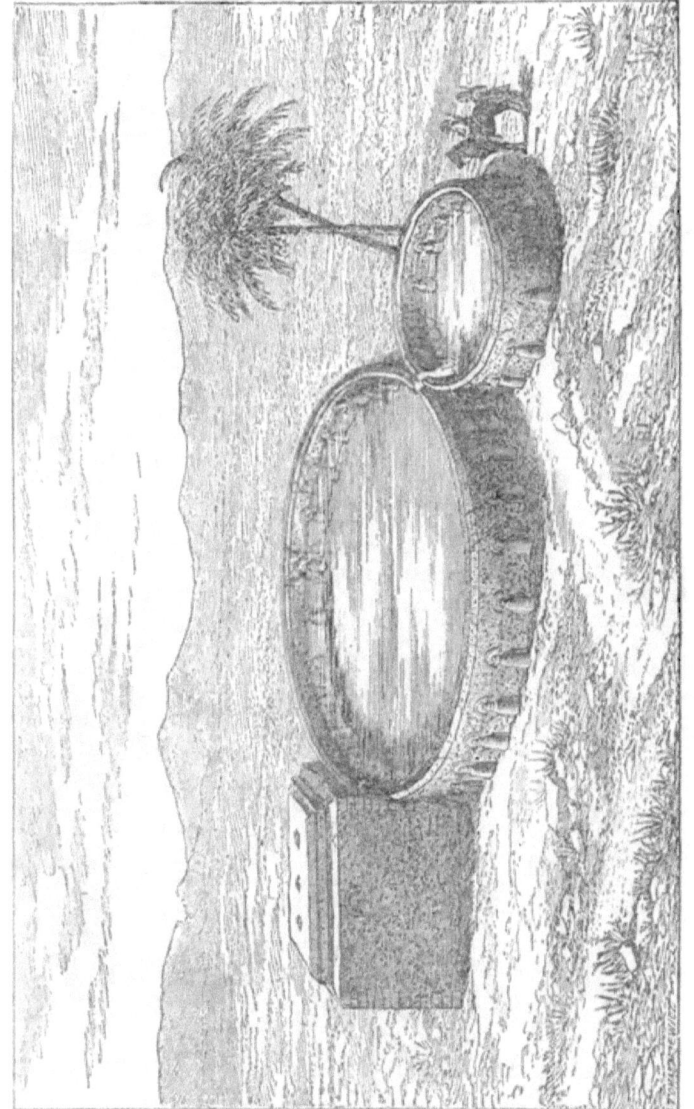

RURAL CISTERNS.

Keeping the remainder, five hundred native Carthaginians and five thousand mercenaries, he proclaimed himself king, and commenced a massacre of all his opponents. If Agathocles outside the walls had known of what was going on, and had arranged an attack for the same time, Carthage was lost. The battle in the streets raged fiercely. Bomilcar and his adherents forced their way into the market-place. But the place could not be held. It was surrounded on all sides by lofty houses, which were occupied by the friends of the government, and from which showers of javelins were discharged on the revolters. Bomilcar was compelled to retreat into the New City. Finally a truce was agreed to. An amnesty was promised, and the rebels laid down their arms. But Bomilcar was too dangerous a person, and had done too much harm, to be allowed to escape. The rulers of Carthage, never much troubled by scruples, moral or religious, broke their oath and crucified him. The tide of success did not turn at once. Agathocles took Utica,[1] the largest of the Phœnician cities in Africa after Carthage, and a number of other towns, till Carthage was almost stripped of allies and subjects.

Agathocles was now recalled by urgent affairs to Syracuse. He left his son Archagathus in command of the African army. Archagathus was too ambitious, and undertook enterprises, especially against the

[1] Another strange story is told of the device which he used in approaching this city. He had captured three hundred of the chief citizens. These he suspended alive on a tower which he brought up close to the gates, and which he had filled with archers and slingers. The defenders of Utica could not defend themselves against this attack without wounding or killing their own countrymen.

wandering tribes of the interior, for which his strength was not sufficient. Carthage, on the other hand, was now under wiser rule. The army was divided into three corps, each of which carried on separate operations against the invaders. Archagathus suffered a great defeat under the walls of the city, and was also weakened by the revolt of many of his allies. His father now returned from Sicily, and for a time restored the balance. But an attack on the Carthaginian camp proved to be a failure. Then occurred a strange succession of changes of fortune. The Carthaginians, in celebrating their last victory after their own hideous fashion with human sacrifice, set fire to their camp. When the confusion was at its highest, some African mercenaries, who had taken service with Agathocles, deserted to the Carthaginians. Their approach was taken as an hostile attack, and a general panic followed. When the mistake was discovered, some were admitted into the city, and there made the very same panic among the Greeks which they had just made among the Carthaginians. Agathocles lost more than four thousand men through this mishap. His African allies now left him, and he began to despair of success. He had no hope of being able to get terms from the enemy, and no means of carrying away his army. His plan was to depart secretly, taking the younger of his two sons with him. But Archagathus the elder discovered the scheme, and revealed it to the army. The soldiers, furious at the thought of being thus deserted, mutinied, seized Agathocles and put him in chains. Everything was now in disorder. Finally, Agathocles contrived to escape from confinement, and

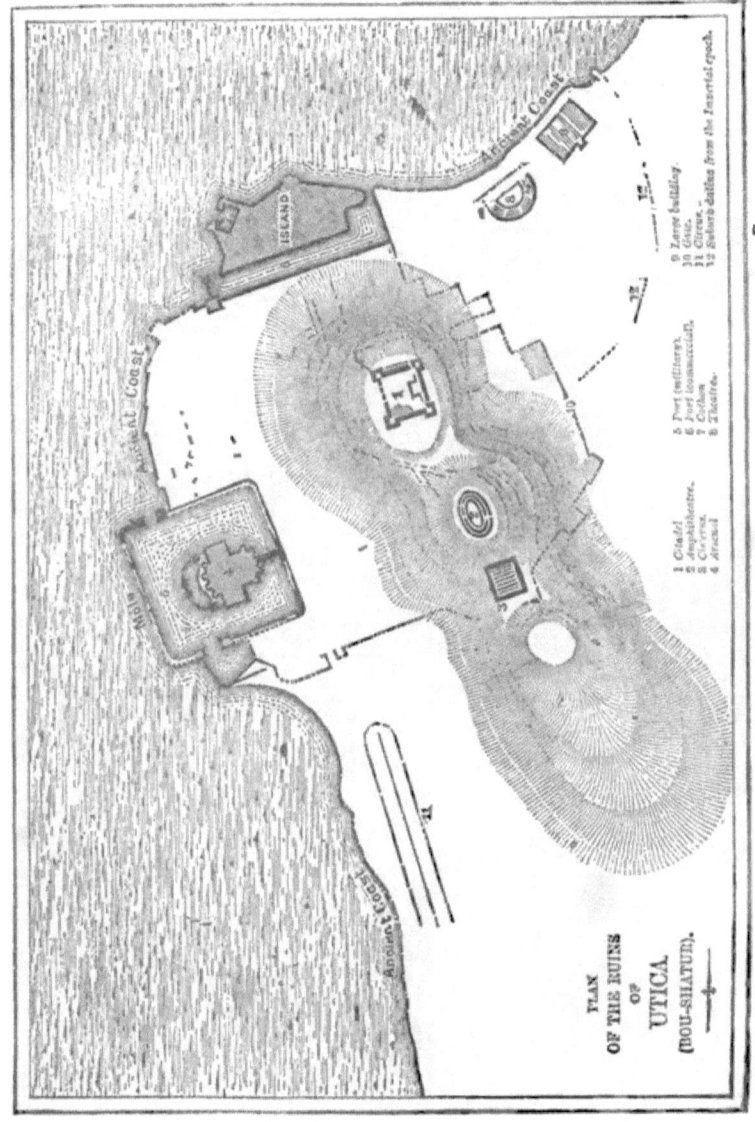

to make his way to Sicily. The army being thus abandoned, revenged itself by murdering his sons, and then made peace with Carthage. They gave up all the towns which they had captured, and received three hundred talents, a free passage for such as wished to go, and service in the army of Carthage for such as preferred to remain. The city had been besieged for four years. It was now safe, and, indeed, seems to have soon recovered her old strength. A few years afterwards we find her helping her old enemy Agathocles—in return, no doubt, for substantial advantages—to make himself supreme over Sicily.

The last Greek antagonist with whom Carthage had to deal might well have been the most formidable of all. Pyrrhus, king of Epirus,[1] was of the kindred of Alexander the Great, through Alexander's mother, Olympias. He had conceived a scheme of conquest which should be like that achieved by his famous kinsman. But as Alexander had gone eastward, so he would go westward. His famous conversation with his philosophical adviser will show us what were his plans, and I will give it, as Plutarch tells it, in dialogue form:

CINEAS. The Romans, my lord Pyrrhus, are said to be great warriors, and to rule over many nations. If, by the favour of God, we conquer them, what use shall we make of our victory?

PYRRHUS. That is an easy question to answer. There will be no city, Greek or barbarian, that, if Rome be once conquered, will be able to withstand us. We shall certainly gain the whole of Italy, of

[1] The modern Albania.

the greatness, excellence, and wealth of which you, of all men, cannot be ignorant.

Cineas (after a brief silence). After gaining Italy, what shall we do next?

Pyrrhus (not yet seeing his drift). Close to Italy is Sicily, stretching out her hands to us, a wealthy island and a populous, and easy to subdue. Since the death of Agathocles it has been all confusion, for lack of government in the city and the folly of them that lead the people.

Cineas. That is like enough. When we have conquered Sicily, shall we come to an end of our wars?

Pyrrhus. Heaven prosper our undertakings so far! Well, then, who would not go on to Africa and Carthage, Carthage which will then be in my grasp? Did not Agathocles, though he had to run away, so to speak, from Syracuse, with only a handful of ships, come very near to taking it?

We are not concerned just now with the rest of the conversation, or with the moral which Cineas drew from it.[1] It was a splendid plan, and Pyrrhus was one who had all the genius that was wanted to carry it out. Hannibal, no mean judge in such a matter, thought him the greatest general[2] that had ever lived. But the beginning of his great enterprise was the hardest part of it—too hard, indeed, for him to accomplish.

---

[1] Briefly it was this: "Master of Carthage," said Pyrrhus, "I shall come and make myself lord of Greece." "Doubtless," said Cineas; "and what then?" "Then," answered the king, with a laugh, "then we will sit down and enjoy ourselves." "Why not sit down now?" was the philosopher's reply.

[2] Another version of the story puts Alexander first and Pyrrhus second.

He spent his strength in vain on Rome. He defeated her armies, but he could not conquer her. Rome, we may say, saved Carthage from conquest. These two were to fight for the mastery of the West.

His own dealings with Carthage may be briefly told. After two campaigns in Italy, in which he had won much glory but little else, he passed over into Sicily in the spring of 278. The Greek cities had invited him to come; they wanted him to help them against their old enemy Carthage. At first he carried everything before him, but Carthage offered him a large sum of money and a fleet which should co-operate with him in his enterprises. He refused these terms. Nothing, he said, would satisfy him—and we cannot but admire his fine feeling for the honour of the Greek name—but that Carthage should quit the island altogether and make the sea the boundary between Greece and herself. After this his good fortune left him. The Greeks grew weary of their ally. They plotted against him, and he retaliated with severities which made them hate him still more. Then he failed in an attempt to storm the fortress of Lilybæum; and even his reputation as a soldier was damaged. At last there was nothing left for him but to go. "How fair a wrestling ring," he said, as he looked back from his ship upon the island; "how fair a wrestling ring, my friends, are we leaving to Rome and Carthage!" In the fourth part of my story I shall tell the tale of this wrestling match.

PART III.

THE INTERNAL HISTORY OF CARTHAGE.

    I.—Carthaginian Discoverers.
    II.—Constitution and Religion of Carthage.
    III.—Revenue and Trade of Carthage.

I.

CARTHAGINIAN DISCOVERERS.

THE "Story of Carthage" is mainly a story of war. Of the people themselves and of their life we hear very little indeed, and that little either from enemies or strangers. But there are some exceptions, and of them the most interesting is the account of the voyage of colonization and discovery made by Hanno, an account which has been preserved; not indeed in his own language—for of the Carthaginian tongue we have but a few words remaining—but in a Greek translation. The date of Hanno is not certain. He is supposed to have been either the father or the son of the Hamilcar who fell at Himera. There is little to make the one supposition more probable than the other. On the whole, I am inclined to accept the earlier time. Carthage was certainly more prosperous, and therefore more likely to send out such an expedition before the disaster of Himera than after it. In this case the date may be put as 520 B.C. Hanno's account of his voyage is interesting enough to be given in full. I shall add a few notes on points that seem to require explanation.

"It was decreed by the Carthaginians that Hanno

should sail[1] beyond the Pillars of Hercules[2] and found cities of the Liby-Phenicians.[3] Accordingly he sailed with sixty ships of fifty oars each, and a multitude of men and women to the number of thirty thousand,[4] and provisions and other equipment.

"When we had set sail and passed the Pillars, after two days' voyage, we founded the first city and named it Thymiaterium. Below this city lay a great plain. Sailing thence westward we came to Soloeis,[5] a promontory of Libya, thickly covered with trees. Here we built a temple to Poseidon;[6] and proceeded thence half-a-day's journey eastward, till we reached a lake lying not far from the sea, and filled with abundance of great reeds. Here were feeding elephants and a great number of other wild animals.

"After we had gone a day's sail beyond the lakes we founded cities near to the sea, of which the names were the Fort of Caricon, Gytta, Acra, Melita, and Arambys. Sailing thence we came to Lixus,[7] a

---

[1] The history of the voyage is called Periplus or "Circumnavigation." The Greek narrative exists in a MS. in the Library of Heidelberg, and was first published in 1533.

[2] The Straits of Gibraltar.

[3] A mixed population springing from marriages of Carthaginians with native Africans, and regarded with much jealousy by the authorities of Carthage.

[4] This number is probably exaggerated. It need not, however, be supposed that all the colonists were conveyed in the sixty ships. These were probably ships of war which convoyed a number of merchantmen, which discharged their cargoes of passengers as the various colonies were founded.

[5] Cape Cantin.

[6] The Latin Neptune, perhaps the Phœnician Dagon.

[7] The Wadi Draa.

great river which flows from Libya. On its banks the Lixitæ, a wandering tribe, were feeding their flocks. With these we made friendship, and remained among them certain days. Beyond these dwell the Inhospitable Æthiopians, inhabiting a country that abounds in wild beasts and is divided by high mountains, from which mountains flows, it is said, the river Lixus. About these mountains dwell the Troglodytæ, men of strange aspect.[1] Of these the Lixitæ said that they could run swifter than horses. Having procured interpreters from these same Lixitæ, we coasted for two days along an uninhabited country, going southwards. Thence again we sailed a day's journey eastward. Here in the recess of a certain bay we found a small island, about five furlongs in circumference. In this we made a settlement, and called its name Cerné.[2] We judged from our voyage that this place lay right opposite to Carthage,[3] for the voyage from Carthage to the Pillars was equal to the voyage from the Pillars to Cerné. After this, sailing up a great river which is called Chretes,[4] we came

[1] Possibly negroes.

[2] Cerné is probably to be placed at the mouth of the Rio de Ouro. Some of the French charts give the name of Herné, which is said to resemble a name used by the natives.

[3] There is some doubt as to the meaning of this expression. Mr. Bunbury suggests that it may mean that the distance from Carthage to the Straits of Gibraltar, and from the Straits again to Cerné being equal, these two would be the sides of an icosceles triangle, of which the base would be the line drawn between Carthage and Cerné. It must be remembered that the ancients had nothing like the correct notions which we have since been enabled to form of the relative positions of the various countries of the world. From Cerné Hanno made two voyages of discovery, which he now proceeds to describe.

[4] The Senegal, which opens out into such an expanse near its mouth.

to a lake, in which are three islands greater than Cerné. Proceeding thence a day's sail, we came to the furthest shore of the lake. Here it is overhung by great mountains, in which dwell savage men clothed with the skins of beasts. These drove us away, pelting us with stones, so that we could not land. Sailing thence, we came to another river, great and broad, and full of crocodiles and river-horses. Thence returning back we came again to Cerné; and from Cerné we sailed again towards the south for twelve days,

VOTIVE STELE FROM CARTHAGE (HIPPOPOTAMUS).

coasting along the land. The whole of this land is inhabited by Ethiopians. These would not await our approach, but fled from us; and their tongue could not be understood even by the Lixitæ that were with us. On the last day, we came near to certain large mountains covered with trees, and the wood of these trees was sweet-scented and of divers colours. Sailing by these mountains for the space of two days, we came

But there is a difficulty about the mountains, which it is not easy to identify with anything in the lower course of this river.

to a great opening of the sea; and on either side of this sea was a great plain, from which at night we saw fire arising in all directions. Here we watered, and afterwards sailed for five days, until we came to a great bay, which the interpreters told us was called the Western Horn.[1] In this bay was a large island, and in this island a lake of salt water, and again in this lake another island. Here we landed; and in the daytime we could find nothing, but saw wood ashes; but in the night we saw many fires burning, and heard the sound of flutes and cymbals and drums and the noise of confused shouts. Great fear then came upon us, and the prophet bade us leave this place. We sailed therefore quickly thence, being much terrified; and passing on for four days found at night a country full of fire. In the middle was a lofty fire, greater than all the rest, so that it seemed to touch the stars. When day came we found that this was a great mountain which they call the Chariot of the Gods.[2] On the third day of our departure thence, having sailed by streams of fire, we came to a bay which is called the Southern Horn.[3] At the end of this bay lay an island like to that which has been before described. This island had a lake, and in this lake another island, full of savage people, of whom the greater part were women. Their bodies were covered with hair, and our interpreters called them Gorillas. We pursued them, but the men we were not able to catch; for being able to climb the precipices and defending themselves with

---

[1] The Gulf of Bissagos.
[2] Mt. Sagres.
[3] Sherboro' Island and Sound, a little distance south of Sierra Leone.

stones, these all escaped. But we caught three women. But when these, biting and tearing those that led them, would not follow us, we slew them, and flaying off their skins, carried these to Carthage. Further we did not sail, for our food failed us."

This account was set, we are told, by Hanno on his return to Carthage in the temple of Chronos or Saturn —the same, as has been already said, as the Moloch of Scripture.

The elder Pliny, after mentioning the voyage of Hanno, which he strangely enough supposes to have extended as far as the borders of Arabia, says, "At the same time Himilco was sent to discover the northern coasts of Europe." Unhappily, we possess no account of Himilco's voyage that can be compared to the "Circumnavigation" of Hanno. All that we know of his narrative comes to us from Avienus, a very indifferent Latin poet, who wrote about geography towards the end of the fourth century of the Christian era. And what Avienus professes to quote from him has a very incredible look. It took him four months to sail from Carthage to a country which was probably Britain; not, as we might suppose, on account of rough seas and stormy winds, but because there are no breezes to make a ship move, or because there were such quantities of seaweed that it was held by them as much as if it were passing through a wood. Perpetual fogs covered everything. Besides these difficulties the sailor had to steel himself against the terrible sight of strange sea-monsters with which these waters abounded. Avienus professes to have seen the narrative of Himilco, and to quote from it directly.

The ancients were not very scrupulous in such matters, and it is just possible that Avienus took his information at second hand. It has been suggested that the Carthaginians, jealous about their trade and afraid that other dealers should meddle with their markets,[1] instructed Himilco to write such an account of his voyage as would deter every one else from following in his steps. It is certainly not sluggish seas and winds not strong enough to move a ship which are the obstacles a traveller sailing north would chiefly have to dread. However this may be, Himilco the discoverer is little more than a name to us.

[1] It may possibly have been one of the reasons why the Carthaginians were ready to attack the Phocæans at Alalia that these bold sailors had visited Tartessus (probably Gades), had made friends with its king, and so intruded into regions which the city of merchants considered to be its own.

II.

THE CONSTITUTION AND RELIGION OF CARTHAGE.

WE know something of the Constitution of Carthage, for Aristotle has given a chapter to the subject in his book bearing the title of "The Politics." This is itself a curious fact. The Greeks had but little esteem for any country besides their own—Egypt, from which they got most of their learning, perhaps excepted. And not only does he write at some length about it, but he praises it highly. He quotes and, on the whole, agrees with a general opinion that "in many respects it is superior to all others." And he gives very excellent reasons for this superiority. It is a sure proof, he thinks, "that a State is well ordered when the commons are steadily loyal to the constitution, when no civil conflict worth speaking of has arisen, and when no one has succeeded in making himself tyrant."

Aristotle speaks of Carthage having "kings," and this name as given to the chief magistrates of the city often occurs in history. But they were not kings in the common sense of the term. They did not resemble, for instance, the kings of the Eastern world, of Assyria, of Persia, or of Egypt. They are, indeed, expressly compared to the kings of Sparta; and these, we know, had but very limited power, and were little more than high priests and permanent commanders-in-chief. One important difference between the two constitutions was that, in Sparta, the dignity was hereditary in two families, while in Carthage it was elective. "They must belong," he says, "to one of certain distinguished families, but they succeed to the throne by election, not by seniority." But it does not appear that this election was annual. On the contrary, once chosen they were chosen for life. These two magistrates were called by the Romans "Suffetes,"[1] a corruption of the word Shophetim, or "Judges."

Next to the kings came the generals. The two offices might be held together, but they were often separate. A king did not command an army or a fleet unless he was specially appointed to the post. Sometimes a general would be made king while he was absent on service. Hanno, who commanded the great exploring and colonizing expedition before described, is said to have been a king.

Below these high officers of State came a legislative body which, to borrow a name made familiar both by ancient and by modern history, we may call the Senate. In this Senate there were two bodies, the smaller[2] and more powerful being chosen out of the larger. Perhaps we may compare this Upper Council

---

[1] Possibly "Suffetes" was a reminiscence of the Latin word *suffectus*, which was used when a magistrate was elected to fill a vacancy occurring at some casual time.

[2] It consisted of a hundred members.

to the cabinet or ministry in the Constitutions of England and the United States of America. We are told that it was called into existence to meet the danger which sooner or later overtook most of the Republics of the ancient world. "When the House of Mago became dangerous to a free state, an hundred judges were chosen from the senators, who, upon the return of generals from the war, should demand an account of things transacted by them, that they being thereby kept in awe, should so bear themselves in their command in the war, as to have regard to the laws at home." The members of the Council seem to have been chosen by what are called Pentarchies, *i.e.*, bodies of five, by the Greek writer. We do not know what these were, but we may guess that they were committees that had the charge of various important parts of government, as finances, trade, military matters, police, etc. Whether they were divisions of the Council or the Senate we cannot say. But one thing is certain,. viz., that the Council was a remarkably unchanging body. It followed one line of policy, we may say for centuries, with extraordinary consistency, and this it could hardly have done except it had kept up the same character by renewing itself. It is clear that there were no regular changes of government, no passings of power such as we see in the United States from Republicans to Democrats, or in England from Liberals to Conservatives.

About the powers of the larger assembly or Senate we know nothing for certain. Probably it was legislative while the Council was executive. It was the

Congress or Parliament, while the Council was the Ministry or Cabinet.

Finally, there was a general assembly of the people. About this, too, we know very little. We may guess that its power was limited to approving or rejecting measures that were brought before it, all such measures being first considered in the Senate. In the same way the people had the right of approving or disapproving of appointments to offices. Aristotle evidently thought that they were in much the same position as the people at Sparta; and of the people at Sparta we know that they had not much to do with the government of the country.

These were the actual "estates of the realm" in Carthage—the Kings or Suffetes, the Senate with its two chambers, so to speak, and the Popular Assembly. It remains to ask, "Was there a nobility?" Probably there was, and probably it was something like that which exists in England. There were, indeed, no inherited titles, but still the same families remained powerful in the State. Probably they remained powerful as long as they remained rich. There was no bar of birth that prevented any one from becoming a member of this nobility. Ability and wealth, perhaps either of these in a very marked degree, would pass any one into it.

Aristotle says that the offices of State were unpaid. This does not of necessity imply that these were not lucrative. They would bring patronage and opportunities of making money. He also says that the highest offices—and he names those of King and General—were put up for sale. Perhaps he means that they were obtained by bribery, though this is not the natural interpretation of his words. As he says afterwards that one of the abuses of the Carthaginian Constitution was that several offices were held by one man, we may suppose that though nominally unpaid, they could be, and often were, made a source of profit. Probably the decay of Carthage was due to the corruption and greed of money, which are sure to be developed sooner or later in a wealthy State. Rome, when the virtue and patriotism of its citizens decayed, fell into the hands of a despotic ruler; Carthage, following the same course of decay, fell under the domination of a few wealthy citizens.

One of the points of the resemblance which Aristotle sees between Carthage and Sparta was the practice of having Common Meals. But Sparta was a comparatively small State. The actual number of citizens living at the capital, when we have deducted those who were under or above the military age, and who were therefore excused from the Common Meals, could not have much exceeded a thousand. Carthage, on the other hand, was one of the most populous cities of the ancient world. When it was taken by the Romans, long after it had begun to decay, it contained seven hundred thousand inhabitants. How many of these were citizens we cannot conjecture; but the number must have been too great to admit of a system of Common Meals. Probably these were limited to the ruling class. Aristotle speaks of them as being held by the "clubs" or "companies." What Livy says quite agrees with this. Hannibal, then in exile, sent an emissary to stir up the war-party at Carthage

VOTIVE STELE TO TANIT.

to action. His coming and the message which he brought, was, we read, "debated first in societies and banquets, and afterwards in the Senate." And we find it stated by another historian that the Carthaginians transacted their State affairs by night, and in the evening and at night-time held their meetings and societies. Perhaps we may say that modern politics furnish an illustration in the "Caucus," a meeting of influential persons by which the action of the party is determined.

Justice seems to have been administered, not by a general assembly of the people, as at Athens, but by special Courts. We know the name of one of these, "The Hundred and Four."[1] Possibly this may have been the title of the whole judicial body, and that this was divided into various Courts for the trial of different kinds of cases.

The Religion of Carthage was naturally in the main that of the great city from which it was founded. The supreme Deity was Baal Hammon, or Moloch. Dr. Davis—from whose excavations among the ruins of Carthage much has, of course, been learnt—tells us that he did not find a single votive tablet in which the name of this god did not appear. He was worshipped with the horrible human sacrifices of which we hear from time to time in Carthaginian history.[2] These

[1] Not to be confounded with the Council of the Hundred.
[2] When Carthage was besieged by Agathocles, a sacrifice of two hundred children belonging to the first families in the country was made to Moloch; and three hundred men also voluntarily devoted themselves in the same way. We hear of these sacrifices as prevailing among the Canaanite, *i.e.* Phœnician, tribes whom the Israelites drove out of Palestine; and special care was taken to forbid this particular

dreadful practices caused the Greeks to identify him with Chronos or Saturn, who, in their own mythology, was said to have devoured his own children.

Next in honour to Moloch was Melcart, the tutelary deity of Carthage, as he was of its mother-city, Tyre

A STELE TO TANIT.

To the Greeks he was known as Hercules. His

kind of rite. So we read in Lev. xviii. 21, "Thou shalt not let thy seed pass through the fire to Moloch." In spite of this prohibition the practice gained ground among the Israelites. Solomon built a temple to Moloch; and the reformer Josiah "defiled the Valley of Hinnom that no man might make his son or his daughter pass through the fire to Moloch."

VOTIVE STELE TO TANIT FROM CARTHAGE.

splendid temple at Tyre was one of the most famous in the world. Missions with gifts and offerings seem to have been regularly sent to it from Carthage. Neither there nor elsewhere does the god seem to have been represented in human form. Herodotus, who describes the Tyrian temple as an eye-witness, says nothing of any image, but describes, among the many rich offerings with which it was adorned, two pillars, one of pure gold, the other of emerald, shining with great brilliancy at night.[1]

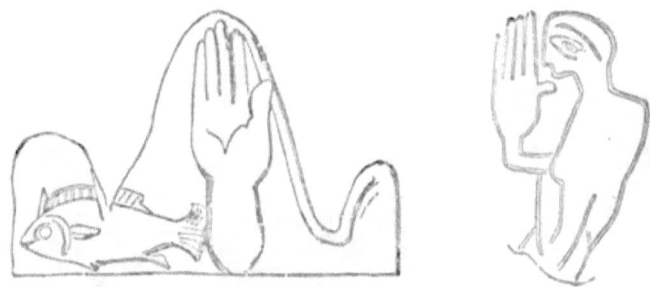

VOTIVE STELES FROM CARTHAGE.

A sea-god, whom the Greeks naturally identified with their own Poseidon, and the Romans with Neptune, was worshipped at Carthage. He was the same probably as Dagon, the fish-god, whom we know to have been worshipped in the cities of the Philistines. Ashtaroth, the Greek form of whose name was Astarte, corresponded to Aphrodite or Venus. Her Carthaginian name was Tanit. Of another Carthaginian deity, known to the Greeks as Triton,

[1] This was probably of green glass, which had long before been manufactured in Egypt, and was lighted from within.

we cannot recover the native name. As the Greek Triton was a god of the sea, possibly this was only another form of Dagon. We do not hear of any separate order of priests; but we find kings and generals offering sacrifice—sometimes, as in the case of Hasdrubal at Himera,[1] while battle was actually going on.

[1] See p. 27

III.

THE REVENUE AND TRADE OF CARTHAGE.

THE revenue of Carthage came from various sources which may be mentioned in order.

1. *Tribute from subject or dependent countries.* The Phœnician towns on the coast of Africa, both those which were older than Carthage and those which had been founded from it, paid tribute in money.

CARTHAGINIAN COIN.

Leptis, for instance, in the rich district of the Lesser Syrtis, is said to have paid as much as a talent per diem.[1] The tribes of the interior paid their tribute in kind, those who were settled and employed in cultivating the ground furnishing corn, the wandering tribes such articles as dates, wild-beast skins, gold,

[1] This would amount to £89,968 15s., or nearly $450,000.

precious stones, etc. The foreign possessions of the empire also paid in kind. Part of the stores which they thus furnished was laid up in the provinces

CARTHAGINIAN COIN (ELECTRUM).

themselves for the use of the army, and part was sent to Carthage. The amount of these contributions is not stated anywhere; but it seems to have varied with

CARTHAGINIAN COIN (SILVER).

the needs of the government, and sometimes to have amounted to as much as a half of the whole produce.

2. *Customs duties* are mentioned in the treaties between Carthage and Rome; and the regulations about

them are precise. In the treaties with the Etrurians, of which we hear from Aristotle, we learn that it was provided what articles might and what might not be imported. Hannibal, when in power at Carthage after the end of the Second Punic War, introduced a great reform into the management of the customs, which we learn from this passage to have been levied on goods imported both by land and by sea; and is said, by putting a stop to dishonest practices, to have improved the revenue so much, that it was no longer necessary to tax individuals. That these duties were heavy, we may learn from the fact that smuggling went on between the Greek towns in the district round Cyrene and the towns dependent on Carthage.

3. *Mines.* Carthage possessed mines in Spain and Corsica. The richest of these were in the neighbourhood of New Carthage. In Polybius' time (204-122 B.C.), when they were worked by the Romans, they produced about £2,000 per day. They are said to have been discovered by a certain Aletes, who was supposed to have done so much for his country by this discovery, that a temple was dedicated to him at New Carthage. We must not suppose, however, that all the mines (Diodorus says that all the mines known in his time were first worked by the Carthaginians) belonged to the State. Many of them were worked by individual citizens to their great profit. The powerful Barca family is said to have derived from their mines much of the wealth by which they were enabled to become so powerful, and Hannibal is specially mentioned as receiving a large income from mines. Probably the State was the owner of some, and re-

ceived a royalty (or sum proportionate to the quantity of metal raised) from the others.

The Commerce of Carthage may be conveniently considered under its two great branches—the trade with Africa, and the trade with Europe.

1. The trade with Africa. This was carried on with the barbarous tribes of the inland country that could be reached by caravans, and of the sea-coast. Of both we hear something from Herodotus, the writer who furnishes us with most of our knowledge about these parts of the ancient world. His story about the dealings with the tribes of the sea-coast runs thus. "There is a certain country in Africa outside the columns of Hercules. When the Carthaginians come hither, they unlade their goods and set them in order by the side of the sea. This done, they embark on their ships again and make a smoke. And the people of the country, seeing the smoke, come down to the sea, and put gold beside the goods and depart to a distance. Then the Carthaginians come forth from their ships and look; and if it seem to them that the gold is of equal value with the goods, they take it and depart; but if it seem not equal, then they return to their ships and sit still. Then the barbarians come and add other gold to that which they put before, until they persuade the Carthaginians. And neither do any wrong to the other; for the one touch not the gold till it be made equal in value to the goods, and the others touch not the goods before the sellers have received the gold."[1] The Caravan routes are

---

[1] Heeren quotes from **Captain Lynn's** " Narrative " a curiously similar account. "In Soudan, beyond the desert, in the countries abound-

described in a very interesting passage. The starting-point is Thebes in Upper Egypt, where Herodotus probably got his information; and the route, in which the stations—always places where water can be found—are given with much detail, extend to the Straits of Gibraltar in the west, and Fezzan, and probably still more inland places, in the south.

The goods with which the Carthaginian merchants traded with the African tribes were doubtless such as those which civilized nations have always used in their dealings with savages. Cheap finery, gaudily coloured cloths, and arms of inferior quality, would probably be their staple. Salt, too, would be an important article. Many of the inland tribes can only get this necessary of life by importation, and the Carthaginians would doubtless find it worth their while to bring it, not necessarily from the sea, but from places on the route where, according to Herodotus, it could be found in large quantities.

The articles which they would receive in exchange for their goods are easily enumerated. In the first place comes, as we have seen, gold. Carthage seems to have had always at hand an abundant supply of the precious metal for use, whether as money or as plate. Next to gold would come slaves. Even then the negro race was the victim of the cruel system which has not yet quite been rooted out of the world,

ing in gold, there dwells an invisible nation, who are said to trade only by night. Those who come to traffic for their gold, lay their merchandise in heaps and retire. In the morning they find a certain quantity of gold-dust placed against every heap, which if they think sufficient, they leave the goods; if not, they let both remain until more of the precious ore is added."

though no Christian nation, at least ostensibly, practises it. The ancients, indeed, had other slaves besides negroes. It was a horrible feature of the slavery of these times that, through the practice of selling, for private or public gain, prisoners of war and the inhabitants of captured towns, men and women of every race were reduced to bondage, and thus the slave might be as well born and as well educated as his master.[1] But these slaves were sure to be discontented, and very likely, therefore, to be dangerous, and the more gentle and docile negro soon came to be prized. Fashion, too, favoured the quaint appearance of the race, so curiously contrasted with the fair complexion and chiselled features of the Greek. Thus in Menander (342–291 B.C.), as he is represented to us by Terence, we find a soldier saying to his lady-love, "Did you ever find my good will to you halt? When you said you wanted a handmaid from Ethiopia, did not I give up all my business, and find one for you?"

Ivory must have been another article of Carthaginian trade, though we hear little about it. The Greeks used it extensively in art, making some of their most magnificent statues partly of it and partly of gold;[2] and it seems to have been employed in early

---

[1] One Latin writer draws a distinction between slaves that were "learned" and that "had a smattering of learning." All the early schoolmasters at Rome, almost without exception, had been slaves. The elder Cato made a profit of taking in noble Roman boys to be taught by an educated slave of his own.

[2] The great statues of Phidias, viz., of Zeus at Olympia, of Here at Argos, and of Athene at Athens, were made of these two materials, and therefore called chryselephantine.

times at Rome for the chairs of state used by the higher magistrates. We do not precisely know where this ivory came from first. Virgil speaks of the substance as coming from India, and the elder Pliny says that the luxury of his times had exhausted all the sources of supply except those of the farthest East. We may be certain, however, that in the flourishing days of Carthage her traders dealt largely in this article, which indeed is found of the largest size and finest quality in Africa. The elephant is still found

VOTIVE STELE FROM CARTHAGE.

over the whole of that continent south of the Sahara, except where it has been driven away by the neighbourhood of man. The Carthaginians had domesticated it, a thing which has never since been done by any African race.

Precious stones seem to have been another article which the savages gave in exchange for the goods they coveted. The carbuncle, in particular, came in such abundance from Carthage into the markets of Europe that it was called the " Carthaginian Stone." Perhaps we may add *dates* to the list of articles obtained from the interior.

The European trade dealt, of course, partly with the things already mentioned, and partly with other articles for which the Carthaginian merchants acted as carriers, so to speak, from one part of the Mediterranean to another. Lipara, and the other volcanic islands near the southern extremity of Italy, produced resin; Agrigentum, and possibly other cities of Sicily, traded in sulphur brought down from the region of Etna; wine was produced in many of the Mediterranean countries. Wax and honey were the staple goods of Corsica. Corsican slaves, too, were highly valued. The iron of Elba, the fruit and the cattle of the Balearic islands, and, to go further, the tin and copper of Britain, and even amber from the Baltic, were articles of Carthaginian commerce. Trade was carried on not only with the dwellers on the coast, but with inland tribes. Thus goods were transported across Spain to the interior of Gaul, the jealousy of Massilia (Marseilles) not permitting the Carthaginians to have any trading stations on the southern coast of that country.

While we are writing of trade, we must not omit to mention a curious statement about what has been called the "leather money" of Carthage. The work from which it comes bears the name of Æschines, a disciple of Socrates. It is certainly not of his time, but it is probably ancient. "The Carthaginians," says this author, whoever he may have been, "make use of the following kind of money: in a small piece of leather a substance is wrapped of the size of a

ART AND LITERATURE.

piece of four drachmæ (about 3s.); but what this substance is no one knows except the maker. After this it is sealed and issued for circulation; and he who possesses the most of this is regarded as having the most money, and as being the wealthiest man. But if any one among us had ever so much, he would be no richer than if he possessed a quantity of pebbles." This unknown substance was probably an alloy of metal, of which the ingredients were a State secret; and the seal was a State mark. We have, in fact, here a kind of clumsy banknote.

Of Carthaginian art and literature there is little to be said. The genius of the Phœnicians did not lead them to distinguish themselves in either way. As for art, whatever grace is to be found in the scanty remains that are left to us of Carthaginian civilization, is clearly due to Greek influence. The coins, for instance, that are figured on pp. 115, 116, are evidently the work of Greek artists. About Carthaginian literature we cannot speak so positively. That there were libraries in the city

WRITING-CASE.

when it was taken by the Romans, we know for certain, as we also know that the conquerors were not sufficiently aware of their value to keep them for themselves, but allowed them to be dispersed among the African princes. But whether these libraries contained a native Carthaginian literature, or were furnished with the production of Greek genius, we do not know. Of one Carthaginian work, indeed, we know something. We have its subject, the name of its author, and, it may also be said, its opening sentence. It was a book on agriculture,

VOTIVE STELE (BULL).

written by one Mago, and it began, it is said, with the remark that he who would make his farm prosper should sell his town-house. So high a reputation had it obtained, that when Carthage was taken, the Roman Senate appointed a committee to look after its translation into Latin. It was afterwards translated into Greek. Roman writers made much use of it, and Cicero speaks of it as the standard work on its subject.

Of the domestic life of the Carthaginians we know almost nothing. Where there is great wealth there is sure to be great luxury. Of this we get, indeed, a few hints from the historians. We have seen, for instance, how, when one of the Carthaginian generals were pressed for arrears of pay by his mercenaries, he was able to give them security in the rich gold and silver drinking-cups which belonged to the Carthaginians on his staff. And Athenæus, a great collector of gossip on all such matters, tells us that Dionysius sold a splendid robe to a Carthaginian millionaire for a hundred and twenty talents—the almost incredible sum of nearly thirty thousand pounds. And it seems to have been also true that in Carthage, as elsewhere, "where wealth accumulates men decay." Political and military talent she could always command, but she trusted more and more to her mercenaries, to those "silver spears" which are sure, sooner or later, to break in the day of need.

PART IV.

CARTHAGE AND ROME.

For the First and Second Punic Wars our chief authorities are Polybius and Livy. The first was a Greek, and a great friend of the younger Scipio, the conqueror of Carthage. He was present at the capture of that city, but unfortunately the part of his work which relates that event, and the history of the Third Punic War generally, is lost. For the First Punic War, which is the chief subject of the introductory chapters of his work, and for the Second, he is our best authority, so far as he goes. Here, again, unfortunately, much is lost; indeed, we have no complete book after the fifth, and this takes us a little farther than the battle of Cannæ. Considerable extracts have, however, been preserved of the lost books, among them one containing a description of the battle of Zama. Polybius was an admirable historian, painstaking and just in the highest degree.

Livy (Titus Livius) lived in the last days of the Roman Republic and the first of the Empire, since he was born B.C. 59, the very time of the first Triumvirate, and died in the fourth year of Tiberius. He wrote a history of Rome in one hundred and forty-two books, of which thirty-five only survive. Happily the ten books, twenty-one to thirty, which give a detailed account of the Second Punic War from the beginning to the end, have been preserved, and epitomes of the lost books exist, from which we get some valuable information about the First and Third wars. Livy is a great writer; some excellent judges have even said that his style is the very best to be found among prose writers ancient or modern. It is certainly full of vigour and beauty; but Livy is not a great historian. He was very careless, never taking the pains, so far as we can learn, to visit the scenes of the events which he describes, though they must often have been within his reach, or attempting to realize them to himself. For the Third Punic War our chief authority is Appian, a native of Alexandria, who wrote there, in Greek, a Roman history, in which he treated the affairs of every country separately.

I.

THE WAR IN SICILY AND ON THE SEA.

WE have heard more than once of Campanians among the mercenaries who were accustomed to fight both for Greece and for Carthage in the Sicilian wars. They seem to have been particularly unscrupulous, for they would change sides when changing sides seemed likely to give them better pay or better prospects of victory. And this habit of theirs agrees with the bad account we get of them in other ways. These Campanians let out their swords for hire, not so much because they were poor (as did the Arcadians in ancient times, and the Swiss and Scotch in modern Europe), as because they liked the life of a soldier of fortune. They were the youth of a dissolute people,[1] and, not able to find the career they liked at home, where they would have had to deal with the Romans, they sought it abroad, and, as we have seen, especially in Sicily. We shall not be surprised, therefore, to find some of these Campanians behaving in a most cruel and unscrupulous way to one of the Greek cities. After the death of Agathocles, who,

[1] Capua, the chief city of Campania, had a very bad reputation in this way.

tyrant as he was, was a man of energy, affairs in Sicily had fallen into a state of great confusion. Among other causes of trouble was a *corps* of Campanian mercenaries, who had been in the service of the tyrant, and who, after his death, asserted their independence, and set up in the trade of brigands. They seized the city of Messana, slew or drove out the citizens, and divided among themselves everything that they possessed. For a time the Mamertines, or "Servants of Mars"[1] (for this was the name that the robbers had assumed), prospered greatly, spreading their power over the neighbouring portion of the island. Then came a check. Syracuse had again fallen into the hands of an able ruler, one Hiero, of whom we shall often hear again. Hiero reduced the Mamertines to great straits, and they looked about in despair for some one who could help them.

There were two parties among them, one favouring Carthage, the other Rome. At first the latter prevailed. An embassy was sent, offering submission and begging for help. The request perplexed the Romans not a little. It was quite a new thing for them to look beyond the limits of Italy. There they were now supreme; but they dreaded undertaking conquests outside it. And to grant this request would of course embroil them with Carthage. On the other hand, Carthage would become a dangerous enemy if it were allowed to possess itself of Messana. It would only have to conquer Syracuse to make itself master of Sicily. The Senate debated the question more than once without coming to any decision.

[1] "Mamers" is an Italian form of "Mars."

Besides their fear of a new enterprise, they had, we may hope, some scruple about taking to themselves such very discreditable allies. From the Senate the matter was referred to the people, and the people felt neither the fear nor the scruple, but resolved that help should be sent, and that the Mamertines should be received as allies.

Meanwhile the other party at Messana had been busy. They applied for help to Carthage; and Carthage at once sent it. A peace was made with Hiero, who was besieging the city. A fleet sailed into the harbour, and a body of troops under Hanno occupied the citadel. When the Romans, who were under the command of Appius Claudius, one of the Consuls of the year, arrived, they found themselves anticipated. Unfortunately for Carthage, both the officers in charge of the fleet and Hanno were wanting in foresight or resolution. The former was seized at a meeting of the citizens to which he had gone in the hope of keeping the peace; the latter consented to give up the citadel if he were permitted to withdraw with his garrison. Then the Romans became masters of Messana without having to strike a single blow for it.

The Carthaginians were not disposed to accept this state of things. Hanno they crucified as having shown in his conduct neither courage nor good judgment. Then, in concert with Hiero, they closely invested the city. Claudius attempted to make terms; he was even willing to depart, if the Mamertines might be allowed to remain. When these terms were rejected he resolved to act. He marched out of the city and offered battle. Hiero accepted it, but after a long fight was driven back into his camp. The next day he returned to Syracuse. Appius followed up his victory, attacking and routing the Carthaginian army, which immediately raised the siege of the city. The next year a larger army was sent; Hiero, who had the sagacity to see with whom the victory was most likely to be, submitted to Rome, becoming one of its most constant and useful allies. Many other cities, both Sicilian and Carthaginian, followed this example. Carthage, on the other hand, increased her forces in the island, making Agrigentum the base of her operations and the place in which her military stores were kept.

The next year the Romans besieged Agrigentum, and kept the garrison closely within the walls. After a blockade which lasted five months, Hannibal, one of the Suffetes, who was in command, found himself sorely pressed by famine, and sent urgent entreaties to Carthage for help. In answer to these requests, a considerable body of troops, with a number of elephants, was sent to Sicily. Hanno, who commanded the Carthaginian army in the field, was rendered superior in force to the Romans by this reinforcement. He cut off their supplies and reduced them to great straits. Indeed, but for the help of Hiero they could not have held out. Hanno now thought it time to attack the enemy. He sent on his African light-horse in advance, with orders to provoke the Roman cavalry to an engagement, and by retiring before them to draw them within reach of his whole army. The stratagem succeeded. The Romans sallied furiously from their camp, drove the Africans before them, and then, finding themselves in presence of Hanno's army, were themselves driven back.

For two months the two armies lay quiet, with a space of about a mile between them. Meanwhile the famine in the city grew worse, and Hannibal, by fire signals from the city (for the Carthaginians seem to have had some system of telegraphing), and by messengers, made his colleague aware that he could hold out no longer. The Romans were scarcely less in need, so that both parties were eager to fight. The battle that followed was long and obstinate. At last the Carthaginian mercenaries, who composed the front line, gave way, fell back upon the elephants behind them, and threw the whole army into disorder. Only a small part of the troops escaped. But Hannibal with the garrison of Agrigentum was more fortunate. Seeing that the Romans, rejoicing in their victory, were guarding their lines very carelessly, he made his way through undiscovered. The next day the Romans marched into Agrigentum, where they found abundance of spoil and many prisoners of war.

After this success the Romans began to think that then it was within their power to make themselves masters of the island. But the great obstacle was that Carthage was still mistress of the sea, and that even their own coasts were not safe from the ravages of her fleet. If their hope was to be fulfilled they must have a fleet of their own. Ships of course they had, for the treaties[1] with Carthage, made hundreds of years before, had set limits beyond which they

[1] See pp. 14-16.

should not go; possibly they had ships of war; but they had nothing which they could match against the great five-banked vessels of the enemy. Fortunately one of these came into their possession, stranded by a storm or in an attack made upon their transports. This they used as a model for their shipbuilders. In the course of a few weeks, a hundred five-banked and twenty three-banked vessels were built—of green wood, it is said, and not likely to last, but still sufficient for their purpose.

The first attempt of the new force was not fortunate. A squadron of seventeen ships was taken at Lipara, with one of the consuls, who was in command. But the Carthaginians soon found that the Romans were quite as formidable by sea as by land. Their admiral, Hannibal, who was reconnoitring with fifty ships, fell in unexpectedly with a superior force of the Romans, lost the greater part of his fleet, and barely escaped himself. Still, the greater experience of their seamen would have given them the advantage but for the device by which their enemies contrived to make a sea-fight very much like a fight on dry land. Every Roman ship was filled with a boarding apparatus. It was like a gangway, eighteen feet long and four feet broad, and was attached to a pillar of wood set up by the bowsprit, from which it was dropped when the two ships came in contact. The further end was furnished with a sharpened bar of iron, which was driven by the force of the fall into the enemy's deck, and held it fast. If the ships were laid broadside to broadside, the boarders jumped from all parts of their own ship on to that of the enemy; if prow only

DUILIAN COLUMN.

touched prow, they went two and two along the gangway.

The new apparatus was soon brought into use. Hannibal (the same commander who had escaped from Agrigentum) encountered the Roman Consul Duilius, and despising his enemy, bore down upon him without taking the trouble to form his fleet in order. The front ships, as soon as they came near the Romans, were grappled by the new machines, and the boarding parties poured in from the Roman vessels. The Carthaginians were taken by surprise and overpowered, and lost all the thirty ships that composed the van. The rest of the fleet fared little better. Whenever they tried to approach, the grappling-irons hung over them. In the end they fled with the loss of fifty more ships; Hannibal escaping in an open boat. This battle of Mylæ was one of the turning points of the long struggle between the two powers. Carthage had ruled the sea for centuries, and now it was beaten by a foe who had first taken to it only a few months before.[1]

It is needless to give all the details of the long struggle that followed. Hannibal met with his end in the year of his defeat at Mylæ. He had sailed to Sardinia, and was there surprised by the Roman fleet, losing many of his ships. As usual he escaped, but this time in vain. He was seized by the survivors and crucified.

[1] Duilius received high honours at Rome, a triumph, a column adorned with the beaks of the captured vessels, and the singular privilege of being accompanied by a torch-bearer and a flute-player when he was coming home from dinner at night.

The next two years the war dragged on in Sicily without any decisive event, though the advantage was for the most part with Rome. But in 256 a great battle was fought. The Roman Government, weary of these tedious campaigns, resolved to carry the war into Africa, and attack their enemy at home. With this end in view they collected a fleet of as many as three hundred and thirty decked ships. On these they embarked their best troops. Each vessel had a crew of three hundred seamen, and carried a complement of one hundred and twenty soldiers. The Carthaginian force was still larger, numbering three hundred and fifty ships, and one hundred and fifty thousand men. The two fleets met at Ecnomus, a promontory of the southern coast of Sicily.

The Roman fleet was formed in the shape of a triangle, with the apex or point towards the enemy. At this point were the two huge ships, each rowed by six banks of oars, in which sailed the two Roman Consuls—Atilius Regulus, of whom we shall hear again, and Manlius. Each side of this triangle was made up of a squadron; a third squadron, which held the transports containing the cavalry in tow, formed the base; and there was yet a fourth, a reserve, ranged in one long line so as to cover both flanks of the squadrons before them.

The Carthaginians adopted very different tactics. They arranged their ships in what may be called open order, extending their line from the shore far out to sea with the view of surrounding the enemy. The shore squadron, or left wing, was under the command of Hamilcar; the rest of the fleet was led by the

Hanno whose army had been defeated before Agrigentum. The Roman fleet began the attack. Seeing that the enemy had but a weak line of single ships, they bore down upon the centre. Hamilcar had foreseen this, and had given orders to his officers to retreat as soon as the attack should be made. This was done, and with the expected result. The Romans eagerly pursued the flying enemy; their order of battle was broken, the two squadrons in advance being separated from the third (that which had the transports in tow) and from the reserve. Then the retreating Carthaginians turned upon their pursuers. An obstinate fight followed; the Carthaginians had the advantage in seamanship and in the speed of their ships. But do what they might, they hardly dared to come to close quarters. The Roman ships were fitted with the dreaded grappling and boarding machines. If these were once brought into use the battle had to be fought by the soldiers, and there was no chance of standing against the soldiers of Rome.

While this struggle was going on, another commenced in the rear of the Roman fleet. Hanno bore down with his ships upon the reserve squadron and threw it into confusion. And then began a third, the left or in-shore wing of the Carthaginian fleet attacking the squadron which had the transports attached to it. But the Roman superiority was maintained everywhere. At close quarters the Carthaginians could not hold their own, and though here and there they might sink a ship by a sudden skilful charge, to close quarters they were bound sooner or later to come. Hamilcar was the first to retreat; then Hanno, who had been pressing hard on the transport squadron and the reserve, was attacked in his turn and forced to fly. Thus the Romans won the second great naval victory. Twenty-six of their ships had been sunk, but none were taken. The Carthaginians lost about a hundred, as many as sixty-four having been captured with all their crews. Those that escaped were scattered in all directions, and there was now nothing to prevent the Romans from invading Africa.

II.

THE INVASION OF AFRICA.

HANNO hastened home with the news of the disaster of Ecnomus (though home, as we have seen, was not the place to which a defeated Carthaginian general would naturally desire to go), and bade his countrymen prepare for defence. But Carthage was, now as ever, almost helpless when attacked in her own dominions. Her subjects were always disaffected and ready to rebel; and even her own colonies were not permitted to protect themselves with walls. No resistance could be offered to the invaders, who found the country much the same as Agathocles had found it fifty years before, a singularly rich and perfectly defenceless region. They collected a rich booty, part of which consisted of as many as twenty thousand slaves. It is possible that if, instead of busying themselves with plunder, they had advanced on Carthage at once, they might have finished the war at a single blow.

If this had ever been possible, it certainly ceased to be so when an order came from the Senate at Rome that one of the consuls was to remain in Africa with such forces as might be necessary to finish the war, while the other was to return home with the rest of the expedition. Regulus was left accordingly with fifteen thousand infantry and six hundred horse and a squadron of forty ships; the rest of the force, with the vast booty that had been collected, Manlius put on shipboard and carried back to Italy.

RESERVOIRS OF CARTHAGE.

The Carthaginians, on the other hand, were doing their best to strengthen their force. They appointed two new generals, and sent for a third from Sicily, who at once came back, bringing with him between five and six thousand men. It seems strange that the Romans, who must now have been masters of the sea, made no attempt to interrupt him. On his arrival the Carthaginians resolved to take the offensive. The wealthy citizens could not bear to see their estates plundered and their country houses burnt to the ground, and resolved to risk a battle. What might have been the result if they had had skilful generals is doubtful; but, unfortunately, skilful generals could not be found. Hamilcar and his colleagues marched out of the city and took up their position upon a hill. As their strength was in cavalry and elephants they

CROSS SECTION OF CISTERN WALL. FROM DAUX.

ought, of course, to have remained on level ground, where both these could have been brought into use. The Roman general, whose military ability was great, saw his advantage. Half the enemy's force was useless in the position which he was occupying, and in that position he resolved to attack him. He ordered a simultaneous advance against both sides of the hill on which the Carthaginian camp was pitched. The cavalry and the elephants were, as he had foreseen, quite useless; and though some of the mercenaries stood firm against the first charge, these too gave way when they were taken in the rear. The Romans won a decided victory, though they were too weak in cavalry to inflict much loss upon the enemy in his retreat. The next day they advanced and took up a position at Tunes, a town which, as we have seen, was not more than five miles from Carthage.

The Carthaginians were in despair. Both their fleet and their army had suffered terrible defeats, and their subjects and allies were in rebellion—the Africans ravaging the territory of their late masters even more mercilessly than did the Romans. In fact they had nothing left to them but the city itself; and this, crowded with the multitude of fugitives that had fled into it from all the country round about, was threatened with famine. Affairs were in this condition when envoys arrived from Regulus, who was afraid that his year of office might expire before the war was finished, offering to treat for peace. Envoys were at once sent from Carthage; but they could do nothing. The Roman general, probably aware that the Senate at home would not sanction any great concessions, demanded terms which it was impossible to grant. The Carthaginian government felt that they could not be more entirely humiliated by absolute conquest, and they broke off the negotiation, resolving to resist to the last.

Then came one of those singular turns of fortune of which history is so full. The pride of the Roman general was "the pride that goeth before a fall." The Carthaginians had not hesitated to use their almost boundless wealth in hiring mercenaries from abroad, and now there came to Africa a body of these troops in command of one of those soldiers of fortune who have had the luck to have great opportunities and to make good use of them. Xantippus came from the best school of soldiers in the world—Sparta. It was a Spartan who had turned the tide when Athens seemed likely to conquer Syracuse; and another Spartan was to do the same service for Carthage against Rome. Xantippus heard the story of the late battle; he saw the strength of the Carthaginian forces, the numbers of their cavalry and of their elephants, and he came to the conclusion—a conclusion which he did not hesitate to announce to his friends—that their disasters had been due, not to the inferiority of their army, but to the unskilfulness of the generals. The Senate sent for him. Introduced into the council-chamber, he set forth the causes of the late defeat, and the strategy which ought to be pursued in the future, with such clearness as to convince his hearers. The generals were displaced, and the "care of the army was committed" to the Spartan.

Every one hoped much from the change, and Xantippus soon began to show himself equal to his task. Even in drilling the troops—and this he began to do at once—his skill was so manifestly superior to that of his colleagues, that the soldiers began to feel the utmost confidence in him. They loudly asked that they might be led against the enemy, and that the general who was to lead them should be Xantippus. The other generals offered to give up their commands to their comrade; and the army, which numbered twelve thousand foot and four thousand horse, and which was accompanied by the enormous number of a hundred elephants,[1] was led out against the enemy. Xantippus arranged the elephants in a single line in front. Behind these he placed what Polybius calls "the Carthaginian phalanx." Probably the desperate condition of the country had brought a force of native Carthaginians into the field. On the right wing were posted the heavy-armed mercenaries. With them were ranged also some of the light-armed troops and of the cavalry. The left wing was made up entirely of the two latter kinds of troops.

Regulus, on the other hand, when he saw that the Carthaginians were bent on fighting, arranged his line of battle with the special view of holding his ground against the elephants, which his men greatly feared. The light-armed troops were, as usual, posted in front; but behind them stood the legions in unusually deep and close order. The cavalry were posted as usual on the wings. These tactics were well contrived to resist the elephants, but laid the army, with its narrow front, open to the flank attacks of the powerful Carthaginian cavalry.

Xantippus began the battle by a forward movement of his elephants against the Roman centre. His cavalry charged at the same time on either wing. The Roman horse, five hundred only against four thousand—

---

[1] It is not easy to imagine how a city which was threatened with famine could support a hundred elephants, each of which must have required a daily ration of at least half a hundredweight of food, some of it at least available for human consumption.

if these numbers are right—was speedily overpowered. The Roman left wing at first fared better. Charging fiercely, with not the less zeal because they were not called to encounter the dreaded elephants, they fell on the heavy-armed mercenaries, routed them, and pursued them as far as their camp. The centre, too, held its own for a time. The front ranks, indeed, were trampled down in heaps by the elephants, but the main body, with its deep, close files, stood firm. But they had to face about to resist attacks in front, on the sides, and in the rear. One part, after driving back the elephants, was met by the phalanx of native Carthaginians, which was fresh and unbroken, and indeed had not been in action at all; another had to resist the furious charges of the cavalry; nor were there any reserves to be brought up. The greater part of the army fell where they stood: some crushed by the elephants, others struck down by the javelins showered on them by the nimble African horsemen, some slain in more equal conflict with the Carthaginian heavy-armed. The few that sought safety in flight died but with less honour. The way to the fortified post which they held upon the sea-coast (it was called Aspis or Clypea from its resemblance to a shield) was over a flat and open country; the cavalry and the elephants pursued the fugitives, and few reached the fort. A solid body of two thousand men, however, which had broken through the mercenaries, was able to make good its retreat to Aspis. Five hundred prisoners were taken, among them the Consul Regulus. All the rest of the army, scarcely less than twelve thousand in number, perished on the field or in the flight. The great historian,[1] from whom I have taken this account, concludes his narrative of the campaign with reflections on the changes of fortune which bring men down in the course of a day from the heights of prosperity to the depths of misery, and on the marvellous results which the genius of a single man can effect; but he says nothing either here or afterwards of the romantic story of the fate of the prisoner Regulus. We are not certain to what year it belongs—we are not even sure that it is true at all; on the other hand, it is too famous, too noble in its meaning and moral, to be omitted. I may therefore tell it now where it will fitly close the career of one of the great soliers of Rome, the simple, frugal men who were called from the plough to command the armies of the republic.[2]

I do not know that the story can be better told than in Horace's noble ode, perhaps the very noblest that he ever wrote. Regulus, we may say, by way of preface, after being kept in prison at Carthage for several years, was sent to Rome to negotiate a peace, under the promise to return if he failed. Among the terms which he was to offer was that of a ransoming

---

[1] Polybius.

[2] The story was told in later times that Regulus was sowing his fields when the messenger came with the tidings of his election to the consulship; and the agnomen (a sort of second surname) of *Serranus* was said to have been given to the family from this circumstance. Among the future heroes of his race whom Æneas sees is in his Elysian fields is "Serranus o'er his furrow bowed." It is cruel to have to say that the first Regulus that bore the name of Serranus was the son of the hero; and still worse to be told that the proper spelling of the word is "Saranus," and that it probably comes from Saranum, an insignificant town of Umbria.

HORACE ON REGULUS.   149

or exchanging of prisoners. When brought into the Senate, which at first he refused to enter as being now a mere Carthaginian slave, he strongly advised his countrymen. At the same time he gave his voice against peace generally.

With warning voice of stern rebuke
Thus Regulus the Senate shook :
He saw prophetic, in far days to come,
The heart-corrupt, and future doom of Rome.
"These eyes," he cried, "these eyes have seen
Unblooded swords from warriors torn,
And Roman standards nailed in scorn
On Punic shrines obscene ;
Have seen the hands of free-born men
Wrenched back ; th' unbarred, unguarded gate,
And fields our war laid desolate
By Romans tilled again.

"What ! will the gold-enfranchised slave
Return more loyal and more brave ?
    Ye heap but loss on crime !
The wool that Cretan dyes distain
Can ne'er its virgin hue regain ;
And valour fallen and disgraced
Revives not in a coward breast
    Its energy sublime.

"The stag released from hunter's toils
From the dread sight of man recoils,
Is he more brave than when of old
He ranged his forest free ? Behold
In him your soldier ! He has knelt
To faithless foes ; he, too, has felt
The knotted cord : and crouched beneath
Fear, not of shame, but death.

"He sued for peace tho' vowed to war ;
Will such men, girt in arms once more
Dash headlong on the Punic shore ?
No ! they will buy their craven lives
With Punic scorn and Punic gyves.

> O mighty Carthage, rearing high
> Thy fame upon our infamy,
> A city eye, an empire built
> On Roman ruins, Roman guilt?"
>
> From the chaste kiss, and wild embrace
> Of wife and babes, he turned his face,
> A man self-doomed to die,
> Then bent his manly brow, in scorn,
> Resolved, relentless, sad but stern,
>   To earth, all silently ;
> Till counsel never heard before
> Had nerved each wavering Senator ;—
> Till flushed each cheek with patriot shame,
> And surging rose the loud acclaim ;—
> Then, from his weeping friends, in haste,
> To exile and to death he passed.
>
> He knew the tortures that Barbaric hate
> Had stored for him. Exulting in his fate,
> With kindly hand he waved away
> The crowds that strove his course to stay.
> He passed from all, as when in days of yore,
> His judgment given, thro' client throngs he pressed
> In glad Venafrian fields to seek his rest,
> Or Greek Tarentum on th' Ionian shore.[1]

What is the truth about the "tortures of barbaric hate" we cannot say. The Romans had a horrible story of how the hero on his return was cruelly put to death. But then they were never scrupulous about the truth when they were writing of their enemies; and about Carthage and its doings they were, we have reason to believe, particularly apt to exaggerate and even to invent. On the other hand, the Carthaginians showed no mercy to their own generals when these

[1] I have availed myself of a translation by Sir Stephen De Vere. (Bell and Sons, 1885.)

were unsuccessful; and it is very probable that they showed as little to an enemy, especially when he had done them such damage and had treated them as haughtily as had Regulus.

But there is at least equal authority for a story not less horrible which is told against the Romans themselves, or rather against a Roman woman. The Senate handed over two noble Carthaginians to the wife of Regulus as hostages for the safety of her husband. When she heard of his death she ordered her servants to fasten the two prisoners in a cask, and to keep them without bread and water. After five days one of them died. The savage creature kept the living shut up with the dead, giving him now a little bread and water that his torments might be prolonged. But the servants themselves rebelled against these horrible doings, and informed the Tribunes of the people of what was going on. By them the poor wretch was rescued; and the people would not allow him to be ill-treated any more.

III.

IN SICILY AGAIN.

THE Romans still retained their superiority at sea. It is, indeed, a very strange thing that the Carthaginians, though they had been sailors, and adventurous sailors too, for centuries, should have been beaten almost at once on their own element by a people that had had little or nothing to do with it.[1] But so it was. News of the disaster that had happened to the army of Regulus was brought to Rome, and a fleet was sent to carry off the garrison of Clypea, which, it was said, still held out against the enemy. It met and defeated the fleet of Carthage, taking, we are told, as many as one hundred and fourteen vessels out of a total of two hundred, and carried the troops. But though the Romans seem to have fought as well by sea as by land, still they were not sailors. We shall hear several times in the course

---

[1] The fleet of Rome must have been, to a great extent, manned by the Italian allies. Indeed, down to just a late period the seamen employed in it were called *socii navales*, "naval allies." Polybius, to show the ignorance of the Romans in these matters, has a curious story of how the crews of the ships first built during the war were taught to row by practising on dry land. The practising, one imagines, would not go very far in teaching them.

of the next few years of terrible losses by shipwreck, losses which we know to have been increased, if not caused, by the obstinacy and ignorance of the officers in command. So it seems to have been in the case of the relieving fleet. The pilots warned the consuls that the south coast of Sicily was dangerous, but warned in vain. The result was a calamity of which Polybius, a sober and sensible writer, says that "history can scarcely afford another example of so great and general a disaster." Out of four hundred and sixty-four vessels little more than a sixth part escaped. The Carthaginians were proportionately encouraged, and, fitting up a new fleet and levying another army, resolved to have another struggle for Sicily. In the first campaign, indeed, they lost Panormus, but in those that followed they had a clear advantage. Again the weather helped them. The Romans lost another fleet, and for a time gave up all hope of being masters of the sea, contenting themselves with keeping only so many vessels afloat as were wanted to carry supplies to their army. In the field, too, Carthage more than held her own. The havoc which the elephants had wrought in the army of Regulus had not been forgotten, and the Roman armies did not venture to offer battle in any place where the ground was suitable for the action of these formidable creatures. It was not till they found out that it was easy to make them as dangerous to their friends as they could be to their foes that they dared to face them. One of the Carthaginian generals was rash enough to use the animals in attacking a town. The archers showered arrows upon them from the walls till, driven to madness by their wounds, they turned round and broke down their own ranks. Many fell into the hands of the Romans on this occasion. A still greater gain was that they were no longer feared.

And now began one of the most obstinate sieges recorded in history. Lilybæum was a strongly fortified town near the Cape of the same name. Its wall was unusually high, and its ditch unusually deep, while the harbour could be approached only by a channel through shallow lakes which stretched between it and the sea. The Romans began by attacking a fort on the south-western wall, and battered down six of the towers upon the wall. Himilco, who was in command of the garrison, was unceasing in his efforts, repairing the breaches, digging countermines, and watching continually for a chance of setting fire to the Roman works. And he averted a worse danger in the threatened treachery of the mercenaries. The leaders of these troops were actually in treaty with the Romans, when Himilco heard of what was going on, and contrived to break it off. A few days afterwards came help from Carthage. No news of the garrison at Lilybæum had reached the city, and it was feared that they were in distress. A fleet of fifty ships was hastily fitted out and despatched to Sicily, with a relieving force of ten thousand men on board. The admiral in command waited for a favourable wind, and then, with all his ships ready for action, sailed straight into the harbour, the Romans being so surprised by their boldness that they did not attempt to oppose. Himilco, encouraged by this reinforcement, resolved

STELE AT LILYBÆUM.

to attack the besiegers. Sallying forth with nearly his whole force, he fell on the Roman works; but he just missed his object: his troops were on the point of setting fire to the engines and towers when he found that they were suffering heavier loss than he could afford, and withdrew them. But a few weeks afterwards he succeeded. The works had been injured by a violent gale, and some of the mercenaries saw in the confusion thus caused an opportunity for destroying them. Himilco approved their scheme. These bands sallied from the gate and set fire to three different places. The Romans were taken by surprise; and the wind blew such volumes of smoke into their faces that they could see and do nothing. In the end everything was destroyed, the towers being burnt to the ground, and the metal heads of the rams melted. After this loss they gave up all hopes of taking the place by storm, and resolved to trust to a blockade.

Meanwhile the Carthaginian fleet lay at Drepanum; and this the new consuls who came into office in the year 249 resolved to attack. Publius Claudius, who was in command, managed to reach Drepanum unobserved. Adherbal, the Carthaginian admiral, was taken by surprise, but did not lose courage. He manned his ships at once, and sailing out of the harbour by the opposite side to that by which the Romans were entering, formed his line on the open sea outside. Claudius had to recall his ships; such as had entered the harbour came into collision in backing out with those that followed them, and there was great confusion. Still the captains ranged them as well as they could along the shore, with their prows turned towards the enemy. But they had lost the choice of ground; the Carthaginians had the open sea and plenty of room to manœuvre. They could retreat when they were hard pressed, and turn again when the opportunity occurred. When the Roman vessels ventured to advance they were attacked in front, on the side, and in rear. But a Roman ship that was in difficulties had nothing behind it but the shore. If it retired, it either grounded in the shallows or was actually stranded. Nor was this disadvantage of place counterbalanced by any superiority in the build of the ships or in seamanship. The ships were clumsy, the seamen unskilful. In the end Claudius suffered a crushing defeat. He made his own escape with thirty ships; but all the rest, nearly a hundred in number, were captured. The crews, too, were taken prisoners, excepting a few who beached their ships and jumped ashore.

Junius, the other consul, was even more unfortunate. He had a hundred and twenty ships of war, with which he had to convey a fleet of eight hundred transports. The Carthaginian admiral forced him to cast anchor on a lee-shore (near Camarina), where there was no harbour within reach. When it came on to blow the blockading squadron put out to sea, and doubling Cape Pachynus escaped the worst of the storm. The Roman fleet had not time, or perhaps was not wise enough, to follow them. Anyhow, it was completely destroyed. "Scarcely a plank remained entire," says the historian. As a few days before most of the ships in the harbour of

Lilybæum had been burnt, Rome was now without a fleet.

Still, the siege of Lilybæum was pushed on. The blockading army had now most of Sicily to draw upon for stores, and was well supplied, while the town could be provisioned from the sea. Though the

COIN: THE TEMPLE AND RAMPARTS OF ERYX.

Romans gained possession by surprise of the strong post of Eryx, the second highest mountain in Sicily the war for some time dragged on without much advantage to either side.

And now appeared upon the scene one of the few great men that Carthage produced. Hamilcar, surnamed Barca,[1] was a very young man when he was appointed to the command of the Carthaginian fleet and army. But he had already made himself a name, and he soon showed that he was fit for his post. He established himself in a strong place in the north-west of the island, between Panormus and Drepanum. It was a lofty rock called Hercta (now *Pellegrino*), and seems to have united every kind of advantage. It was so difficult of approach from the land that it could be defended by a very small force. There was some productive land in the neighbourhood. The climate was cool and healthy; and there was a deep and spacious harbour. In this place, though the Roman forces held all the neighbourhood, he maintained himself for three years. His fleet—for Rome had given up for the present the attempt to command the sea—ravaged the southern coasts of Italy, and helped to furnish him with supplies. On land he kept his enemies engaged by perpetual surprises and stratagems. He won, indeed, no great victory over them, but he kept them from doing anything else, and the siege of Lilybæum made no progress. So anxious were the Romans to drive him out of this stronghold, that they at one time assembled as many as forty thousand men to carry on their attacks upon him. All, however, was in vain, and it was of his own free will that at the end of three years he took up another position. This was Eryx, the capture of which by the Romans has been mentioned above. He put his army on board the fleet, and suddenly carried it to the place which he had fixed upon, and though the

[1] See page 11.

enemy still held the fort upon the top of the hills, got possession of the town. Here he maintained himself for two years, getting little help, it would seem, from home, for one of his chief difficulties was with his mercenaries, who were clamouring for the

PHŒNICIAN WALL AT ERYX.

pay which he could not give them, and whom he was obliged to put off with promises. Still the Romans could make no impression on him, and of course made no advance in the siege of the Carthaginian fortresses.

If Hamilcar could have been everywhere the war might have had a different result, or, in any case, might have been prolonged still more than it was. But he could not be sure that his lieutenants would be as able as himself. In 241 Rome made a great

POSTERN IN THE WALL OF ERYX.

effort to recover her supremacy at sea. The public treasury was exhausted, as it might well be after neary five and twenty years of war, but private citizens came forward to supply what was wanting. Some of the richest undertook to build each a ship; or

BATTLE OF ÆGATES ISLAND.

two or three of smaller means would join together. Thus a fleet of two hundred five-banked vessels were got together, and these of the very best construction. With this Lutatius Catulus, the consul, sailed to Sicily. The Carthaginians seem to have been unprepared, not expecting indeed that the enemy, who had abandoned the sea for several years, should now seek to recover the command of it. Catulus was therefore able to possess himself unopposed of the harbours of Lilybæum and Drepanum. He pressed the siege of the latter place with much vigour, and meanwhile kept his crews busy with training and exercise, till he made them expert and ready.

The Carthaginians, on the other hand, prepared to act. The plan of Hanno, who was in command of the fleet, was this. To take stores for the supply of Hamilcar's army at Eryx, and, after landing these, to take on board some of the best troops and Hamilcar himself, who alone was equal to an army; and thus engage the Romans. It was the object of the Romans, on the other hand, to force an action before this could be done. Catulus accordingly put some of his best troops on board his ships and sailed to Ægusa, an island opposite Lilybæum. Hanno was at Hiera, another island, a little further out to sea, The whole front was known by the name of the Ægates (a word that has probably something to do with the Greek word for a goat). Catulus intended to give battle at once. Then, when the day for action came, he began to doubt. The wind was stormy, and was blowing from the west, and so would help the movements of the enemy and hinder his own. On the other hand, there was much to be lost by delay. At present the Carthaginian ships were burdened with the stores which they were carrying. If he did not engage them at once they would rid themselves of these, would take on board some first-rate troops from the army at Eryx, and, above all, would have the presence of the dreaded Hamilcar himself. These thoughts made him resolve on battle. The Carthaginians were already on their way eastward when he put out to sea. His crews, become strong and dexterous by practice, got their ships between the enemy and the point for which he was making, and, ranged in a single line, prepared to receive them. The conflict was short and decisive. Hanno's ships were encumbered with stores; his crews were unskilled, for the fleet had been neglected, and the troops on board were nothing better than raw levies. In all these points the Romans were superior; they had nothing on board but what was wanted for the battle; their rowers were well trained, and their fighting men of the best quality. At the very first meeting they showed their superiority. Fifty of the Carthaginian ships were sunk and seventy more taken with all their crews; the rest were saved by a sudden change of the wind to the east which took them back to their anchorage at Hiera.

The battle of the Ægates Islands brought the war to an end. Carthage could no longer provision her army in Sicily, and felt that it was useless to prolong the struggle. Accordingly, Hamilcar was empowered to make peace. The Romans were ready enough to meet him, for they too were exhausted by the long struggles, and after some negotiations a treaty was made. The chief condition was that Carthage was to give up all her positions in Sicily, and engage to leave the island alone for the future. She had had a hold on the island for at least four centuries, and for nearly two had cherished hopes of winning it. Sometimes she had been very near their accomplishment. Now they had to be finally given up. This was undoubtedly a great blow. We may call it the first great step downward. A war indemnity of nearly £800,000 was imposed. But Hamilcar was resolved to save his honour. The Romans demanded that the troops at Eryx should surrender. This demand he resolutely refused, and it was given up. They marched out with all the honours of war and were carried back to Carthage; and so, after a duration of four and twenty years, the First Punic War came to an end.

IV.

CARTHAGE AND HER MERCENARIES.

WE have seen more than once that Carthage had much trouble with her mercenary troops. This trouble now came upon her again, and in a worse form than ever. The fact was that five and twenty years of war had exhausted even her vast wealth, and she could not meet her engagements with the soldiers whom she had hired. These, on the other hand, were more powerful than they had ever been before. They were not troops hired for a campaign, and discharged after a few months' service, but a standing army trained by a long war to know each other and to act together; and many of them had been taught the art of war by a great soldier, Hamilcar Barca.

As soon as peace was concluded, Gesco, Governor of Lilybæum, had begun sending the mercenaries to Carthage in small detachments. He hoped that as they came they would be paid off and dismissed to their homes. Had this been done, all would have been well. But the government either would not or could not find the money. Shipload after shipload of the men arrived till the city was full of them. After a while, so troublesome and disorderly were they, they were collected in a camp outside the walls, and left there with nothing to do but talk over their grievances and plot mischief.

When at last the money, or part of the money, was forthcoming, it was too late. The troops had found leaders, and the interest of these leaders was not peace but war. One of them was a certain Spendius, a runaway slave from Campania, who dreaded, of course, that when everything was settled he might be sent back to his master, that is to torture and death. He is said to have been a man of enormous strength, and brave even to rashness. The other was a free-born African, of the name of Matho. He had been a ringleader in all the disturbances that had taken place since the return of the mercenaries, and he dreaded the vengeance of his employers. Matho found his fellow Africans ready to listen to him; and there was probably much truth in what he said. "The Carthaginians," he told his comrades, "are going to send to their homes the troops belonging to other nations; when you are left alone they will make you feel their anger." A pretext for open revolt was soon found. Gesco, who had been sent to settle with the troops, handed over the arrears of pay, but put off the question of allowances for corn, horses, etc., to another time. At this proposal there were loud cries of discontent, and in a few minutes a noisy crowd of troops was assembled. Spendius and Matho harangued the assembly, and were received with shouts of applause. Any one else that attempted to speak was killed. "Kill," says the historian, was the only word that every one in this motley crowd, gathered from almost every country of Western Europe, could understand. The two speakers were chosen generals. Gesco and his staff were seized, fettered, and thrown into prison. There was now open war between Carthage and her mercenaries.

The African towns at once joined the rebels. They were always discontented with their masters, and this discontent had now reached its height. The necessities of Carthage during the war just ended had compelled her to increase the taxes of her dependencies, and to exact these taxes to the uttermost farthing. The rent in kind paid by the cultivators of the soil had been raised to a half of the produce, and the tribute paid by the towns had been doubled; and any default in payment had been cruelly punished. So fierce was the wrath raised by this oppression that the very women brought their ornaments—and her ornaments were no small part of an African woman's wealth—and threw them into the common stock. From these and other sources, Spendius and Matho received so much money that they settled all the claims of the troops, and had still abundance of means for carrying on the war.

Two towns only, Hippo and Utica, remained loyal. These were at once besieged. The mercenaries had three armies in the field. One was before Hippo, another before Utica; the third held an entrenched camp at Tunes. Carthage was thus cut off from all communication by land with Africa: but she still retained command of the sea.

The Carthaginian commander-in-chief, Hanno,[1]

---

[1] This Hanno seems somehow to have got the title of "The Great," but to have done very little to deserve it.

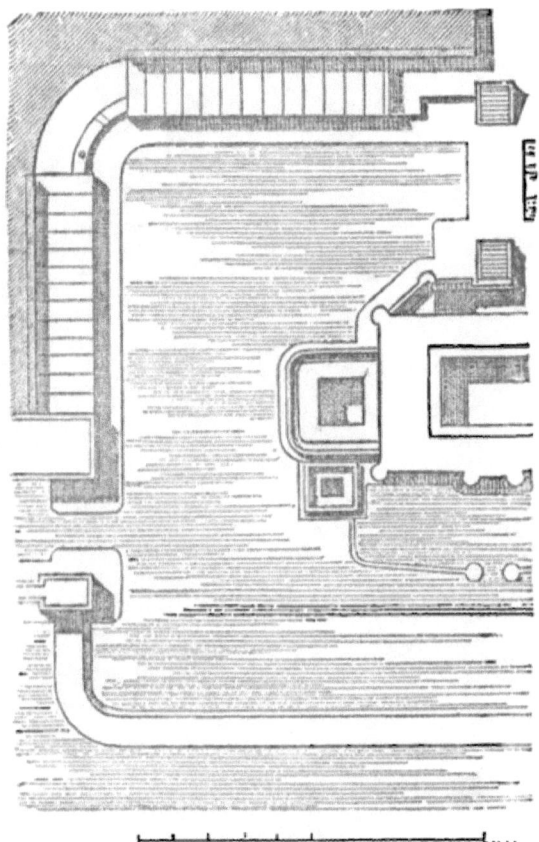

PLAN OF HARBOUR AT UTICA.

marched against the rebel force that was besieging Utica. He had as many as a hundred elephants with him. These broke through the entrenchments of the rebel camp, and the mercenaries fled in confusion. Hanno, accustomed to have to do with half savage enemies, who, once defeated, could not easily be rallied, thought that the victory was won, and, while he was amusing himself in Utica, allowed his troops to be as idle and as careless as they pleased. But the enemy were soldiers trained by Hamilcar Barca, and accustomed to retreat and rally, if need was, more than once in the same day. They rallied now, and seeing that the Carthaginian camp was left unguarded, attacked it, and got possession of a quantity of stores, and, among them, of some artillery which Hanno had sent for out of the city.

The conduct of the war was now committed to Hamilcar. The strength of his force was a corps of ten thousand native Carthaginians. Besides these he had a body of mercenaries, a number of deserters from the enemy, and seventy elephants. His first operation was to relieve Utica. The chief difficulty was to break the blockade which the rebel general Matho had established round Carthage. The hills at the land end of the isthmus on which the city stood were held in force by the rebels; as was the only bridge over the river Macar. But Hamilcar had noticed that a certain wind brought up such quantities of sand to the bar of the Macar as to make it easily fordable. Taking advantage of this, he marched his army across the river by night, and, to the surprise of both friends and enemies, appeared in the morning on the other side, and hastened to attack the rear of the rebel force that was guarding the bridge. A strong detachment from the besiegers of Utica advanced to support their comrades. Hamilcar was marching with his elephants in front, his light-armed troops behind them, and his heavy-armed in the rear. On coming in sight of the enemy, he changed this disposition. Spendius mistook the movement for a flight, and ordered a charge. The rebels found the heavy troops quietly waiting to receive them, while the cavalry and the elephants fell upon their flanks. They were soon broken. Six thousand were slain upon the field of battle, and two thousand taken prisoners. Hamilcar had broken the blockade; but Hippo and Utica were still besieged, and the rebels were still in force at Tunes.

His success, however, had a good effect on the African tribes. One of the chief Numidian princes came into his camp with a force of two thousand men, and Hamilcar felt himself strong enough again to offer battle. The fight that ensued was long and obstinate. At last the Carthaginians prevailed, chiefly by the help of the elephants. Ten thousand rebels were killed, and four thousand taken prisoners. To these latter Hamilcar, with a wise mercy, offered liberal terms. They might take service with Carthage, or they might go home. But if they were found in arms again, they must expect no further mercy.

The rebel generals were dismayed when they heard of this politic act. Their only plan was to commit their followers to deeds which could not be pardoned.

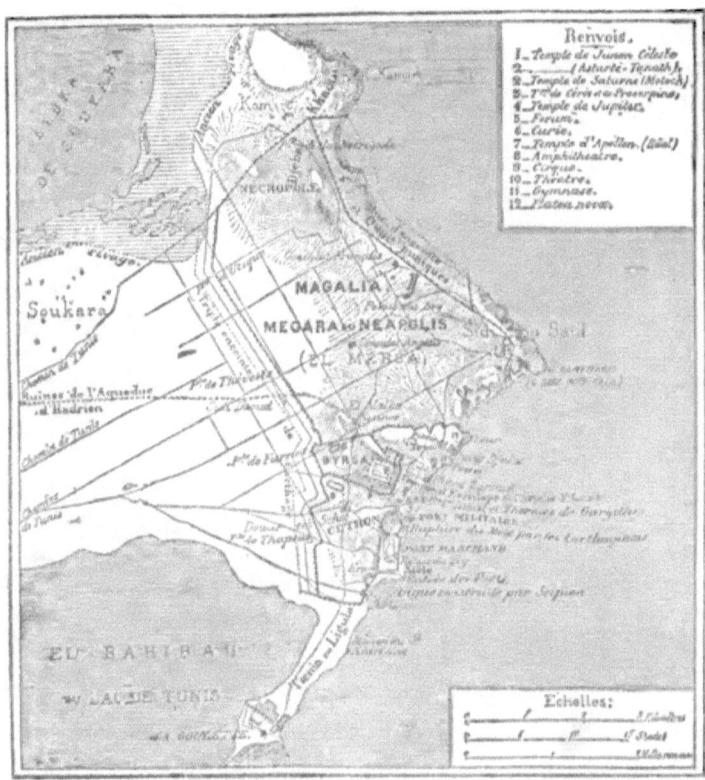

MAP OF PENINSULA OF CARTHAGE.

Accordingly they called an assembly of the soldiers. Into this was brought a courier who professed to come with a despatch from the rebels in Sardinia. This despatch contained a warning of a plot that was being hatched in the camp for setting Gesco and the other prisoners free. Then Spendius stood up to speak. "Do not trust Hamilcar," he said. "His mercy is a mere pretence. When he has got you all in his power, he will punish you all. And meanwhile take care that Gesco, who is a most dangerous man, does not escape you." When he had finished speaking, a second courier arrived, this time professing to come from the camp at Tunes, and bearing a despatch to much the same effect as the first. On this Antaritus, a Gaul, who had shared the command with Spendius and Matho, rose to address the assembly. He had the advantage of being able to speak in Carthaginian, a language of which most of his hearers, from long service with the State, knew something. He told his hearers that it was madness to think of concluding peace with Carthage. Any one who advised such a thing was a traitor, and they had better make it impossible by putting the prisoners to death.

This horrible advice was followed. Gesco and his fellow-prisoners, seven hundred in number, were cruelly murdered, and from that time till the end of the war no mercy was showed on either side.

For a time everything went ill with the Carthaginians. Hanno had been joined with Hamilcar in the command; but the two could not agree, and the army suffered greatly in consequence. Sardinia was lost to Carthage, and now Utica and Hippo revolted, after massacring their Carthaginian garrisons. At this crisis the foreign allies of the State stood faithfully by it. Hiero of Syracuse gave them help. It was not to his interest that Carthage should be destroyed. Rome left without a rival would be too powerful, and Syracuse would soon be swallowed up. And Rome, without the same reason, behaved equally well. She would not take possession either of Sardinia or of Utica, though both were offered to her by the rebels. And she allowed traders to send supplies into Carthage, while she forbad them to have any dealings with the rebels.

And now the tide turned against the mercenaries. They were besieging Carthage, but they were also besieged themselves. Naravasus, a Numidian prince, with his cavalry cut off all supplies from the country, and they were reduced to the most frightful extremities. Spendius and his colleagues endeavoured to make terms. Hamilcar agreed to let the rebels go free, with ten exceptions such as he should choose. When the treaty was concluded, he said, "I choose among the ten those that are now present." Spendius and Antaritus were two of them.

The siege of Carthage was now raised, and Hamilcar advanced against the camp at Tunes. He posted himself on one side, while his lieutenant, Hannibal, took up his position on the other. Spendius and his fellow-prisoners were crucified before the walls. Unfortunately Hannibal was an incompetent general. Matho, who was in command of the rebels, made a sally, stormed the camp, and took Hannibal himself prisoner. In retaliation for the death of Spendius he was fastened alive to the same cross on which the body of the rebel leader was still hanging.

Carthage now made a last effort to bring the war to an end. Every citizen that was of an age to bear arms was forced to serve. Hamilcar and Hanno agreed to forget their differences and to act together. And now everything went well. Matho was compelled to risk a battle, and was defeated and taken prisoner. All the African towns, except Utica and Hippo, at once submitted, and these, finding themselves alone, did not long hold out.

"Such," says Polybius, "was the conclusion of the war between Carthaginians and their mercenaries, after a continuance of three years and about four months; a war by far the most impious and bloody of any that we find in history."

Carthage came out of the struggle much weakened. Besides men and money she lost her province of Sardinia. The Romans seem to have repented of their moderation, and did not refuse the island when it was offered them by the rebel mercenaries a second time, and when Carthage prepared to retake the island by force, Rome declared war. The unfortunate State had to give way, and to pay besides an indemnity of twelve hundred talents.

V.

CARTHAGE AND SPAIN.

WHEN the war of the mercenaries was at last over, Hamilcar Barca was left the greatest man in Carthage. It was he who had saved the State at its greatest need; and it was to him the people looked for guidance. For the next forty years, or thereabouts, he and his family, or the party that was led by them, called by their opponents the "Barcine Faction," had the government in their hands. Hamilcar's one object was to recover what Carthage had lost; but it was an object which it was difficult to attain. To reconquer Sicily and the other islands of the Western Mediterranean was hopeless. For four hundred years and more Carthage had spent her strength in these regions, and had never quite got them into her grasp. Now they had passed for ever into hands which were stronger than hers. Not only must no action be taken directly against Rome, but nothing must be done to rouse her jealousy. Another war with Rome would be fatal, at least till Carthage had got back her strength, and war had already been threatened. Hamilcar had to look elsewhere, and he looked to Spain. Carthage had already had dealings with this country. She had trading ports along its coasts, and she had got some of her best troops from its tribes. Hamilcar now conceived the idea of building up here an empire which should be a compensation for that which his country had lost elsewhere. This idea he kept secret till he had begun to carry it into action. He set out with the army, of which he seems to have been permanent commander-in-chief, on an expedition to complete the conquest of the African tribes dwelling westward of Carthage. Little or nothing was heard of him till the news came that he had crossed over into Spain, and was waging war on the native tribes. For nine years he worked on, making a new empire for his country. We know little or nothing about his campaigns, except that they were successful. Not only did he make war support itself, but he sent home large sums of money with which to keep up the influence of his party, and he had still enough to spare for bribing native chiefs. At the end of the nine years he fell in battle. But he left an able successor behind him in Hasdrubal, his son-in-law, who had been his colleague in his campaigns. Hasdrubal carried out his plans, and completed the work which he had begun. Here, too, we know nothing of details. That he was a good soldier we are sure, for when the restless tribes of the African coast had risen in arms after Hamilcar had crossed over into Spain, he had been sent back by his chief, and had soon reduced them to submission. But he seems to have been still greater as a manager and ruler of men. By pleasing manners, by politic dealing with the native tribes, and by friendship formed with their petty chiefs—he is said to have married a Spanish princess—he furthered the cause of his country more than by force of arms. The foundation of New Carthage was his work. It had the best harbour on the coast; it was near the rich silver mines discovered by Aletes, and it soon became the capital of the new province. So powerful, indeed, was Hasdrubal that he was suspected of a plan for making himself absolute master of Carthage; while the treaty with the Romans by which the boundaries of the two empires were fixed at the river Ebro is spoken of as having been made with Hasdrubal.

The jealousy of the Romans had indeed by this time been roused. They saw with some alarm the wonderful progress that the Carthaginian general was making with the Spanish tribes, and they looked about for friends for themselves. Saguntum, a town partly Greek in origin (its name seems to have been connected with that of Zacynthos, one of the islands off the western coast of Greece), applied to them for protection, and they readily promised it. A treaty was concluded by which the river Iberus (now the Ebro) was to be the eastern boundary of the Carthaginian province, but it was stipulated that Saguntum, which lay about fifty miles within these limits, should be independent. Hasdrubal met his death by assassination. He had executed a Spanish chief for some offence against his government, and one of the man's slaves in revenge struck him down. He had held the chief command in Spain for a little more than eight years.

And now the greatest man that Carthage ever produced comes to the front. Some seventeen years before, when Hamilcar was about to cross over into Spain, his son Hannibal, then a boy of nine, begged to be allowed to go with him. The father consented, but first he brought the boy up to the altar on which, in preparation for the expedition he was about to make, he was offering sacrifice, and bade him lay his hand upon the victim, and swear eternal hatred to Rome. We shall see how the lad kept his oath.

He was present at the battle in which his father met his death; and though then but eighteen years of age, was put by his brother-in-law, Hamilcar's successor, in high military command. "There was no one," says Livy, "whom Hasdrubal preferred to put in command, whenever courage and persistency were specially needed, no officer under whom the soldiers were more confident and more daring." And indeed he was the very model of a soldier. He was bold, but never rash, cool in the presence of danger, and infinitely fertile in resource. To fatigue he seemed insensible. He could bear heat and cold equally well. Of food and drink he cared only to take so much as satisfied the needs of nature. To sleep he gave such time as business spared him; and he could take it anywhere and anyhow. Many a time could he be seen lying on the ground, wrapped in his military cloak, among the sentries and pickets. About his dress he was careless; it was nothing better than that of his humblest comrades. But his arms and his horses were the best that could be found. He was an admirable rider, a skilful man at arms, and as brave as he was skilful. With such a man in the camp, there could be no doubt as to the successor of

Hasdrubal: the army at once elected him to the command. His strong resemblance to his father, whom many of the soldiers still remembered, was not the least of his many claims. And the government at home could do nothing but confirm the election.

Hannibal's first operations were against some Spanish tribes in the interior, occupying the country on both banks of the Upper Tagus (the western portion of what is now New Castile). A great victory over a native army, which is said to have numbered as many as a hundred thousand men, brought to an end these campaigns, which occupied the autumn of 221 and the greater part of the following year.

In the spring of 219 Hannibal laid siege to Saguntum. His first operations were successful. His quick eye had spied the weak place in the town's fortifications, and he at once made it the object of his attack; but the Saguntines were prepared to receive him. Indeed they more than held their own, and Hannibal himself was dangerously wounded by a javelin thrown from the wall. But he had the advantage of vast numbers—his army amounting, it is said, to as many as 150,000—while the garrison had not men enough to guard the whole circuit of their walls. The battering-rams were used with effect, and a breach was made. Then came an attempt to storm, furiously made, and furiously resisted. The townspeople are said to have made great havoc among the besiegers by a curious missile, which is described as having had a heavy iron point and a shaft which was wrapped in tow and set alight. In the end the storming party was beaten back.

Meanwhile an embassy arrived from Rome. Hannibal refused to receive it. He pretended that it would not be safe for the envoys to enter his camp. He could not, he said, undertake to protect them from his barbarian allies. The ambassadors proceeded, as their instructions directed, to Carthage. Hanno, the leader of the peace party, pleaded earnestly with the Senate to yield to the demands of Rome. He advised that the army should be withdrawn from before Saguntum, that compensation should be made to that town, and even that Hannibal should be surrendered as having broken the treaty. But he scarcely found a seconder, and the ambassadors were sent away with a refusal.

The siege meanwhile was being pressed on with vigour. The garrison hastily built a new wall at the spot where the breach had been made, but this was easily thrown down; and a party of the besiegers now established itself actually within the city. The defence was still continued, but it was manifestly hopeless. Hannibal was willing to give terms. The Saguntines might withdraw with their wives and children, each person to have two garments, but leaving all their property behind. While this offer was being discussed in an irregular assembly, for a number of people had crowded into the Senate-house, some of the chief citizens gradually withdrew. They lit a great fire, and collecting all the public treasure and all the private property on which they could lay their hands, flung it into the flames, and then, with desperate resolution, leaped into them themselves. While this was going on, the Carthaginians forced their way into the town. Every grown-up male was slain. The booty was enormous. Enough was left, besides all that the soldiers took, to bring a great sum into the public treasury.

There could be now no doubt that war would follow. The Romans, indeed, made all preparations for it. Still, anxious, it would seem, to do all things in order, they sent another embassy to Carthage. The envoys were instructed to put to the Carthaginian Senate the simple question, "Was it by the order of the government that Hannibal attacked Saguntum?" The Carthaginian Senate refused to give a direct answer. The speaker who represented their opinion pleaded that the regular treaty between Carthage and Rome made no mention of Saguntum, and that they could not recognize a private agreement made with Hasdrubal. "Upon this," says Livy, "the Roman gathered his robe into a fold and said, 'Here we bring you peace and war: take which you please.' Instantly there arose a fierce shout, 'Give us which you please!' The Roman, in reply, shook out the fold, and spoke again, 'I give you war.' The answer from all was, 'We accept it; and in the spirit with which we accept it, will we wage it.'"

Thus began the Second Punic War.

VI.

FROM THE EBRO TO ITALY.

AFTER the capture of Saguntum, Hannibal went into winter quarters at New Carthage. He gave a furlough to any of his Spanish troops that wished to visit their homes. "Come back," he said, "in early spring, and I will be your leader in a war from which both the glory and the gain will be immense." The winter he spent in maturing his great plan, which was nothing less than to invade Italy. Carthage, he knew, had been brought to the brink of destruction by being attacked at home; and this because her subjects had been raised against her. Rome, too, had subjects who were doubtless ill-content with her rule. Within the last hundred years she had added the greater part of Italy to her Empire. It was in Italy that he hoped to find his best allies. We shall see how far his hopes were fulfilled, how far they were disappointed.

In the spring he made a disposal of his forces. Some fifteen thousand, chiefly Spaniards, he sent into Africa. With his brother Hasdrubal he left an army of between twelve and thirteen thousand infantry, two thousand five hundred cavalry, five hundred slingers, and twenty-one elephants, besides a fleet of fifty-seven ships, chiefly of the largest size. His policy in making these arrangements was to garrison Africa with Spanish, and Spain with African troops. The force with which he himself crossed the Ebro consisted of ninety thousand infantry and twelve thousand cavalry.

To cross the Ebro, which was still nominally the boundary between Rome and Carthage, was formally to commence hostilities. On the night before he made the passage, Hannibal, who had lately returned from a solemn visit to the temple of Melcarth at Gades, had a dream. He saw a youth of godlike shape, who said, "Jupiter has sent me to lead your army into Italy. Follow me, but look not behind." Hannibal followed trembling, but could not, after a while, keep his eyes from looking behind. He saw a serpent of marvellous size moving onwards, and destroying the forest as it went. When he asked what this might mean, his guide answered, "This is the devastation of Italy. Go on and ask no more, but leave the designs of fate in darkness."

Hannibal's numbers, indeed, were much diminished before he reached the foot of the Alps, which was to be the first stage in his journey. He had to conquer the country between the Ebro and the Pyrenees, and leave a large force to hold it; and he felt it wise to dismiss to their homes a number of men who were unwilling or afraid to go on with him. It was with fifty thousand foot and nine thousand horse that he crossed the Pyrenees. From the Pyrenees he marched with little opposition to the Rhone. His route seems to have led him to Nemausus (now Nismes), while the point at which he touched the river was probably Roquemaure. Polybius describes it as being four

PASSAGE OF THE RHONE.

days' march from the mouth. He found the further bank occupied by a strong force of the neighbouring Gauls. His guides informed him that some twenty-five miles higher up the river there was an island, and that when the stream was divided it was shallow and comparatively easy to cross. Accordingly he sent Hanno, son of Bomilcar, with a party of his army to cross at this place, and to take the enemy in the rear. Hanno found no one to oppose him. His Spanish troops, men accustomed to the water, put their clothes and arms on bladders, and swam to the further bank, pushing these before them; the Africans, who had not had the same experience, crossed upon rafts. Hannibal meanwhile was making his own preparations for the passage. He had collected from friendly tribes on the right bank of the river a number of small boats. These he used for his infantry. Larger vessels and rafts constructed by his own men were reserved for the cavalry, and were put higher up the stream, to break the force of the current against the lighter craft. When all was ready he gave the signal to start. The enemy, though startled by his boldness in thus crossing in face of their opposition, would doubtless have stood firm, and, perhaps, successfully resisted him, but for the force which had already made the passage higher up the river. At the critical moment they saw behind them the smoke of the fires which, by a concerted plan, Hanno and his infantry had lighted. They found themselves taken in the rear, a danger which no undisciplined troops can brave. Hannibal, familiar with this fact, pushed boldly on. He was himself in one of the foremost boats, and, leaping to shore, led his men to the charge. The Gauls broke and fled almost without striking a blow. He had still to get his elephants across. A large raft was covered with earth and moored firmly to the bank, and to this again a smaller raft, similarly disguised, was attached. The elephants, led by two females, were taken first upon the larger, then upon the smaller raft, and, fancying themselves still upon dry ground, made no objection. Then the smaller raft was detached, and propelled across the stream. The great beasts were frightened when they found themselves afloat, but their very terror kept them quiet; and two that plunged into the water, though their unfortunate drivers were drowned, got safely to the opposite shore.

Hannibal marched up the left bank of the Rhone till he reached the Isére. Here he made a valuable ally in a chief of the Allobroges, whom he supported against a younger brother that was claiming the throne. This prince supplied his army with stores of all kinds, among which shoes are especially mentioned, and escorted him as far as the foot of the Alps.

But, it will be asked, were the Romans doing nothing to defend themselves against this invasion? They had other work on their hands, for they were at war with the Gauls in what is now Northern Italy, but was then called Cisalpine or Hither Gaul. The first armies they could raise were sent against them; but Publius Cornelius Scipio (a name of which we shall hear much hereafter) was despatched with a force to the mouths of the Rhone. Had he moved up the river at once he might have hindered Hannibal's passage, but he sat still. A proof that the

Carthaginians were near was soon given him. Hannibal had sent a squadron of African horse to reconnoitre, and this fell in with some cavalry which Scipio had sent out for the same purpose. A sharp skirmish followed. It was the first occasion on which the two enemies crossed swords, and the Romans won the day. When his cavalry had returned, Scipio marched up the river; but he found Hannibal gone, and did not think it well to follow him. Returning to the sea, he sent the greater part of his army under his brother Cnæus into Spain, and sailed back with the rest to Italy. This policy of strengthening the Roman force in Spain, in face of what seemed a greater danger nearer home, was masterly, and was to bear good fruit in after time.

Hannibal's route across the Alps has been the subject of much controversy, into which I do not intend to enter. The view which seems to me the most probable is that he marched up the left bank of the Rhone as far as Vienne; then, leaving the river, struck across the level country of Upper Dauphiny, and met the river again at St. Genix. Thence he marched up the valley of the Upper Isére, and crossed by the pass of the Little St. Bernard, descending into the Valley of Aosta.

The dangers and difficulties of the passage are described in vivid language by the historians, and indeed they must have been terrible. To take an army, with all its stores and baggage, the horses, and the elephants, across the Alps, was indeed a wonderful task; still more wonderful when we consider how late it was in the year when the attempt was made

It was almost the end of October before the summit of the pass was reached, and the seasons, there is little reason to doubt, were colder then than they are now.

If Hannibal had only had natural obstacles to contend with he would have had plenty to do; but he found the mountain tribes fiercely hostile. They resented the intrusion of this formidable force into their country, and they saw an excellent opportunity for plundering. Their attacks began as soon as he commenced the ascent, and were continued till he had nearly reached the highest point. The first stage of the march was at the pass which leads to the Lake of Bourget. Every mile of this had to be won by hard fighting. The road was steep and narrow, and the barbarians attacked the army from points of vantage. It was only Hannibal's foresight in occupying a still higher position, which the enemy had left during the night, that prevented a most serious loss. When the plain at the upper end of the pass was reached, the disciplined army had nothing to fear. The mountaineers' fortified town was stormed, and much of the property that had been lost was regained. The next three days' march was made without opposition; and then the mountain tribes, seeing that force had failed, tried what treachery could do. Their chiefs came into the camp, offered hostages, sent in supplies, and promised to guide the army by the best and shortest route. Hannibal did not wholly trust them, and took precautions against a sudden attack. But he allowed the guides to lead him into a dangerous defile, where the longer road would have been safer.

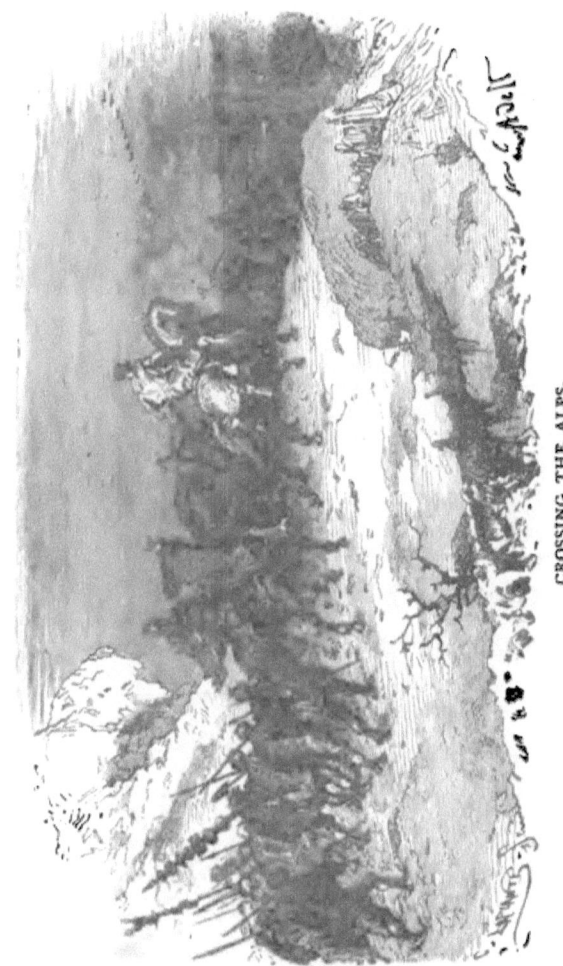

CROSSING THE ALPS.

At the most critical point of the march the enemy attacked, rolling down great rocks or sending showers of stones from the cliffs. The loss was great, but the army struggled through. The elephants, difficult as they must have been to drive up those narrow and slippery roads, were of great service. The mountaineers were terrified at the sight of them, and wherever they were visible did not venture to approach.

The story of how Hannibal split with fire and vinegar the rocks which his men could neither remove or climb over is so famous that it cannot be omitted, though it is not easy to imagine how the vinegar came to be there. Had his foresight, wonderful as it was, extended so far as to provide this most unlikely kind of store? But without further criticism I shall quote Livy's own words. "Having to cut into the stone, they heaped up a huge pile of wood from great trees in the neighbourhood, which they had felled and lopped. As soon as there was strength enough in the wind to create a blaze they lighted the pile, and melted the rocks, as they heated, by pouring vinegar upon them. The burning stone was then cleft open with iron implements."

Livy represents this incident as occurring in the course of the descent. By that time the work, of course, was really done. The army took nine days, we are told, to make its way to the top. That once reached, they were permitted to rest two days. When they resumed their march a fall of snow almost reduced them to despair. But Hannibal told them to keep up their courage. He would show them the end of their toils. And indeed, a little further on, they came to a point from which they could look down on the rich plains of Italy. "You are climbing," he cried to his men, "not the walls of Italy only, but of Rome itself. What remains will be a smooth descent; after one or, at the most, two battles, we shall have the capital of Italy in our hands."

Six days sufficed for the descent. It was more than four months since Hannibal had started from New Carthage. His losses on the way had been terrible. He brought down with him into the plains of Italy not more than twenty thousand infantry (three-fifths of them Africans and the remainder Spaniards) and six thousand cavalry; and he had left thirty-three thousand, most of them victims of disease and cold, upon his road. This was the force, if we are to reckon only his regular troops, with which he was to undertake the conquest of Italy. The numbers rest on the authority of a Roman who was a prisoner in the Carthaginian camp, and who heard them from the lips of the great general himself.

VII.

THE FIRST CAMPAIGN IN ITALY.

HANNIBAL gave a few days' rest to his troops. They greatly needed it, for their toils and sufferings had given them, we are told, a look that was "scarcely human." Then he struck his first blow. If he was to succeed he must have the people of the Italian peninsula on his side against Rome. In one way or another they must be made to join him. Accordingly, when the Taurini, a tribe of Gauls, refused his proposals of alliance—they were at feud with another tribe which was friendly to him—he attacked and stormed their stronghold.[1] After this almost all the tribes of Hither Gaul joined him. They furnished him with supplies and with a number of excellent recruits.

Meanwhile Publius Scipio had landed his army at Pisa, had marched over the Apennines, and, crossing the Po at Placentia, was advancing against the invaders. Hannibal scarcely expected to meet him so soon; Scipio had never believed that the Carthaginian army would be able to make the passage of the Alps. Both made ready for battle. Among the preparations

---

[1] Probably the town afterwards called *Augusta Taurinorum* and now known as Turin.

of Hannibal was a spectacle which he exhibited to his army. Some of the mountaineers who had been taken prisoners in crossing the Alps were matched to fight against each other. The conquerors were to have a set of arms and their liberty; the conquered would, at all events, be released from their chains by death. All the prisoners eagerly accepted the offer when it was made to them, and fought with the greatest courage, whilst those who had not been chosen looked envyingly on. Hannibal meant the exhibition as a parable to his own men. "This," he said, "is exactly your situation. You have this same choice—a rich reward and liberty on the one side, and death on the other. See how gladly these barbarians accept it. Do you be as cheerful and as brave as they are."

Scipio crossed the Ticinus by a bridge which he had built for the purpose. Both armies were now on the north bank of the Po, the Carthaginians moving eastward and having the river on their right, the Romans coming westward to meet them. At the end of the second day's march both encamped, and on the morning of the third the cavalry of both advanced, Hannibal and Scipio commanding in person. The Romans had their light-armed troops and their Gallic horsemen in front, and the rest of their cavalry in the second line. Hannibal had skilfully arranged his heavy cavalry in a solid body in the centre; while the light and active African troopers, men who rode their horses without a bit, were on either wing. The Roman light-armed, after a single discharge of their javelins, retired hastily through the spaces of the squadrons behind them.

Between the heavy cavalry on both sides there was an obstinate struggle, the Romans having somewhat the advantage. But the clouds of Africans had outflanked the Roman line, and had fallen first on their light-armed troops and then on the rear of the heavy cavalry. A general rout followed. Not the least serious disaster of the day, as we shall see, was that Scipio himself received a disabling wound. Indeed, it was only the bravery of his son, a youth of seventeen, of whom we shall hear again, that saved his life. A body of horsemen formed round the consul, and escorted him off the field.

Hannibal waited awhile to see whether his antagonists meant to risk a general engagement. As they made no sign, he advanced, and finding that they had left their camp, crossed first the Ticinus, and afterwards the Po, where he captured six hundred men who had been left behind by the Romans. Scipio was now encamped under the walls of Placentia. Hannibal, after vainly offering him battle, took up a position about six miles off. The first result of his late victory was the crowding into his camp of the Gallic chiefs from the south side of the Po. Before long he had a stronger proof of the change of feeling in this people. A Gallic contingent that was acting with the Roman army left the camp at night, carrying with them the heads of a number of their comrades whom they had massacred, and took service with him. Scipio was so alarmed by this general movement among the Gauls that he left his camp, and moved southward to the Trebia, where he could find a strong position and friendly neighbours. Hannibal immediately sent his African horse in pursuit; and these, if they had not stopped to plunder and burn the deserted camp, might have greatly damaged the retreating army. As it was, all but a few stragglers had crossed the Trebia before the Africans came up. Scipio took up a strong position on the hills, and resolved to wait till his colleague Sempronius, who was on his way northward, should join him. Hannibal, who had followed with his whole force, pitched his camp about five miles to the north. He had received meanwhile a most welcome gain in the surrender of Clastidium, a fortress near Placentia, where the Romans had accumulated great stores of corn. The place was given up to him by the commandant, a native of Brundusium, who received, it is said, four hundred gold pieces as the price of his treachery.

It was not long before Sempronius and his army arrived. The numbers of the Romans were of course greatly increased by this reinforcement; but the result was really disastrous. Scipio was a skilful general; Sempronius was nothing but a brave man, whom the accident of being consul for the year had put in command of the army. And, unfortunately, Scipio was disabled by the wound which he had received at Ticinus. His colleague could not believe but that the Romans must win a pitched battle, if the enemy should be rash enough to fight one; and he was anxious to get the credit of the victory for himself. If he was to do this he must force a battle at once. Winter was coming on, and before the beginning of another campaign he would be out of office.

If he had any doubt about success, it was dispersed

by the result of a skirmish which took place between the Roman and Carthaginian cavalry. Hannibal had sent some horsemen, Africans and Gauls, to plunder the lands of a tribe which had made terms with Rome. As these were returning, laden with booty, some Roman squadrons fell upon them, and drove them to their camp with considerable loss.

Sempronius was now determined to fight, and Scipio could not hinder him. As Hannibal was at least equally anxious for a battle, which was as much to his interest as it was against the interest of his antagonists, the conflict was not long delayed. Sempronius had forty thousand men under his command, and Hannibal's army, reinforced as it had been by the Gauls, was probably equal.

Hannibal's first care was to place an ambuscade of two thousand men, picked with the greatest care, in some brushwood near the river. His brother Mago had chosen a hundred foot-soldiers and as many troopers; and each of these again had chosen nine comrades. They were to play, we shall see, an important part in the battle. Early the next morning he sent his African cavalry across the river, with orders to skirmish up to the Roman camp, and provoke an engagement. Sempronius eagerly took the bait. He sent out of his camp, first his cavalry, then his light-armed, and finally his legions, and he sent them before they had been able to take any food. It was now far on in the winter; the snow was falling fast, and the Trebia, swollen by rain, was running high between its banks. The water was up to the men's breasts, as they struggled, cold and hungry, across it. The Carthaginians, on the other hand, had had their usual meal, and had warmed themselves before fires. With ample time on his hands and perfectly at his ease, Hannibal drew up his army. Twenty thousand infantry, Africans, Spaniards, and Gauls, formed the centre; the cavalry, numbering ten thousand, were on the wings, with the elephants in front of them. The light-armed troops had been sent on in advance to support the African horse. The Roman line of battle was similarly arranged.

And now again, as before at the Ticinus, the weakness of the Romans in cavalry was fatal. This arm was inferior both in numbers and in quality. The Carthaginian horse charged on both wings, and routed their opponents almost without a struggle. The flanks of the great body of infantry which formed the Roman centre were thus uncovered, and were exposed to fierce attacks both from the cavalry and from the light-armed troops of the enemy. Still they held their own for a long time with all the courage and tenacity of Romans. But everything was against them, and when Mago's ambuscade leapt out from the watercourse, in which it had been hiding, and fell furiously upon their rear, the day was lost. If anything was still wanting to complete their rout, it was found in the elephants, strange and terrible creatures which few of the Romans or their allies had ever seen before. The rear of the army suffered worst. Indeed it was almost destroyed. The front ranks cut their way through the Gallic and African infantry that was opposed to them, and made their way to Placentia. These numbered about ten thousand. Some stragglers

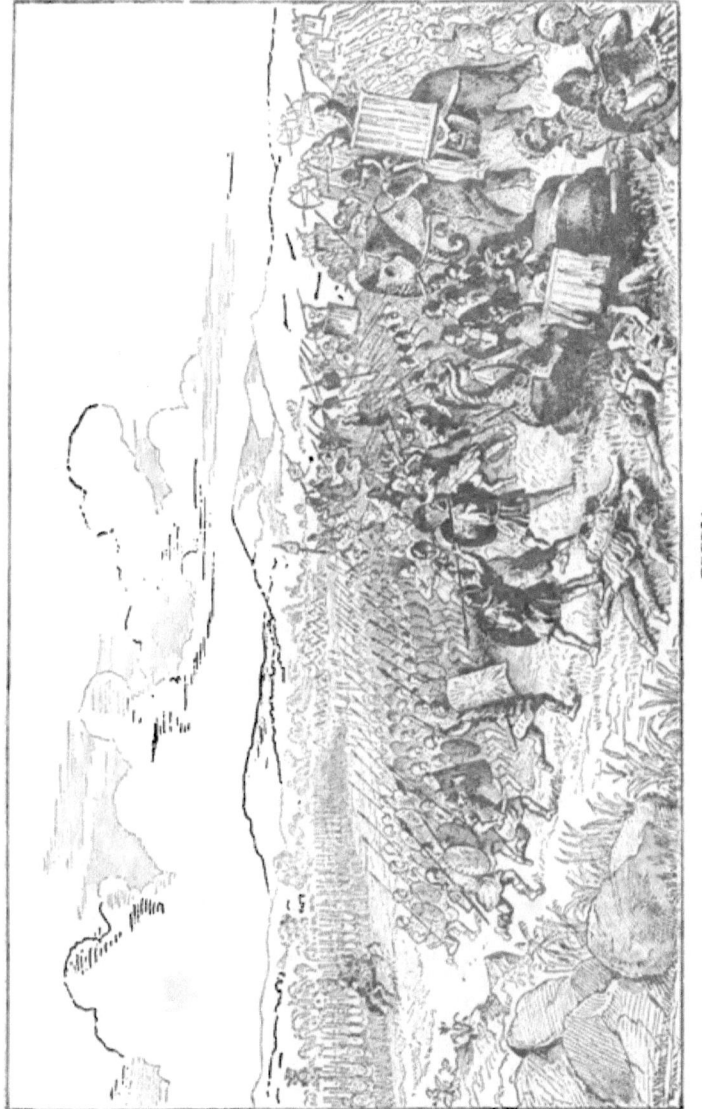

TREBIA.

from the rest of the army afterwards joined them. Others made their way back into the camp, for the conquerors did not pursue beyond the river. But it is probable that the Romans lost nearly half their force in killed, prisoners, and missing.

The Carthaginians did not win their victory without some loss. But the slain were chiefly from among the Gauls, whom Hannibal could most easily spare. His best infantry, the Spaniards and Africans, suffered little, except indeed from the cold—which the latter, of course, felt very much. The cold, too, was fatal to all the elephants but one.

With the battle of the Trebia the first campaign of the Second Punic War came to an end.

VIII.

TRASUMENNUS.

HANNIBAL spent the winter among the Ligurian Gauls. They had welcomed him among them as the successful enemy of Rome, but grew weary, we are told, of his presence, when they found that they had to support his army. He was even in danger of being assassinated, and had to protect himself by frequently changing his dress and even his wig. The winter was scarcely over when he took the field, making his way through the marshes of the Arno into the heart of Etruria. This way was the shortest that he could have taken, and by following it he avoided the Roman armies that were watching for him. But it cost him and his army dear. The floods were out everywhere, and not a spot of dry ground could be found on which his men could rest themselves. All that they could do was to pile up the baggage in the water and to rest upon that, or even upon the heaps of dead horses. Weary, without food, and without sleep, for this was their worst trouble, numbers perished on the march. Hannibal himself, who rode upon the one elephant that was left, to keep himself as far as possible above the water, was attacked with ophthalmia, and lost the sight of one of his eyes. When he reached the higher ground he gave his troops a short rest, and then marched boldly towards Rome, wasting the country, which was one of the richest parts of Italy, most cruelly as he went. One of the Roman Consuls, Flaminius, was at Arretium with about thirty thousand men; the other was at Ariminum on the east coast with as many more. Hannibal ventured to leave them in his rear, and now there was no army between him and Rome. Flaminius, who had found it hard to sit still and see the country of his allies wasted with fire and sword before his eyes, could not allow Rome itself to be attacked without striking a blow for it. He broke up his camp, and followed the Carthaginians. This was exactly what Hannibal expected and wished. And he laid an ambush for his pursuer. The road from Cortona to Perusia, along which he was marching, passed close to the northern shore of the Lake Trasumennus. Near the north-west corner of the lake the hills on either side of this lake approach close to each other; at the north-east corner again there is a still narrower passage formed by the hills on the north, and the lake itself on the south. Between these two is a level plain, somewhat like a bow in shape, if we suppose the edge of the water to be the string, and the retreating hills the bow itself. In front of the hills which commanded the eastern end of the pass Hannibal posted his African and Spanish troops; and here he himself remained. At the end of the pass itself, behind some rising ground which conveniently concealed them, he stationed his Gallic cavalry. The rest of his army he placed on the further slopes of the hills which enclosed the plain upon the north.

Flaminius reached the western end of the lake at sunset, and pitched his camp there for the night. The next morning, while the light was still dim, and without, it seems, attempting to reconnoitre his route, he continued his march. When his whole army had passed through the defile into the plain beyond, Hannibal gave the signal which had been arranged, and the Numidian cavalry with the Gallic infantry descended from the hills, and occupied the western outlet. The Roman army was hemmed in. They were surrounded, too, with mist, which rose from the lake and lay thick upon the level ground, while the sunshine was bright upon the slopes down which the enemy was moving to the attack. Before they could form their ranks in order of battle, almost before they could draw their swords, the enemy was upon them.

Flaminius did his best, but it was very little that he could do. There was no scope for a general's skill, even if he had possessed it. It was a soldiers' battle, where every man had to fight for himself; but the soldiers of Rome, newly recruited ploughmen and vinedressers, were scarcely a match for the veterans of Carthage, and were now taken at a terrible disadvantage. Still, for a time, they held their ground. For three hours the battle raged, so fiercely that none of the combatants felt the shock of an earthquake which that day laid more than one Italian city in ruins. Then the Consul fell. Conspicuous in his splendid arms, he had kept up the Roman battle, till one of Hannibal's troopers, an

SLAUGHTER OF THE ROMANS.

Insubrian Gaul, recognizing his face (for Flaminius had conquered the Insubrians eight years before), fiercely charged him. "See!" cried the man to his comrades, "this is he who slaughtered our legions and laid waste our fields. I will offer him a sacrifice to the shades of my countrymen." The Consul's armour-bearer threw himself in the way, but was struck down; and Ducarius (for that was the trooper's name) ran the Consul through with his lance. Then the Romans ceased to resist, even as the English ceased at Senlac when Harold was slain. Some sought to escape by the hills, others waded out into the lake, which is shallow to some distance from the shore. Men weighted with heavy armour could not hope to escape by swimming; yet some were desperate enough to try it. These were either drowned in the deeper water, or struggling back to the shallows were slaughtered in crowds by the cavalry, which had now ridden into the water. About six thousand of the vanguard cut their way through the enemy at the eastern end of the pass, and halted on the high ground beyond to watch the result of the battle. When the mist lifted, as the sun gained strength, from hill and plain, they saw that their comrades were hopelessly defeated, and, taking up their standards, hurried away. But without provisions, and not knowing which way to turn, they surrendered themselves next day to Hannibal. About ten thousand contrived to escape from the field of battle. These made the best of their way to Rome. Nearly fifteen thousand fell on the field or in the flight. The Carthaginians lost two thousand and five hundred, a proof that for a time at least the Romans had not sold their lives for nothing. The body of the Consul was never found, though Hannibal, anxious to give so brave a foe an honourable burial, ordered a careful search to be made for it.

A few days afterwards Hannibal had another success. Maharbal surprised a body of cavalry which Servilius was sending to help his colleague, killed half, and took the other half prisoners. He then marched south, but not, as one might expect, on Rome, though it had no army to protect it. He was afraid of undertaking the siege of such a city; indeed, when he attempted to take Spoletium, a colony, or military settlement, in Umbria, he was beaten back with great loss. He marched on in a south-easterly direction, wasting the country as he went, and gathering an immense booty, till he came to the eastern sea near a town called Hadria. There he took a few days rest and refreshed his army, for both men and horses were terribly exhausted with toil and privation. We are told that the horses, which were covered in ulcers, were bathed in old wine, and that this treatment cured them. From this place, too, he sent despatches to Carthage with an account of what he had done. They were the first that he had written since he crossed the Ebro. Soldiers say that the most dangerous thing that a general can do is to cut himself off from his base, to launch himself into the air, as it is sometimes called—that is, to leave nothing behind him on which he can fall back. Hannibal had done this so boldly that he had never been able even to send a messenger back with a letter. Now he was at the sea, and letters could be sent to and fro without hindrance. He is also said at this time to have armed some of his African infantry with arms of the Roman fashion. From Hadria he moved still southward, ravaging the eastern part of Italy as far down as Apulia, but always showing that it was with Rome and not with the Italian subjects of Rome that he was waging war. Any Roman citizen, or child of a Roman citizen that was of age to carry arms, he ordered to be slain.[1] The Italians that fell into his hands he not only spared, but treated with the utmost kindness.

[1] So goes the Roman story, but the frequent mention of Roman prisoners seems to prove that it was false.

IX.

FABIUS AND HIS TACTICS.

At Rome, after the first feeling of grief and terror had passed away, everything was being done to carry on the war with vigour. No one spoke of surrender, or even of peace. The chief command of all the armies of the State was given to a veteran soldier, Quintus Fabius Maximus by name, who had won the honour of a triumph nearly twenty years before. Fabius' first act was to consult the books of the Sibyl.[1] They were found to prescribe various acts of worship of the Gods, as the offering of prayers and sacrifices, the building of temples, and the celebrating public games. These were either done at once or promised for some future time. The Dictator (for this was his title) then ordered the levying of two new legions, and of a force which was to defend the city and man the fleet. He also directed that everything in the line of Hannibal's march should be destroyed. The Carthaginians were to find nothing but a desert wherever they came. He then marched north. At

---

[1] Books of prophecy, said to have been written by one of the Sibyls, sold to Tarquinius Priscus, fifth king of Rome, and afterwards preserved in the temple of Jupiter of the Capitol, to be consulted in any great need of the State. See "The Story of Rome," p. 59.

Ocriculum in Umbria he met Servilius, who was on his way to Rome, and took over his legions from him. Servilius he sent to command the fleet, which was being got ready at Ostia for the defence of the Italian seas. He himself, with an army numbering about fifty thousand men, followed in pursuit of the enemy. Hannibal found that he gained no friends in Apulia, and marched westward into Samnium, which, less than a hundred years before, had been the fiercest enemy of Rome. But here again he met with no success in making strife between Rome and its allies. He moved on into what was, perhaps, the very richest part of Italy, the great Falernian plain, where wines were grown that were to become famous over all the world. Fabius still followed him, watching every movement, cutting off stragglers, and harassing him in every way that he could devise, but always refusing a battle. When he saw his enemy below him in the Falernian plain—for Fabius kept his own army on the hills—he believed that he had him in a trap. To the north, the passes into Latium and the way to Rome were barred; the sea was in front of him; and to the south the deep stream of the Volturnus. On the east the hills, with their passes held by Roman troops, seemed to shut off his escape. Then Hannibal showed what a master of stratagem he was. He not only escaped, but carried off the booty which he had collected. His plan was this. About two thousand oxen were chosen out of the vast herds which had been collected out of the plundered districts. To their horns were fastened bundles of dry twigs. Then one day, as the dusk of evening came on, he silently struck his camp, and moved eastward towards the hills, the oxen being driven a little in front of the vanguard. When the army reached the foot of the hills it was dark; and then Hannibal ordered the bundles to be lighted. The drivers of the oxen started them up the slope of the hills; the animals, maddened by fear and pain—for the light flashed all about them, and the heat reached the flesh at the roots of their horns—rushed wildly on. The four thousand Romans who had been posted to guard the principal pass were dismayed at the sight. What it meant they could not understand; but that it meant danger they were sure. Probably they fancied that they were being surrounded—for this is always the first fear of all but the very best and bravest troops. Anyhow they left their post, and made for the heights. Fabius, in his camp, saw the strange sight, and was equally puzzled; nor did he venture out till it was light.[1] Meanwhile Hannibal had quietly marched his army through the pass, taking all his plunder with him, and pitched his camp next day at Allifæ, on the other side of the hills. Fabius followed him. He marched northwards through Samnium, as far as the country of the Peligni, ravaging as he went. Fabius still moved along, keeping his army between him and Rome.

---

[1] "This story of Livy," says Niebuhr, "represents the Romans in a foolish light. The truth is told by Polybius. Nothing was more common among the ancients than the march by night with lanterns; and when the Roman outposts saw the lights between themselves and the unoccupied district, they thought that the Carthaginians were forcing their way, and quickly advanced towards the supposed danger to shut the road against the enemy" (Lecture lxxiv.).

The effect of Hannibal's escape was twofold. Not only did he get out of a difficult position, carrying the greater part of his plunder with him, but he made it very hard for Fabius to carry out his policy of delay. This policy of course had many enemies. The allies, who saw their country ravaged without being able to strike a blow for it, were furious; and the wealthy Romans, whose estates were suffering in the same way, were loud in their complaints. And Hannibal's cunning plan of leaving Fabius' estates untouched, while all the neighbourhood was plundered, increased their anger. This change of feeling soon became evident. Fabius had to go to Rome on business for a time, and left his army in the charge of Minucius, Master of the Horse (this was the title of the Dictator's second-in-command), with strict orders not to fight. Minucius did fight, and won something like a little victory. When news of his success came to Rome, the opponents of Fabius persuaded the people to divide the army, and give the command of one half to the Dictator, and of the other to the Master of the Horse.

There were now two Roman armies encamped about a mile apart. Hannibal, who knew what had happened, immediately took advantage of the situation. Minucius, if he wished to satisfy his friends was bound to fight, and Hannibal soon gave him what looked like a favourable opportunity. He occupied some rising ground between his own camp and that of the Romans with what looked like a small force. The Romans hastened to dislodge it. But there were five thousand men in ambush, who, when the fighting had been going on for some time, fell upon the Roman rear. This gave way, and another great disaster would have been the result, had not Fabius, who was on the watch, led out his troops, and changed the fortunes of the day. After all no great harm was done; and there was this good result, that Minucius confessed his error, and gave up his command. The rest of the year passed without any further disasters, except that the Consul Servilius, landing on the coast of Africa, and ravaging the country, was attacked by the Carthaginians, and lost a thousand men.

Hannibal spent the winter at Geronium, in the north of Apulia. It was a mountainous country; and it was close to the sea. (This part of Apulia, indeed, is like an elbow projecting out into the Adriatic.) He had ample supplies, and he was in communication with Carthage. Probably new troops were sent to him. Anyhow, when the next year came (216) he was stronger than ever. It was late in the spring when he took the field. His first movement was to march round the Roman army, which had been watching him during the winter, and to seize a great magazine of stores which the enemy had collected. It was still his policy to provoke them to fight a battle, and this successful movement helped him. The Romans had gathered a great force, but found it difficult to feed it. They were afraid, too, lest they should lose their allies, if they allowed Hannibal to march up and down through Italy and plunder as he pleased. And the party of fighting had had a great success at the elections. C. Terentius Varro, a man of the people, after loudly proclaiming that the nobles were prolonging the war for their own purposes, had been chosen Consul by an immense majority. It was resolved to fight, but not to do so till the newly-levied legions should have joined the army of the year before. This was done about the beginning of June; and the whole army, now numbering about ninety thousand men, marched in pursuit of Hannibal, who was gathering in the early harvests on the seaboard of Apulia. The two consuls (Varro's colleague was a noble, Æmilius Paullus by name) had command on alternate days. Æmilius, an experienced soldier, was doubtful of the result of a battle, and anxious to put it off. Varro, on the other hand, was confident and eager, and on his first day of command brought matters to a crisis by taking up a position between Hannibal and the sea.

X.

CANNÆ.

THE great battle was still delayed for a few days. But when Hannibal's cavalry cut off the Roman watering-parties from the river, and left the army without water at the very height of an Italian summer, the impatience of the soldiers could not be restrained. On the morning of the 1st of August,[1] Varro, who that day was in command, hoisted on his tent the red flag as a signal of battle. He then ordered the army to cross the river Aufidus, and to draw up their lines on the right bank. Hannibal at once took up the challenge, and fording the stream at two places, drew up his army opposite to the enemy. His army was but half as large; if he should be defeated his doom was certain; but he was confident and cheerful. Plutarch tells us a story—one of the very few which show us something of the man rather than of the general—of his behaviour on the morning of the battle. He seems to have been one of the soldiers whose spirits rise in danger, and who become cheerful, and even gay, when others are most serious. "One of his chief officers, Gisco by name, said to him: 'I am

[1] The Roman reckoning was six or seven weeks in advance of the real year, and the time was really about midsummer.

astonished at the numbers of the enemy.' Hannibal smiled and said: 'Yes, Gisco; but there is something more wonderful still.' 'What is that?' said he. 'That though there are so many of them, not one of them is called Gisco.' The answer was so unexpected that everybody laughed." And he goes on to tell us that the Carthaginians were mightily encouraged to see this confident temper in their chief.

The Aufidus, bending first to the south, and then again, after flowing nearly eastward for a short distance, to the north, makes a loop. This loop was occupied by Hannibal's army. The left wing consisted of eight thousand heavy cavalry, Spaniards and Gauls. Hasdrubal (who must not be confounded with Hannibal's brother of the same name) was in command. They had the river on their left flank and on their right. Behind them was one half of the African infantry. "One might have thought them a Roman army," says Livy, "for Hannibal had armed them with the spoils of Trebia and Trasumennus." Next in the line, but somewhat in advance so as to be about on a level with the heavy cavalry, were posted the Spanish and Gallic infantry, with their companies alternately arranged, and under the immediate command of Hannibal himself and his brother Mago. These troops were still armed in their native fashion. The Spaniards wore white linen tunics, dazzlingly bright, and edged with purple. Their chief weapon was the sword which they used, of a short and handy size, and with which they were accustomed to thrust rather than strike. Nevertheless it was fitted for a blow, for it had, of course, an edge. The

Gauls were naked from the hips upwards. They used very long swords, without a point. Both had oblong shields, and both seemed to the Romans and Italians, whose stature seldom exceeded the average height of men, to be almost giants in size. Still further to the right, but thrown back somewhat so as to be on a level with their countrymen on the left wing, stood the other half of the African infantry. And then on the extreme right wing of the whole army, were the African light horsemen under the command of Mago. These, to use the military phrase, "rested upon nothing;" that is, they had nothing to support their right flank. There were but two thousand of them, for they had had some of the hardest of the fighting since the army had entered Italy; but they were confident of victory. The whole army numbered fifty thousand, but ten thousand had been detached to guard the camp. The right wing of the enemy consisted of the Roman horse, who thus fronted the heavy cavalry of Carthage; next to these came the infantry of the legions, more than seventy thousand strong, yet drawn up in so dense an array—in column, in fact, rather than in line—that they did not overlap the far smaller force of their adversaries. On the left wing were posted the cavalry of the allies. It was here that Varro commanded. Paullus was on the right of the army. The whole force numbered about eighty thousand, allowing for the detachment which had been told off to guard the camp. Their faces were turned to the south. This was a great disadvantage to them, not so much on account of the glare of the sun, for it was yet early in the day, but because the hot wind, which the country people called Vulturnus, rolled such clouds of dust in their faces that they could scarcely see what lay before them.

The battle began as usual with the skirmishers. Here the Carthaginians had the advantage. The slingers from the Balearic islands[1] were more expert and effective than any of the Roman light-armed troops. The showers of stones which they sent among the legions did much damage, wounding severely, among others, the Consul Paullus. Then the heavy-armed cavalry of Carthage charged the Roman horse that was ranged over against them. The Romans were some of the bravest and best born of their nation; but they were inferior in numbers, in the weight of men and horses, and in their equipment. They wore no cuirasses; their shields were weak; their spears were easily broken. Probably they had no special skill in cavalry tactics; had they possessed it, there was no opportunity of showing it, for there was no room to manœuvre. It was a fierce hand-to-hand fight; many of the Spaniards and Gauls leapt to the ground, and dragged their opponents from their horses.

In the centre of the field where the Roman legions met the Gallic and Spanish infantry, Hannibal seemed for a time to be less successful. He had advanced these troops considerably beyond the rest of his line. When charged by the heavy columns of the enemy they were forced to fall back. The Romans pressed

---

[1] Majorca, Minorca, and Ivica. The reader must not be tempted by the plausible derivation from the Greek βάλλω (ballo), to throw or strike. The name seems to have been derived from some form of Baal.

on in a dense and unmanageable mass. And in what seemed the moment of victory they found themselves assailed on both flanks and in the rear. On either side the two bodies of African infantry, who had hitherto taken no part in the battle, fell upon them. Almost at the same time came Hasdrubal with his heavy horsemen. After routing the Roman cavalry of the right wing, he had charged that of the allies upon the left. These had been already thrown into confusion by the stealthy attack of five hundred Africans, who had pretended to surrender, but came up in the critical moment and hamstrung their horses. Hasdrubal completed their rout, and leaving the Africans to pursue the fugitives, charged the rear of the Roman infantry. These were now surrounded on all sides, for the Gauls and Spaniards in their front had rallied, and checked their advance. Upon this helpless mass the Carthaginians used their swords till they were fairly weary of slaying. How many men lay dead upon the field when darkness came on it is impossible to say. Polybius gives the number at seventy thousand, and he is probably a better authority than Livy, who reduces it to fifty thousand. Among them were one of the consuls, the ex-consul Servilius, twenty-one military tribunes (officers of a rank about equal to that of a colonel), and eighty members of the Senate. Varro had fled from the field with seventy horsemen. Hannibal's loss was something under six thousand.

The question was, "What was he to do?" He had destroyed the enemy's army, for even the force left to guard the camps had surrendered, and there was no other army in the field. Most of his officers, while they crowded round to congratulate him, advised him to give himself and his army some rest. Maharbal, who was in chief command of the cavalry, thought otherwise. "Do you know," he said, "what you have done by this day's victory? I will tell you. Four days hence you shall be supping in the Capitol of Rome. Let me go on in front with my cavalry. They must know that I have come before they know that I am coming." Hannibal was not so sanguine. He praised Maharbal's zeal, but must take time to consider so grave a matter. Then Maharbal broke out: "I see that the gods do not give all their gifts to one man. Hannibal, you have the secret of victory, but not the secret of using it."

It will never be decided whether Hannibal, with his cautious policy, or the bold Maharbal was in the right. But one is disposed to believe that so skilful a general, one, too, who was not wanting in boldness (for what could be bolder than this whole march into Italy?), knew what could and what could not be done better than anybody else. He could not hope to succeed unless the allies of Rome deserted her, and he had to wait and see whether this would happen. Till he was sure of it he could not, we may well believe, afford to risk an advance. One defeat would have been fatal to him. It would have been almost as fatal to sit down in vain before the walls of Rome. But, however this may be, it is certain that the opportunity, if it was an opportunity, never came back to him. He did indeed come near to Rome, as I shall have to tell hereafter, but this was a feint rather than a serious attack. That midsummer day in the year 216 saw the highest point which the fortunes of Carthage ever reached. Then only, if even then, she might have been the mistress of the world.

XI.

AFTER CANNÆ.

THE victory of Cannæ had great results, though it did not make Hannibal feel strong enough to strike a blow at Rome. First and foremost among these results was the alliance of Capua, the second city in Italy. The Capuans, indeed, were not all of one mind in the matter. It was the people that favoured Carthage; the nobles were for the most part inclined to Rome. It was a noble, however, and one who was married to a lady of the great Roman house of Claudius, that took the lead in this movement. The people rose against the Senate, stripped it of its power, massacred a number of Roman citizens who were sojourning in the town, and sent envoys to invite Hannibal to their city. He was of course delighted to come; Capua, which had more than thirty thousand soldiers of her own, was almost as great a gain as the victory at Cannæ. He was near to being assassinated, indeed, on the night of his entering the city, for the son of his entertainer had resolved to stab him at the dinner-table. The next day he was present at a meeting of the Senate. He was full of promises; he undertook that Capua should thereafter be the capital of Italy. Meanwhile he demanded that a leading citizen who had been specially active on the Roman side should be given up to him. The man was arrested, and was sent by Hannibal to Carthage.

The greater part of Central and Southern Italy followed the example of Capua. All the Samnites, with the exception of a single tribe, revolted from Rome; so did Lucania and Bruttii, and so did many of the Greek cities in the south, the chief among them being Crotona. These cities had passed the height of their prosperity, but they were still populous and powerful towns.

It was only the extraordinary tenacity and courage of Rome that enabled her to hold out. The Senate never lost its courage, and, after the first panic was over, the people were ready to stand by their rulers to the last. When Varro, whose rashness and folly had almost ruined his country, returned to Rome, the Senate went out to meet him, and publicly thanked him that he "had not despaired of the commonwealth." As he was of the opposite party in politics, this was a way of saying that all Romans, whatever their way of thinking, must join together to made the best of everything. Nothing that could be done to raise an army was neglected. Bands of brigands were induced to enlist by promises of pardon for past offences; even slaves were recruited. As many as eight thousand soldiers were gained in this way. But when a proposal came from Hannibal that the prisoners of Cannæ should be ransomed, the horsemen at £17, the infantry at £10 each, the offer was refused. By great exertions an army was raised, and put under the command of Marcellus, who was probably the best soldier that Rome possessed at the time.

Hannibal had sent his brother Mago to Carthage from the battle-field of Cannæ. Introduced into the Senate, he gave a glowing account of what had been done, of the four victories which had been gained, of the two hundred thousand men that had been slain, the fifty thousand that had been taken prisoners. As a practical proof of the truth of his story, he poured out on the floor of the Senate-house a peck of gold rings which had been taken, he said, from Roman soldiers that had been slain in battle. It was only the horsemen, indeed only the upper class of the horsemen, he explained, that were accustomed to wear them. But the practical conclusion of his speech was a demand for help. "The nearer the prospect," he said, "of finishing the war, the more you are bound to support your general. He is fighting far away from home. Pay is wanted for troops; provisions are hard to obtain. And though he has won great victories, he has not won them without some loss. He asks, therefore, for help in men, money, and stores."

The war-party was delighted. One of them turned to Hanno, leader of the opposite faction, and asked him, " Does Hanno still repent of having made war on Rome?" "Yes," replied Hanno, "I still repent, and shall do so till I see peace made again. Your invincible general makes as great demands upon you as if he had been beaten. And as for his prospects for the future, has any Latin city joined him? Has a single man of the thirty-five tribes of Rome deserted to him?'

To these questions Mago could only answer "No!" Hanno asked again, "Has Rome said a word about peace?" Mago could only answer that it had not. Then said Hanno, "We are as far off from the end of the war as we were when Hannibal crossed into Italy. I vote that no help should be sent to prolong a war which can have no good end."

This protest, of course, was useless. The Senate resolved to send four thousand African troops, forty elephants, and a sum of money. And Mago was to go into Spain and raise 20,000 troops to fill up the gaps in the armies there and in Italy. As a matter of fact little was done; at this crisis the Carthaginian government showed but little energy, and Hannibal was left, for the most part, to help himself.

The winter of 216-5 he and his army spent in Capua. Ever since he had started from New Carthage, more than two years before, his men had lived in tents, satisfied with the hard discipline and scanty fare of the camp. Doubtless, they had lost something of their vigour by the time that they took the field again; but there were other and weightier reasons why Hannibal's great plans should end in failure than that his army was spoilt by the luxury of a winter in Capua.

In the next year little was done. Hannibal gained some small successes, and met with some small losses. His chief venture had been the siege of Nola, which, after Capua, was the chief city of Campania. In this he failed, owing chiefly to the skill and energy of Marcellus. To have let a year pass without making a decided advance was in fact to fall back. Still his prospects in some directions had improved. At Syracuse the wise old King Hiero, who had continued to be loyal to Rome, without making an enemy of Carthage, was dead. Hieronymus, his grandson and successor, was a foolish youth, who thought he could do better for himself by joining what seemed to be the winning side. He offered his help to Carthage, asking as the price the supremacy over the whole of Sicily. Philip, King of Macedon, again, seemed ready to join an alliance against Rome. Little advantage, however, was gained in this way. Of what happened to Hieronymus I shall soon have to speak. Philip's action was delayed, first by the accident of his envoys falling into the hands of the Romans as they were on their way back from Hannibal's camp, and afterwards by causes which we have no means of explaining. Anyhow, at the time when his help would have been most valuable to Hannibal and most damaging to Rome, he did nothing.

On the other hand, Carthage suffered a great loss in the complete conquest by their enemies of the island of Sardinia, which had again fallen into their hands. On the whole, at the end of 215 Hannibal, though he had received no serious check in the field, was in a much worse position than he had been in at the beginning.

The next year also (214) had much the same result. Hannibal made an attempt to seize Tarentum, but failed. There were in this town, as elsewhere, a Carthaginian and a Roman party. The latter got to know what their opponents were planning, and took such precautions, that when Hannibal appeared before the walls of the city he found it prepared for defence; and after vainly lingering in the neighbourhood for a few days, was obliged to depart. In another part of Southern Italy he suffered a serious loss. Hanno, one of his lieutenants, had raised a force of twenty thousand Lucanians. This was defeated at Beneventum by the Roman general Gracchus, who was in command of an army of slaves. Hanno's Lucanian infantry either perished on the field of battle, or dispersed to their own homes; but he escaped himself with about a thousand African cavalry.

The next great event of the war—its exact date is uncertain—was a great gain to Hannibal. The friends of Carthage in Tarentum, though overpowered for the moment, had never given up their plans; and now they found an opportunity for carrying them out. The city had sent hostages to Rome. These had attempted to escape, had been captured, and executed. This act of cruelty roused their fellow-citizens to fury; communications were at once opened with Hannibal, and the ringleaders of the plot were not, as might have been supposed, popular leaders, but nobles—relatives, it is probable, of the unfortunate hostages. Hannibal marched towards the town with a picked force of ten thousand men, and halted a few miles off, while his friends within the city completed their preparations. One party was told off to deal with the governor. a Roman of the house of Livius. He had been giving a banquet to some of the citizens; the conspirators paid him a visit after it was over, laughed and joked with him, and finally left him in such a state that they had nothing to fear from his watchfulness. Another party had arranged to admit Hannibal himself by a gate which opened out of the quarter of the tombs, which in Tarentum—we might almost say alone among Greek cities—were within the walls. A fire signal was given by Hannibal and answered by the conspirators. The latter fell upon the guards of the gate, and Hannibal was at hand outside to support them. A third party was busy at another of the gates. They had been accustomed for several days to go out on what seemed to be hunting parties, to return late at night, to talk over their sport with the guard, and to give them some of the game. On this occasion they brought back with them a particularly fine wild boar. While the animal was actually in the passage of the gate, and the sentry was busy admiring it, thirty African soldiers, who had been stealthily approaching, rushed up, cut the man down, and, securing the gate, let in a large body of their comrades. The city of Tarentum was taken, but the citadel was hastily secured by the Roman garrison. The Tarentines were not harmed. It was sufficient if any citizen wrote over his door, "This is a Tarentine's house." But all the dwellings in which Romans had been quartered were given up to plunder.

XII.

THE TURN OF THE TIDE.

FROM Trebia to Cannæ the tide of success rose with Hannibal. For three years or thereabouts after Cannæ it may be said to have remained at its height. His gains and losses about balanced each other. This, of course, really meant that his chances of victory were growing less, for his was an enterprise to which delay, even without defeat, was fatal.

In 212 the tide manifestly turned. The Romans felt themselves strong enough to besiege Capua. The city was already in distress for want of food, for with the Roman armies so near the rich Campanian plains could not be cultivated. And Hannibal's first attempt to provision it failed. A second succeeded; but shortly after the place was regularly invested. Three Roman armies sat down before it, and then drew a complete line round it with a strong rampart and ditch, and with forts at intervals. The townspeople were not strong enough to make sallies with effect, and all that they could do was to send messenger after messenger to Hannibal, begging earnestly for help, if he did not wish to see them perish. Early in the year 211—that is, after the siege had lasted some months—he made a determined effort to relieve the city. He marched rapidly with a picked force from Tarentum, where the citadel was still holding out against him, and took up a position on Mount Tifata, a hill which overlooked the city. He had contrived to warn the Capuans of his coming, arranging that they should make a sortie from their walls while he was attacking one of the camps of the besiegers. The sortie was easily repulsed; Hannibal's attack seemed at one time likely to succeed, but ended in failure. His elephants—he had thirty-three of these animals with him—forced their way into the Roman camp, and made great havoc with the tents, while they caused a stampede among the horses. In the midst of the confusion voices were heard bidding the Romans make the best of their way to the hills. The camp, they said, was lost, and each man must save himself. The speakers used the Latin tongue, and spoke in the name of the consuls; but they were really Hannibal's men. This was one of the tricks with which this great general was always so ready. Ingenious as it was, it does not seem to have had much effect.

Then he tried his last resource. He would march on Rome itself. With forces so large engaged in this siege, the city could have but few to defend it. It was possible that by a sudden movement he might get within the walls; in any case it was likely that a part of the investing force would be withdrawn for the protection of the capital. The Capuans were informed of what he was intending to do, and encouraged to hold out. He made his way through the rich wine-producing region of Northern Campania, ravaging the country as he went. At Fregellæ he found the bridge over the Liris broken down, and lost some time in consequence. Crossing into Latium, he passed through the town of Anagnia to Mount Algidus. After a vain attempt to seize Tusculum, he continued his march northwards, and pitched his camp at a distance of eight miles from Rome. Fulvius, the proconsul, had made his way meanwhile from Capua with a force of fifteen thousand men. Marching through a friendly country, and finding all that he wanted supplied by the towns through which he passed, he had been able to outstrip the Carthaginian army. Nevertheless the terror in the city was great. The women crowded to the temples, and, with their long hair unbound, threw themselves before the images of the gods and implored their protection. The next day Hannibal advanced still nearer to the walls. He pitched his camp on the bank of the Anio, at the third milestone from Rome; and then, taking with him a force of two thousand cavalry, rode up and reconnoitred the southern wall of the city. On the morrow he crossed the Anio with his whole army, and offered battle. But no engagement was fought. Livy tells us a story of how, that day and the next, so fierce a storm of rain came on that neither army could keep the field, the weather clearing immediately when they returned to camp; and how Hannibal exclaimed, "Once I wanted the will to take this city, and now I want the fortune." We are told that he was greatly discouraged by two proofs of the indifference with which the Romans regarded his presence. Soldiers, he heard, were being actually sent away from the city to reinforce the armies in Spain; and the very land on which he had pitched his camp had easily found a purchaser. By way of retort to this last affront—for so he is said to have regarded it—he ordered the bankers' shops round the Roman market-place to be put up to auction. But he found that his move had failed, and marched back to Campania, and from thence to the extreme south of Italy.

Capua, thus left to itself, could do nothing but surrender. Of its punishment by Rome it is needless to speak in detail. The nobles were executed; the rest of the population sold into slavery. In a play that was acted at Rome some twenty years afterwards we find a brutal jest on their cruel fate. "There," says one of the characters, speaking of some unhealthy spot, " even a Syrian—and the Syrians are the toughest of slaves—cannot live six months." "Nay," says the other, "the Campanians have learnt by this time to bear more than the Syrians."

The next year (210) passed with little incident, as far as Italy was concerned (I shall speak of Sicily and Spain hereafter). The Romans had never been able to vanquish Hannibal in the open field; they scarcely even ventured to meet him. He had shown that he could march from one end of Italy to the other without hindrance, and that he could send his plundering parties up to the very walls of Rome; but he had not been able to save the great city which had come over to him; and there was small temptation to any other to join him. Not only was Capua a great actual loss to him, but the fact that it had fallen in spite of all his efforts to relieve it was a terrible blow to his reputation. For all his skill as a general—and that showed itself more and more as the war went on—he was clearly wanting in power.

In Sicily, the course of events went against the cause of Carthage. Hieronymus, the foolish youth who had succeeded the wise old Hiero at Syracuse, had been murdered after a reign of thirteen months by an assassin who professed to be acting in the interests of Rome. A series of dreadful acts of cruelty followed. Here also, as elsewhere, the popular party favoured Carthage, while the aristocrats were inclined to Rome, and there was a fierce struggle between them. In the end the former triumphed, and Syracuse became the ally of Carthage. As such it was besieged by the forces of Rome, Appius Claudius commanding the army and Marcellus the fleet. The narrative of the siege does not fall within the scope of this book. The story of how the defence was prolonged by the engineering skill of Archimedes is full of interest, but it may be found elsewhere. The efforts which Carthage made to save her new ally were fruitless. A large army, indeed, was collected under Himilco, and this was reinforced from various Sicilian cities, which had been enraged by the savage cruelty which the Romans had shown in their treatment of such places as fell into their hands. But the Roman lines could not be broken; and when Himilco encamped outside them, intending, it is probable, to blockade them as they were blockading the city, a pestilence broke out among his troops. So fearful were its ravages that the army was literally destroyed. The fleet under Bomilcar did no more.

It did not even make an attempt at relieving the city. Though it numbered as many as a hundred and thirty vessels of war, it declined an engagement with the Romans, and instead of attempting to enter the harbour of Syracuse, sailed away to Tarentum. In 212 Syracuse was taken by Marcellus.

Hannibal, however, was not willing to give up the island as lost. He sent one Mutines, a Liby-Phœnician, or half-caste Carthaginian, to take command of the forces ; and Mutines, fixing his headquarters at Agrigentum, carried on for many months a guerilla warfare. Unfortunately his appointment had caused great annoyance to the pure-blood Carthaginian officers in the island, especially to Hanno, who was the commander-in-chief. Hanno at last suspended him, and handed over the command to his own son. The loyalty of Mutines did not stand firm under such provocation, and the Numidians who comprised his force were furious at his disgrace. Communications were at once opened with Lævinus, the Roman general. A force was sent to Agrigentum ; the Numidians cut down the guards of one of the city gates, threw it open, and admitted the Roman soldiers. Hanno, who had come to the place probably to make arrangements for the change of commanders, saw that something had taken place, and, supposing that it was nothing more than some riotous proceedings of the Numidians, went down to restore order. He discovered the truth just in time to save himself by flight. Lævinus executed the principal citizens of Agrigentum, and sold the rest of the population as slaves. Of the sixty-six Sicilian towns that had taken the side of Carthage, six were taken by force of arms and twenty were betrayed; the remainder capitulated. Before the end of 210 Sicily was finally lost.

In Spain affairs had not reached the same point, but they were tending the same way. Hannibal had left, we have seen, his brother Hasdrubal in command, and the war was carried on for several years with varying success between him and the two brothers, Cnæus and Publius Scipio. Cnæus Scipio had been left in Spain in temporary command when Publius left the country to face Hannibal in Italy, and he gained some considerable successes, if Livy's account is to be trusted. We cannot help noticing, however, that the Roman generals are again and again credited with great victories which mostly are found to lead to nothing. Unfortunately we have no other accounts to fall back upon, and we can only tell the story as it is told to us, and believe whatever seems credible.

In 218 Cnæus Scipio fought a battle with Hanno, who had been left in command of the country between the Ebro and the Pyrenees, vanquished and took him prisoner, and almost annihilated his army. The soldiers found a great prize in his camp, for Hannibal had left with him the heavy baggage which he could not carry across the Alps. Hasdrubal moved to help his colleague, but finding himself too late, re-crossed the Ebro. The next year, after wintering at Tarraco, Cnæus defeated the Carthaginian fleet off the mouth of the Ebro. Shortly afterwards he was joined by his brother Publius; and the two generals continued to act together for several years. Their first step was to march to **Saguntum.** The hostages given to the

Carthaginian government by the Spanish tribes were kept in the citadel of this town; the Scipios contrived to get possession of them by the treachery of the officer who had the charge of them. They sent them back to their friends, and of course gained great popularity throughout Spain by the act. In the following year (216) they are said to have defeated Hasdrubal on the banks of the Ebro so completely that he fled from the field of battle with but a few followers. In 215 they relieved Illiturgis, which Hasdrubal and two other Carthaginian generals were besieging. The Romans, we read, had but sixteen thousand men under arms, the Carthaginians sixty thousand; but the result of the battle was a complete victory. The Romans killed more than their own number, captured three thousand men, nearly a thousand horses (Livy is careful not to overstate the number), sixty standards, and seven elephants. Moving on to Intibilis the Scipios fought another battle, killed thirteen thousand of the enemy, captured two thousand, two and forty standards, and nine elephants. The result of these brilliant victories was that nearly all Spain came over to the Roman side. So we read, but find that for all this it was necessary to win two more great victories in the following year (214).

We may be sure, however, that during these years and the two following years (213, 212) the balance of success inclined to the Roman side. And this superiority became more evident when Hasdrubal Barca had to be recalled to Africa, where the Numidian king Syphax had declared war against Carthage. The Scipios had sent envoys to him, promising him immediate help and future reward if he would persevere in his hostility. One of the envoys remained behind to assist in drilling his new levies. The Carthaginians found an ally in King Gala, Syphax's neighbour and rival. King Gala had a son, Masinissa, a youth of but seventeen years, but of extraordinary capacity. Young as he was, he was put in command of his father's army and of the Carthaginian troops which served with it, and defeated Syphax so completely that the war was ended by a single battle. We shall hear of Masinissa again.

Hasdrudal was now able to return to Spain. He took with him large reinforcements, two lieutenants, another Hasdrubal, the son of Gisco, and Mago, the youngest brother of Hannibal, and Masinissa. After this the fortune of war changed. The Scipios had made a great effort to complete the conquest of Spain, raising a native force of twenty thousand to act together with their own troops. In view of the fact that three Carthaginian armies were now in the field, they determined to divide their own forces. Publius with two-thirds of the army was to act against Mago and Hasdrubal Gisco, Cnæus against Hasdrubal Barca. Publius, hearing that his opponents were likely to have their strength largely increased by native allies, resolved to attack them at once. He was himself attacked on his march by the African light horsemen under Masinissa, and when he faced about to receive their charge, found the Carthaginians assailing his rear. He was himself killed early in the day, and after his death his troops soon took to flight. Few, however, could escape when the pursuers were the

DEATH OF THE SCIPIOS.

light African horsemen, and an infantry that was almost as fleet of foot. The camp, however, with its garrison was still safe.

Cnæus did not long survive his brother. His native allies had been bribed to leave him; and he now found himself in the presence of the united forces of the three Carthaginian generals. He drew his forces together on some rising ground that was near. The place was incapable of being defended. The ascent was easy. There was no timber for a rampart; no earth with which the soldiers could make an entrenchment. All that could be done was to make a poor defence out of the pack-saddles of the horses and mules and the baggage. This was almost immediately broken down. Many of the soldiers made their escape to the camp of the other army; but the general perished. He had survived his brother only twenty-nine days. Lucius Marcius, the officer left in command of the camp, contrived to keep together what was left of the Roman forces, and even to inflict some losses on the enemy. His command was taken over by Claudius Nero, who was sent from Rome for that purpose, but who seems to have effected but little good. Livy tells a strange story of how Hasdrubal was surrounded; how he promised to evacuate Spain; how he amused the Roman general by conferences about the terms of agreement, and in the meanwhile contrived to get his army out of their dangerous situation, so that Nero, when the negotiations were broken off, found nothing but an empty camp. The death of the two Scipios seems to have happened in the year 211.

The next year the son of Publius, whom we have

seen saving his father's life at the battle of the Ticinus, came into Spain as commander-in-chief. It was an office which no one had desired to hold, for when the election was held at Rome not a single candidate presented himself. At last the young Scipio came forward. He was not twenty-four years old, and therefore below the legal age for even the lowest office; but the people received him with applause. His high reputation, the beauty of his person, and his charm of manner, spoke for him. When he promised that he would conquer not only Spain, but Carthage itself, what would have seemed in any other man but a foolish boast was received with delight, and he was unanimously chosen.

He began his campaign by a great achievement—the capture of New Carthage, the capital of the Carthaginian province. A night march brought him up to the walls of the city before any one knew that he had even arrived in Spain. With the keen eye of a great general he spied the weak spot in the defences, a place where the sea came up to the wall. Taking advantage of an unusually low tide—for he seems to have had the curious good fortune which goes to make a great general—he led his men through the water, which was barely up to their knees, and found his way into the city. Mago, who was in command, retreated into the citadel; but, finding it impossible to hold out, surrendered himself and his garrison in the course of a few hours. Within four days after coming into this province, Scipio had thus justified his appointment by capturing the Carthaginian capital. It will be convenient if we take this opportunity of finishing the story of the Carthaginian rule in Spain, though it will carry us beyond the time up to which we have followed the course of events elsewhere.

During the remainder of the year which he had begun by the capture of New Carthage Scipio remained quiet, but was busy in preparing for future action. He made friends of the Spanish chiefs. This was a business which he could do better than any other man, for no one could withstand the singular charm of his manner. When he took the field in the following year (209) the natives joined him in large numbers. In the course of this campaign he fought a great battle with Hasdrubal Barca. He is said to have defeated him, but as he did not hinder him from carrying out his great plan (of which I shall have to speak hereafter) of marching into Italy to the help of Hannibal, the defeat was evidently not serious. The next year passed with few incidents, but in 207 a decisive defeat of the Carthaginian armies at Silpia made Scipio master of nearly the whole of Spain. Only Gades was left to Carthage. Scipio had not forgotten his promise that he would conquer not only Spain but Carthage also. One part of it was now nearly fulfilled, and he now saw a chance of fulfilling the other. He crossed over with only a couple of war-ships to Africa, and presented himself at the court of King Syphax. His object was to persuade the king to desert Carthage, and enter into alliance with Rome. Curiously enough Hasdrubal Gisco had come on a similar errand. The two opponents spent several days together, and conversed, we are told, in a most kindly fashion. The king seems to have made promises to both. He was greatly charmed with Scipio, and even promised to make the alliance which he desired. But he was still more charmed with Sophonisba, the lovely daughter of Hasdrubal. She became his wife, and under her influence he remained faithful to Carthage.

Things had not gone well in Spain during Scipio's absence. Mago, who was still at Gades, induced some of the Spanish tribes to revolt against Rome. These had to be again subdued. When this was done, Scipio himself fell ill. During his illness a part of the Roman army broke out into open mutiny. Their pay was in arrear, and Scipio's strict discipline forbad them to make it up by plundering the natives of the country. But when the general was sufficiently recovered to be able to deal with them in person, he contrived to bring them back to their duty. The Carthaginian cause in Spain was now lost. Mago, the brother of Hannibal, transported what forces remained to him into Liguria, and Gades surrendered to the Romans. This was in the year 205.

XIII.

THE LAST CHANCE OF VICTORY.

In Italy Hannibal still remained unvanquished in the field, though his hopes were gradually growing less. Early in the year 210 he won at Herdonia in Western Apulia a victory which may almost be reckoned with those that had made his early campaigns so famous. Cnæus Fulvius, who had been Consul the year before, had made a sudden march on the town. It was one of those that had revolted after the defeat at Cannæ, and he understood it to be badly guarded. He was the bolder because he believed Hannibal to be in the extreme south of Italy. But Hannibal had heard everything from his spies, and was there to meet him. Fulvius, as might be expected, was out-generalled. His army was unskilfully posted, and could not resist the attacks which were directed against it from several points at once. The end was a complete rout. Even the Roman camp was taken. Fulvius himself fell in the battle, and the Roman loss was estimated by some at eleven, by others at seven thousand. It was evidently a great disaster. Nothing like an army was left; only some scattered fugitives made their way to Marcellus in Samnium. It was from Marcellus, not from any officer who had been present at Herdonia, that the Senate received a despatch describing what had happened.

During the rest of the campaign but little happened, though Marcellus is said to have fought a drawn battle with Hannibal, which was claimed as a victory when the next day he found that the enemy had decamped. The following year (209) was one of disaster to Hannibal, for he lost the second of the great gains which he had secured in Italy, the city of Tarentum. It was betrayed to the Romans by the commander of the Bruttian garrison which Hannibal had placed in it. The veteran soldier Fabius, now in his eightieth year and consul for the fifth time, had the great delight of finishing his many campaigns by this piece of good fortune. A happy jest which the old man is said to have uttered on the occasion has been recorded. Livius, when his carelessness had lost the city, had taken refuge in the citadel. The citadel had never passed out of the hands of the Romans, and this fact of course made the recovery of the town somewhat more easy. Livius was disposed to get some credit for himself out of this circumstance. "You may thank me," he said, "Quintus Fabius, for having been able to recover Tarentum." "Quite so," replied Fabius, "for if you had not lost it, I never should have recovered it." Hannibal had heard of the advance of the Romans, and had hastened by forced marches to save the city. He was too late. He pitched his camp close by, and after a few days returned to his headquarters at Metapontum. He made an attempt to entrap Fabius, who might, he thought, be tempted, after his success at Tarentum, into making a similar attempt on Metapontum. A forged letter, purporting to come from some of the principal citizens, was conveyed to him, offering to betray the place into his hands. The old Roman is said to have been deceived, but to have been deterred from making the attempt by some unfavourable signs in the sacrifices. Notwithstanding this loss, Hannibal seems to have held his own during the rest of the campaign. Livy tells us, indeed, that Marcellus fought three battles with him, and that after being beaten in the first, he drew the second, and won the third. But as it was made a complaint against him afterwards that he had kept his troops for the greater part of the year within the walls of Venusia, and had allowed the enemy to plunder the country at his pleasure, we may well doubt whether any victory was won. Rome was now showing great signs of exhaustion, for twelve out of the thirty Latin cities refused to furnish any further supplies; and the Etrurians were beginning to waver in their fidelity.

The next year (208) is chiefly marked by the death of Marcellus. Chosen consul for the sixth time, he marched with his colleague Crispinus to act against Hannibal. He was never content, we are told, except when he was engaged with the great Carthaginian leader himself. The two consuls had ridden out of the camp with an escort of two hundred cavalry, some of them Etrurians, who had been compelled to serve to ensure the fidelity of their cities. Some African horsemen under cover of a wood which was between the two camps, crept unobserved to the rear of the Roman party, and then charged them from behind. The Etrurians fled; the rest of the escort, who were Latins, were overpowered. Marcellus was killed on the spot; Crispinus was wounded so seriously that he died not long afterward. Hannibal gave honourable burial to the body of his brave opponent.

And now came on of the critical years of the war. Hasdrubal, of whose departure from Spain I have spoken before, was now in Italy. He had found little difficulty in crossing the Alps; the native tribes had learnt that no harm was intended to them, and probably received some consideration for their neutrality. And some of the engineering works which Hannibal had constructed were doubtless still in existence. Anyhow, Hasdrubal made his appearance in Italy before the Romans, and even, it would seem, before his brother expected him. Rome made a great effort to meet this new danger. She had lost some of her best generals. Marcellus was dead, and Fabius was too old for active service. Livius, an old soldier who had distinguished himself twelve years before, but had since been living in retirement, and Claudius Nero, were chosen consuls, and fifteen legions were raised to form their armies. Livius was sent to act against Hasdrubal; Nero watched the army of Hannibal.

And now we come to one of the boldest and most skilful achievements in the history of Roman war. A despatch from Hasdrubal to his brother, announcing his intention of joining him, fell into the hands of some Roman scouts and was brought to Nero. It was written in the Carthaginian language, but there were, of course, prisoners in the camp who could read it to the consul. He conceived at once a bold design. He would take his best troops, join his colleague by forced marches, and crush Hasdrubal before he could effect the junction with his brother. The force which he selected numbered seven thousand men. Even they were not at first let into the secret. They were to surprise a garrison at Lucania, he told them. It was only when they were well on their way that he discovered his real design. He reached the camp of Livius in safety, and it was agreed between the two consuls that battle should be given at once.

But the keen eyes of Hasdrubal had discovered what had happened. The Romans seemed more numerous than before; his scouts noticed that of the watering-parties which went down to the river some were more sunburnt than the rest. Finally it was observed that the clarion was sounded twice in the camp, showing that both consuls were present. He resolved to avoid, if he could, an engagement, and left his camp during the night. But when he attempted to march southward his difficulties began. His native guide escaped, and he could not find the ford over the river Metaurus, which lay in his route. He thus lost the start which he had gained by his stealthy departure, and the Romans came up with him. He had begun to fortify a camp, but seeing the enemy advance prepared to give battle. He put his elephants in front. The Gauls, recent levies whom he could not trust, he posted on his left, protecting them as much as he could by the elephants. His own place was on the right wing. Here he had his Spanish infantry, veteran soldiers whom he had often led to victory. The left wing of the Romans which was opposed to him was led by the Consul Livius. Here the struggle was long and obstinate. The elephants at first did good service to their side. Afterwards, maddened by the wounds which they received, they trampled down friend and foe alike. After a while, Nero, repeating the same tactics which had made him leave his own weakened army facing Hannibal to help his colleague, withdrew some of the troops from the Roman right wing, and charged the flank of the enemy. The Spaniards could not resist this new attack. The Gauls, who had broken into the stores of wine and had drunk to excess, were cut down where they stood, or lay helpless on the ground. The rout was complete. Hasdrubal would not survive so terrible a defeat. He set spurs to his horse, charged the Roman line, and fell fighting with the courage that became the son of Hamilcar and brother of Hannibal. The loss of the Carthaginians is said to have been 56,000. This is a manifest exaggeration, for Hasdrubal could not have had so many in his army. Whatever were the numbers, it was a decisive victory. There could now be no doubt that Rome, not Carthage, was to be the conqueror of the Second Punic War. I may conclude this chapter by quoting part of the splendid ode in which Horace, singing the praises of another Nero,[1] dwells on the achievement of his great ancestor.

[1] Tiberius Claudius Nero, afterwards the Emperor Tiberius.

ODE FROM HORACE.

What thou, Rome, dost the Neros owe,
    Let dark Metaurus river say,
And Hasdrubal, thy vanquished foe,
    And that auspicious day
Which through the scattered gloom broke forth with smiling ray.

When joy again to Latium came,
    Nor longer through her towns at ease
The fatal Lybian swept, like flame
    Among the forest trees,
Or Eurus' headlong gust across Sicilian seas.

Thenceforth, for with success they toiled,
    Rome's youth in vigour waxed amain,
And temples, ravaged and despoiled
    By Punic hordes profane,
Upraised within their shrines beheld their gods again.

Till spoke forth Hannibal at length:
    "Like stags, of ravening wolves the prey,
Why rush to grapple with their strength,
    From whom to steal away
Our loftiest triumph is, they leave for us to-day?

"That race, inflexible as brave,
    From Ilium quenched in flames who bore,
Across the wild Etruscan wave,
    Their babes, their grandsires hoar,
And all their sacred things to the Ansonian shore;

"Like oak, by sturdy axes lopped
    Of all its boughs, which once the brakes
Of shaggy Algidus o'ertopped,
    Its loss its glory makes,
And from the very steel fresh strength and spirit takes.

"Not Hydra, cleft through all its trunk,
    With fresher vigour waxed to spread,
Till even Alcides' spirit shrunk;
    Nor yet hath Colchis dread,
Or Echionean Thebes more fatal monster bred.

> "In ocean plunge it, and more bright
>   It rises; scatter it, and lo!
> Its unscathed victors it will smite
>   With direful overthrow,
> And Rome's proud dames shall tell of many a routed foe:
>
> "No messenger in boastful pride
>   Shall I to Carthage send again;
> Our every hope it died, it died,
>   When Hasdrubal was slain,
> And with his fall our name's all-conquering star did wane."[1]

Nero returned in haste to his army, and ordered the head of Hasdrubal to be thrown in front of the Carthaginian outposts. It was carried to Hannibal, and recognized by him. "I see," he said, "the doom of Carthage." The next day he retreated into the extreme south of Italy.

[1] I have borrowed the version of Sir Theodore Martin.

XIV

THE LAST STRUGGLE.

FOR more than three years after the fatal day of Metaurus, Hannibal maintained himself in Italy. It was only the extreme south of the peninsula, the mountainous country of Bruttii, that he held; and even here, though the Roman generals were content to leave him alone, knowing well how formidable he still was in the field, he was obliged to draw his defences within still narrowing limits. His headquarters were at Crotona. Near this place he built an altar to Juno, and placed on it a tablet with an inscription in Carthaginian and Greek, giving a summary of his campaigns in Italy, with the number of battles won, towns taken, and enemies slain. Livy bestows hearty praise on his conduct at this time. "I know not," he says, "whether the man was more admirable in prosperity or in adversity. For thirteen years, far away from home, he waged war, and waged it not with an army of his own countrymen, but with a miscellaneous crowd gathered from all nations—men who had neither laws, nor customs, nor language in common, with different dress, different arms, different worship, I may say, different gods. And yet he kept them together by so close a tie that they never quarrelled among themselves or mutinied against him, and this though he was often without money for their pay. Even after Hasdrubal's death, when he had nothing but a corner of Italy left to him, his camp was as quiet as ever."

Hannibal was of course unwilling finally to give up the great scheme of his life. He hoped against hope that something might yet happen which would give him a chance of carrying it out. Rome had other enemies besides Carthage who might yet be united against her. There was Antiochus in Syria, and Philip in Macedonia. He lived to see them both engaged in war with Rome, and both conquered. If he could only have given them something of his own foresight, and united them against the common enemy, he might even yet have succeeded in his great scheme. But want of wisdom, or want of energy, or want of courage, made them hold back, and the opportunity was lost.

One effort, indeed, was made to help him. His youngest brother Mago, seeing that nothing could be done in Spain, landed with all the forces that he could raise, and with what were sent him from home, in Liguria. On his way he possessed himself of the island now called Minorca, where Port Mahon (Mago's Harbour) still preserves the memory of his visit. He had some success in rallying the Gauls to his standard, but he accomplished nothing of importance. So far as his object was to make a diversion in favour of Hannibal, he failed.

In 204 Scipio crossed over from Sicily to Africa. His first movements were not very successful. He

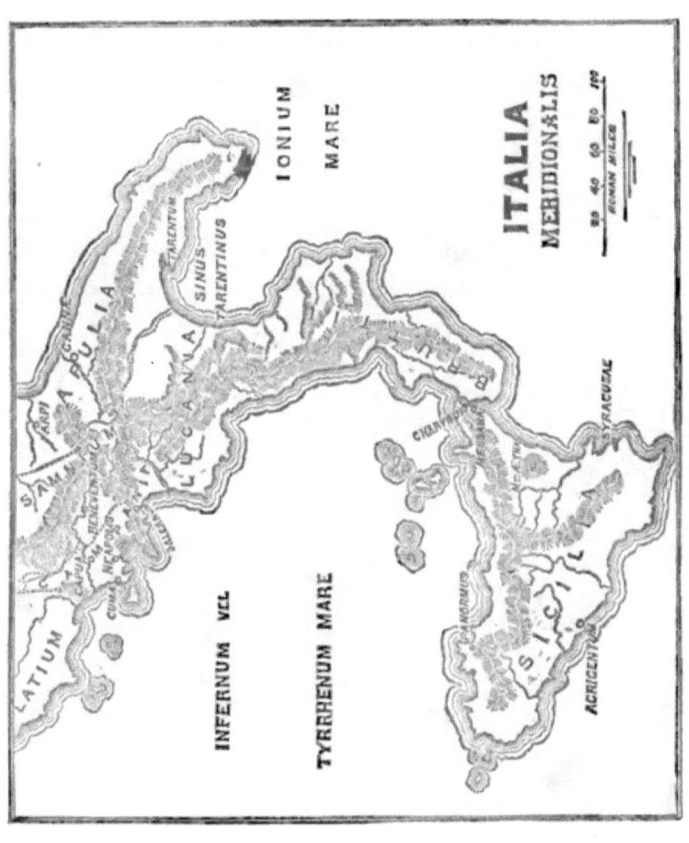

began the siege of Utica, but was compelled to raise it, and to retire to a strong position on the sea-coast, where he was protected by the united strength of his fleet and his army. Here he wintered, and early the following year began again active operations. He had two armies opposed to him—that of Carthage, commanded by Hasdrubal, the son of Gisco, and that of King Syphax. In his own camp was Masinissa, who, though he had lost his kingdom, and indeed had barely escaped with his life, was without doubt a very valuable counsellor and ally.

King Syphax had conceived the hope that he might be able to act as mediator between Rome and Carthage. He now proposed a peace, in which the chief condition was that Hannibal should evacuate Italy and Scipio Africa. Scipio answered that these were terms which could not be accepted, but gave him to understand that he was ready to listen to other proposals. Envoys went backwards and forwards between the two camps. On the part of the king there was, it would seem, a genuine belief that peace might be made; Scipio's envoys were really nothing else than so many spies. He was waiting for the opportunity of carrying out a scheme which had possibly been invented by himself, or, as is more probable, suggested by Masinissa. This scheme was to set fire to the camps of the two hostile armies. These camps consisted of huts which would readily burn, and the chief thing wanted was to put the enemy completely off his guard. Scipio can scarcely be acquitted of something like treachery in this affair. There was virtually a truce between him and Syphax. While negotiations for peace were going on, the king naturally supposed himself to be safe from attack.

When all his preparations were complete, Scipio divided his army into two. With half he was himself to attack the Carthaginian camp; the other half he put under the command of his friend Lælius, who was assisted by Masinissa. The two armies marched out of the camp at night, and Lælius and Masinissa advanced to the camp of Syphax. While the former of these two remained in reserve, the latter undertook the work of setting the camp on fire. The scheme succeeded perfectly. "The camp seemed framed," says Polybius, who doubtless heard the story from Lælius himself, "for the very purpose of being set on fire." The flames spread rapidly; and no one had any suspicion but that the fire had happened by accident. Some perished in their tents; many were trampled to death in the confusion; and nearly all who contrived to escape out of the camp were cut down by the Romans.

At first the Carthaginians in the neighbouring camp thought, as their allies had thought, that the fire was accidental. Some of them ran to help; others stood gazing at the sight. None had any notion that the enemy was at hand; they were therefore actually unarmed when the Romans fell upon them. In a few minutes the second camp was in the same condition as the first. Hasdrubal, with a small body of cavalry, escaped; Syphax also contrived to save himself, but the two armies were virtually destroyed.

Syphax had thought of reconciling himself to Rome; but his wife Sophonisba prevailed upon him to give them up. He raised another army, which was soon joined by Hasdrubal, who had also contrived to get together a new force, among them being four thousand mercenaries from Spain. A battle followed, in which Scipio was again victorious.

There was now only one course left to Carthage, and that was to recall Hannibal and Mago. Mago, who had been defeated by the Roman forces just before this summons reached him, set sail with what was left of his army, but died of his wounds before he reached home. Hannibal received the command to return with indignation and grief. Livy gives—we know not on what authority—the very words in which, "gnashing his teeth and groaning, and scarcely able to restrain his tears," he answered the envoys of the Carthaginian Senate. "They call me back at last in plain words; but they have long since implicitly called me by refusing me reinforcements and money. Hannibal has been conquered, not by the Roman people, which he has defeated and routed a hundred times, but by the jealousy of the Senate of Carthage. It will not be Scipio that will exult in the disgrace of my return so much as Hanno, who, having no other means of overthrowing the power of my family, has done it by the ruin of his own country." Hanno, it will be remembered, was the leader of the peace-party. Wrathful, however, as he was, he made no delay in obeying the summons. He had his ships, indeed, ready prepared for this service. "Seldom," says Livy, "has an exile left his country with a sadder heart than was Hannibal's when he departed from the land of his enemies. Again and again he looked back on the shores which he was leaving, and cursed himself that he had not led his soldiers dripping with the blood of Cannæ to Rome itself. 'Scipio,' he said, 'has ventured to attack Carthage; but I wasted my time at Casilinum and Cumæ and Nola.'"

When the news of his departure reached Rome, a public thanksgiving was ordered. The veteran soldier Fabius had bestowed upon him the unexampled honour of a wreath of oak leaves, given, not as was commonly the case, for having saved the life of a citizen, but for having saved his country. A few months afterwards he died, in extreme old age, having been spared to see the dearest wish of his heart, Italy freed from the invader.

Hannibal's movements after his landing in Africa—from which he had been absent more than thirty years—are not easily followed. Indeed the whole history of this time is somewhat obscure. We hear of a truce between Carthage and Rome, which the former treacherously violated; of favourable terms of peace offered by Scipio, and of a fruitless interview between the two rival generals; but it is difficult to make out of our authorities a clear and consistent account. I shall pass on at once to the great battle which brought the Second Punic War to an end. Of this we have full details. It was fought at Zama, on October 19th according to some authors, according to others in the spring.[1] Scipio arranged his army

---

[1] Possibly the discrepancy may be partly accounted for by the derangement of the Roman calendar of this time. The months and the seasons were not by any means in accordance.

according to the usual Roman fashion, but did not fill up the intervals between the cohorts or companies,¹ and he put more space than usual between the lines. His object was to lessen the danger from the elephants. Lælius with the Roman cavalry was posted on the left, Masinissa with the African horse on the right. The light-armed troops were placed in front, with orders to retire, if they found themselves hard pressed by the elephants, through the intervals between the lines.

Hannibal posted his elephants, of which he had eighty, in front. Behind these was a mixed multitude of mercenaries; behind these, again, the native Carthaginian troops, who now, in the extremity of danger, appear again in the field; and in the third line the veterans whom he had brought with him from Italy. On the left wing he posted his African, on the right his Carthaginian cavalry.

The battle was begun by the elephants. These creatures did at least as much harm to friends as to foes.² They are said, indeed, to have caused so much confusion among the Carthaginian cavalry that Lælius was easily able to rout this part of the hostile army.

In the centre of the two armies the day at first went in favour of Hannibal. His mercenaries, tried and skilful soldiers, were more than a match for the unpractised Romans. If they had been properly

---

¹ The intervals of the first line were usually filled up in the second, and those of the second in the third.

² The trained animals had long since been used up. We hear, not long before this time, of one Hauno being sent to hunt for fresh ones.

supported by the second line they might have won the day. But the citizen-soldiers made no attempt to advance. It was only when they were attacked by the advancing Romans, and even, Polybius adds, by the mercenaries, now infuriated at being thus deserted, that they began to defend themselves. This they did with the greatest fury, striking indiscriminately at friend and foe. Hannibal's own force, which had closed its lines against the fugitives from the routed divisions, had still to be dealt with. Here the battle was long and obstinate. The combatants fell where they fought. But Lælius and Masinissa (for the Numidian prince had also been successful in his part of the field) returned from their pursuit of the Carthaginian cavalry, and fell upon the rear of Hannibal's troops, and broke their lines. A general rout ensued. Hannibal made his way with a small body of cavalry to Adrumetum. Of the rest few escaped. Twenty thousand were killed on the field of battle; as many more were taken prisoners. The Roman loss was fifteen hundred. "Such," says Polybius, "was the battle between Hannibal and Scipio; the battle which gave to the Romans the sovereignty of the world."

Hannibal collected about six thousand men, the remains of his army, and with this force made his way back to Carthage. The government had opened negotiations for peace, and their envoys had just returned, bringing back Scipio's terms. They were briefly these:

1. Carthage was to retain its African possessions; was to be independent; was not to be compelled to receive a Roman garrison.

2. All prisoners and deserters were to be surrendered.

3. All ships of war, except *ten*, were to be given up, and all elephants.

4. Carthage should not make war on any state outside Africa; nor on any within it, without leave first obtained from the Romans.

5. King Masinissa should have restored to him all that he or his ancestors had possessed.

6. The Roman army was to be provisioned and paid till peace was formally concluded.

7. An indemnity of ten thousand talents, and an annual tribute of two hundred, to be paid.

8. One hundred hostages, to be chosen by the Roman commander-in-chief, to be handed over as security.

When these terms were recited in the Carthaginian Senate, a senator rose to speak. Hannibal laid hold of him, and dragged him down. The assembly received this act with angry shouts. "Pardon me," said Hannibal, "if my ignorance has led me to offend against any of your forms. I left my country at nine years of age, and returned to it at forty-five. The real cause of my offence was my care for our common country. It is astonishing to me that any Carthaginian who knows the truth should not be ready to worship his good fortune, when he finds Rome ready to deal with us so mercifully. Do not debate these conditions; consent to them unanimously, and pray to all the gods that they may be ratified by the Roman Senate."

Ratified they were, though not, it would seem, till the

following year. We catch a glimpse of the old days before men had learnt the use of iron, when we read how the heralds went to Carthage carrying with them the knives of flint with which the animals offered in sacrifice were to be slain. The Carthaginians surrendered all their ships of war, their elephants, the deserters who had come over to them, and as many as four thousand prisoners. The ships of one kind and another numbered five hundred. Scipio ordered them to be towed out to sea and burnt. "The sight of the flames was as terrrible," says Livy, "to the vanquished people as would have been that of their city on fire."

When the indemnity came to be paid it was difficult to find the money; and there were loud murmurs in the Senate at the sacrifices which it would be necessary to make. One of the members complained to the House that Hannibal had been seen to laugh; and this though he was really the cause of all their troubles. Then the great man spoke out. "If you could see my heart as easily as you can my face, you would know that my laughter comes not from a joyful heart, but from one almost maddened by trouble. And yet my laughter is not so unreasonable as your tears. You ought to have wept when our arms were taken from us and our ships were burnt. But no; you were silent when you saw your country stripped; but now you lament, as if this were the death-day of Carthage, because you have to furnish part of the tribute out of your private means. I fear me much that you will soon find that this is the least of the trouble you will have to bear."

XV.

HANNIBAL IN EXILE.

It was true that, as the discontented senator had said, Hannibal had been the cause of the troubles of Carthage; still he was too great a man to be anywhere but in the first place; and for some years he practically governed the State. He seems to have done this new work well. The Court of Judges at Carthage had usurped a power which did not belong to them. Every man's property, character, and life were at their disposal; and they were unscrupulous in dealing with it. Hannibal set himself to bring about a change; he carried the people with him; the office of judge became annual, and it was filled up by election. It is a change that does not altogether commend itself to us; but it was probably required by the peculiar condition of the country.

Another reform concerned the public revenue. Hannibal made a searching inquiry into what came in, and what was spent, and he found that a very large proportion of the whole was embezzled. He stated these discoveries in a public assembly. The expenses of the country might be met, the tribute to Rome paid, and taxation nevertheless lightened, if only the revenue were honestly collected and honestly spent. It was only too natural that these proceedings should make many enemies. And besides those who were furious at the loss of their unjust gains, there were doubtless some who were honestly afraid of what Hannibal was aiming at. If he was making Carthage richer and more powerful, it was that he might plunge her again into a war with Rome. So, from one cause or the other, a strong party was raised against him. His enemies had, it is said, the meanness to accuse him to the Roman Government. He was planning, they said, a new war in concert with Antiochus, king of Syria. The Romans were on the point of war with this prince, and were ready to suspect their old enemy. An embassy was sent to Carthage, in spite of the opposition of Scipio, to demand that he should be given up. Ostensibly the object of their invasion was to settle a dispute between Carthage and Masinissa.

Hannibal knew the truth, and resolved to fly. To put his enemies off their guard, he showed no kind of alarm, but walked about in public as usual. But he took horse at night, reached the coast, and embarked in a ship which, in anticipation of such a need, he had kept in readiness, and sailed to Cercina (Kerkena). It was necessary to conceal the fact of his flight, and he gave out that he was going as ambassador to Tyre. But the harbour of the island happened to be full of merchant-ships, and the risk of discovery was great. He resolved accordingly to escape. The captains were invited to a great entertainment, and were asked to lend their sails and yards for the construction of a tent. The revel was long and late. Before it was over Hannibal was gone, and the dismantled ships could not be made ready for several hours. From Cercina he sailed to Tyre, where he was received with great honours, and from Tyre again to the port of Antioch. Antiochus had left that place and was at Ephesus, and thither Hannibal followed him.

Antiochus of Syria, fourth in descent from Seleucus, one of the Macedonian generals who had shared between them the empire of Alexander, has somehow acquired the title of the "Great." He had little that was great about him except, perhaps, his ambition. His treatment of Hannibal, whether it was the result of weakness or of jealousy, was foolish in the extreme. He did not take his advice, and he would not employ him. His advice had been to act at once. Rome at this time (195 B.C.) had to deal with many enemies. The Gauls especially were giving her much trouble. If Antiochus could have made up his mind to attack her immediately, the result might have been different to what it was. As it was he lingered and delayed, and when at last, two years afterwards, he made up his mind to act, the opportunity was lost. In 192 he crossed over into Greece, and was defeated with heavy loss the following year at Thermopylæ. Hannibal was not employed in this campaign. But he was sent to equip and to command a fleet. There was nothing strange in this variety of employment; for then—and indeed the same has been the case till quite recent times—the same men would command fleets and armies indifferently. He was attacked by a greatly superior fleet belonging to the island of Rhodes, then a great naval power, and, though successful where he commanded in person, was defeated.

In the same year (190) was fought the great battle of Magnesia. Whether Hannibal was present at it we do not know; but an anecdote is told of him which belongs to this time. Antiochus had collected a great army—some sixty or seventy thousand in number—to do battle with the Romans. It had been gathered from the cities of Greece and from Western Asia, and their dress and armour was as splendid as it was various. The king looked with pride on the ranks glittering with gold and silver. "Will not this be enough for the Romans?" he asked of Hannibal who was standing by his side. "Yes," said he, with a grim jest, "yes, enough even for them, though they are the greediest nation on the earth!" But it was of the spoils, not of the fighting strength of the army, that he was speaking.

The battle of Magnesia ended, as Hannibal had expected, in the utter defeat of the Syrian army. Antiochus was advised to sue for peace. Two years afterwards (188) it was granted to him, one of the conditions being that he should give to Rome such of her enemies as he had received at his court. He accepted the condition, but gave his guest an opportunity of escaping.

Various stories are told of Hannibal's movements after his flight from the court of Antiochus. According to one account he sought refuge for a time in Crete. A story is told of him here which very likely is not true, but which shows the common belief in his ingenuity and readiness of resource. He suspected the Cretans of coveting the large treasure which he carried about with him. To deceive them he filled a number of wine-jars with lead, which had over it a thin covering of gold and silver. These he deposited with much ceremony in the presence of the chief men of the island in the temple of Diana. His real treasure meanwhile was hidden in some hollow brazen figures which were allowed to lie, apparently uncared for, in the porch of his house. From Crete he is said to have visited Armenia, and to have founded in that country the city of Artaxata. It is certain, however, that he spent the last years of his life with Prusias, king of Bithynia. Prusias was at war with Eumenes of Pergamus, a firm friend of Rome, and Hannibal willingly gave him his help. We need not believe the story which he tells us how he vanquished enemies in a sea-fight by filling a number of jars with venomous snakes and throwing them on board the hostile ships.

For some years he was left unmolested in this refuge. But in 183 the Romans sent an embassy to Prusias to demand that he should be given up. The demand was one which the king did not feel able to resist, and he sent soldiers at once to seize him. Hannibal had always expected some such result. He knew that Rome could never forgive him for what he had done, and he did not trust his host. Indeed he must have known that a king of Bithynia could not refuse a request of the Romans if it was seriously made. The story of his end, ornamented as such stories commonly are, tells us how he made seven ways of getting out of his house, and that finding them all beset with soldiers, he called for the poison, which was kept always ready for such an emergency, and drank it off. Some writers say that he carried the poison with him in a ring—the ring which Juvenal, when he uses the example of Hannibal to show the vanity of a soldier's ambition, describes as "the avenger of the day of Cannæ." Livy gives us what profess to be his last words. "Let me free the Roman people from their long anxiety, since they think it tedious to wait for an old man's death. Flaminius [this was the Roman ambassador] will gain no great or famous victory over a helpless victim of treachery. As to the way in which the Roman character has changed, this day is proof enough. The grandfathers of these men sent to King Pyrrhus, when he had an army fighting against them in Italy, warning him to beware of poison; but they have sent an ambassador to suggest to Prusias the crime of murdering a guest." He was in his sixty-fourth or sixty-fifth year when he died.

Of Hannibal's character, as of the history of his country, we have to judge from the narratives of enemies. His military skill is beyond all doubt. In that, it is probable, he has never been surpassed. His courage also was undoubted, though he is expressly praised for the discretion with which he avoided any needless exposure of his life. The testimony to the temperance of his habits is equally clear. The chief charges brought against him are treachery, cruelty, and avarice. From personal avarice he was certainly free, but a general who has to make war support itself, who has to feed, clothe, and pay a great army in a foreign country, with but rare and scanty supplies from home, cannot be scrupulous. About the charge of cruelty it is not easy to speak. What has been said about Hannibal's alleged avarice applies in a way to this other accusation. A general situated as was Hannibal could not but be stern and even merciless in his dealings with enemies. As to treachery, we know that "Punic faith" passed among the Romans into a proverb for dishonesty; and "faithless" is the epithet, as we have seen, which Horace applies to the great general. But we find no special grounds for the charge, while we may certainly doubt whether the Roman generals showed such conspicuous good faith as to be in a good position for censuring others. There was no more honourable Roman than Scipio, but Scipio's treacherous attack on Syphax during the progress of the negotiations is at least as bad as anything that is charged against Hannibal.

XVI.

THE BEGINNING OF THE END.

THE death of Hannibal did not remove the suspicion of Rome that Carthage might be plotting some mischief. The conditions imposed upon her by the Peace of Hannibal (as the treaty made after the battle of Zama was called) had not permanently disabled her. She had lost her dominions but not her trade; her war-ships had been destroyed, but not the ships of her commerce; and she had always in her treasury the gold with which to hire new armies. Only twenty years had passed since the conclusion of the peace, when she offered to pay up at once the balance of the indemnity which was to have been spread over fifty years. The Romans preferred keeping this hold over their ancient enemies to receiving the money, but they were alarmed at this proof of how completely the wealth of Carthage was restored. Some ten years later, when war with Macedonia was threatening, news came to Rome that the envoys of the Macedonian king had been received at Carthage. Doubtless the envoys had been sent; and it is probable that they found some powerful persons ready to listen to them—for there was still a war-party in Carthage—but there is no reason to believe that the

CATO'S HOSTILITY TO CARTHAGE.

government had had any dealings with the enemies of Rome. There was one Roman statesmen by whom these suspicions were very strongly felt. This was Marcus Porcius Cato, commonly called the Elder Cato, to distinguish him from his great-grandson, Cato of Utica, the republican who killed himself sooner than live under the despotism of Cæsar. Cato had served throughout the campaigns of the Second Punic War, and had not forgotten his experiences of that time. He had been sent to inquire into the causes of a war that had broken out between Carthage and King Masinissa, and he had been much struck by the proofs of wealth and power that he saw during his visit, the crowded population of the city and territory, the well-appointed fleet. and the well-filled armouries. Returning to Rome, he related in the Senate what he had seen. "This people," he said, "is stronger than ever. They are practising war in Africa by way of prelude to war against you." As he spoke, he threw down from a fold in his robe a bunch of ripe figs. "The country that bears these," he cried, as the senators admired the beautiful fruit, "is but three days' journey from here." One is not certain whether he meant that it was so near as to be dangerous, or that it could be easily reached. Anyhow, from that time he never ceased to take every opportunity that occurred of expressing his opinion in the Senate. Whatever the matter might be that was being voted upon, he added the words, "And I also think that Carthage ought to be blotted out." With equal pertinacity one of the Scipios (surnamed Nasica, or "Scipio of the Pointed Nose), a near kinsman of the conqueror of Zama, added to every vote, "And I also think that Carthage ought to be left."

Carthage had a dangerous enemy at home in King Masinissa. He had begun life, as we have seen, by serving with Hasdrubal Barca in Spain, had then changed sides, and fought on the side of the Romans at the battle of Zama. He had been handsomely rewarded for these services. His father's dominions had been restored to him, and to these had been added the greater part of the kingdom of Syphax. For more than fifty years he was continually engaged in enlarging his borders at the expense of Carthage, and he always felt that he could rely on the help, or at least the countenance, of the Romans. Carthage was forbidden to make war on her neighbours in Africa without the leave of Rome, and all that she could do in return for Masinissa's aggressions was to send to appeal to that power to protect her against the wrongs that she was compelled to suffer. More than once the Romans sent commissioners to inquire into her complaints. Once, indeed, possibly oftener, these commissioners decided against Masinissa, but they generally left the matter unsettled. Anyhow, the king went on with his encroachments, and generally contrived to keep what he had laid his hands upon.

In 151 this quarrel broke out into open war. Masinissa had a party of his own in Carthage. The democratic or war party expelled forty of its principal members, imposing at the same time an oath upon the people that they would never allow them to return. The exiles fled to the king and urged him to make war. He was willing enough, for he had his eye on a town which he particularly coveted; but he first sent one of his sons on an embassy to Carthage to demand redress. The prince was not admitted within the works, and was even attacked on his way home. Masinissa then laid siege to the town. The Carthaginians sent Hasdrubal, their commander-in-chief, against him. They were joined by two of the king's chief officers, who deserted, bringing with them as many as six thousand horse. In some slight engagements that followed Hasdrubal was victorious; and the king made a feint of retreat, and drew Hasdrubal after him into a region where supplies could not easily be obtained. A battle soon followed. The old king —he was eighty-eight years of age—commanded in person, riding after the fashion of his country, without saddle or stirrup. No very decided result followed, but the king, on the whole, had the advantage. There was present that day, as spectator of the conflict, a young Roman who had much to do with the conclusion of the story of Carthage. To give him the full title which he bears in history, this was Publius Cornelius Scipio Æmilianus Africanus Minor. He was a son of a distinguished Roman general, Æmilius Paullus, the conqueror of Pydna,[1] and grandson of the Æmilius Paullus who fell at Cannæ. He was adopted by the elder son of the Scipio Africanus, the conqueror of Zama, whose weak health prevented him from taking any part in public affairs.[2] He had

---

[1] Pydna was the great battle (fought in 169) by which the Macedonian kingdom was brought to an end. See "The Story of Rome," p. 163.

[2] The young reader may observe that he took the names of the family into which he was adopted, adding to them that of his own *gens*, altered from Æmilius into Æmilianus, according to the practice in case of adoption.

been serving with a Roman army in Spain, and had come to Masinissa for the purpose of purchasing elephants. He had privilege of seeing the battle from a hill that overlooked the plain, and afterwards said (we probably get the story from his friend Polybius) that, though he had been present at many battles, he had never been so much pleased. "I saw," said he, "one hundred and ten thousand men meet in combat. It was a sight such as two only have seen before me, Zeus from the top of Ida, and Poseidon from Samothrace, in the Trojan war."

Scipio undertook to arbitrate between the two parties. The Carthaginians offered to give up the country round Emporia, or the Markets (now Gabes and Terba), and to pay two hundred talents down and eight hundred more in instalments; but when the king demanded also the surrender of the fugitives, the negotiations were broken off. Hasdrubal ought now to have taken up a position which it would have been possible for him to hold, but he neglected to do so. He expected another offer from Masinissa, and he also had hopes that the Romans would interfere in his favour. His delay was fatal to him. Famine, and the fever that always follows on famine, wasted his army. In the end he was obliged to accept the most humiliating terms. The exiles of Masinissa's party were to be taken back into the city; the fugitives were to be surrendered; an indemnity of five thousand talents was to be paid, and he and his soldiers were to pass through the hostile camp, unarmed and with but a single garment apiece. The helpless fugitives were attacked by one of the king's sons at the head of a force of cavalry, and cruelly slaughtered. Only a very few, among whom was Hasdrubal himself, returned to Carthage.

But worse remained behind. The Carthaginian government condemned to death Hasdrubal and those who had been most active in promoting the war. But when the ambassadors whom they sent to Rome pleaded this proceeding as a ground for acquittal, they were asked, "Why did you not condemn them before, not after the defeat?" To this there was no answer; and the Roman Senate voted that the Carthaginian explanation was not sufficient. "Tell us," said the unhappy men, "what we must do?" "You must satisfy the Roman People," was the ambiguous answer. When this was reported at Carthage, a second embassy was sent, imploring to be definitely told what they must do. These were dismissed with the answer, "The Carthaginians know this already." Rome had accepted the pitiless counsel of Cato, and Carthage was to be blotted out. If there was any doubt, it was dismissed when envoys came from Utica offering the submission of that city. The consuls of the year, Manilius and Censorinus, were at once dispatched with a fleet and an army. Their secret instructions were that they were not to be satisfied till Carthage was destroyed. The forces which they commanded amounted to nearly a hundred thousand men. The expedition was popular; for the prospects of booty were great, and volunteers of all ranks thronged to take part in it. The news that the fleet had sailed was the first intimation that Carthage received that war had been declared.

The Carthaginian government still hoped that an absolute submission might save them. They sent another embassy to Rome with full powers to grant any terms that might be asked. The answer that they received was this: "If the Carthaginians will give three hundred hostages from their noblest families, and fulfil all other conditions within thirty days, they shall retain their independence and the possession of their territory." But secret instructions were also sent to the consuls that they were to abide, whatever might happen, by their first instructions.

The hostages were sent, after a miserable scene of parting from their friends. But few believed that submission would be of any avail. And indeed it was soon seen to be useless. The consuls demanded that the arms in the city should be given up. The demand was accepted. Two hundred thousand weapons, more darts and javelins than could be counted, and two thousand catapults were given up. Then the consuls spoke again. "You must leave Carthage; we have resolved to destroy this city. You may remove your furniture and property to some other place, but it must be not less than ten miles from the sea." And they added some reasons, which must have sounded like the cruellest mockery, why they should be content with this decision. "You will be better away from the sea," they said in effect; "it will only remind you of the greatness which you have lost. It is a dangerous element, which before this has raised to great prosperity and brought to utter ruin other countries besides yours. Agriculture is a far safer and more profitable employment. And," he added, "we are keeping our promise that Carthage should be independent. It is the men, not the walls and buildings of the city, that constitute the real Carthage."[1]

The return of the envoys had been expected at Carthage with the utmost impatience. As they entered the gate of the city they were almost trampled to death by the crowd. At last they made their way into the Senate-house. Then they told their story, the people waiting in a dense throng outside the doors of the chamber. When it was told, a loud cry of dismay and rage went up from the assembly; and the people, hearing it, rushed in. A fearful scene of violence followed. Those who had advised the surrender of the hostages and of the arms were fiercely attacked. Some of them were even torn to pieces. The envoys themselves were not spared, though their only offence had been to bring bad news. Any unlucky Italians, whom business had happened to detain in the city, fell victims to the popular fury. A few more wisely busied themselves with making such preparations for defence as were possible, for of course there was but one alternative now possible. Indeed the Senate declared war that same day.

[1] It is difficult to believe that these abominable sophistries were ever really uttered. But we have good reason for supposing that Appian, from whom we get the report of the Consuls' speech, copied it from Polybius, an excellent authority. The historians of antiquity, however, had a passion for putting speeches into the mouths of their characters, and were not always particular about their authenticity.

XVII.

THE SIEGE AND FALL OF CARTHAGE.

THE Carthaginian government did their best to defend their city. One Hasdrubal, the same that had been condemned to death in the vain hope of propitiating the Romans, was appointed to command the forces outside the city; another had the control of those within the walls. The manufacture of arms was carried on night and day, by men and women alike, even the temples and sacred enclosures being turned into workshops. A hundred shields, three hundred swords, a thousand javelins to be thrown by the catapults, were made daily. The women are said to have cut off their hair for the cords of the catapults, for which the horsehair that was commonly used was wanting.

The wall of Carthage had a circumference of about eighteen miles. It was about forty-six feet high, and thirty-four feet thick. The height is that of what is called the *curtain* of the wall, *i.e.* the portions between the towers. The towers were of four stories, and much higher. Where the sea came up to the fortifications—and as the city was built upon a peninsula, this was the case with the greater part of the circuit—a single wall was deemed sufficient; but on the land side, *i.e.*

THE WALLS OF CARTHAGE.

to the north and south, the wall was triple. Appian tells that the three walls were of equal height and breadth. This is incredible, because such an arrangement would have been useless. The first wall once taken would have given the besiegers such an advantage that the second would have soon become untenable. No trace of any such kind of fortification can be discovered either at Carthage or in any ancient town. The real meaning of the author — possibly Polybius — from whom Appian quoted, seems to have been this. There were three ditches. Behind the inner of the three, the wall proper was built.

THE TRIPLE WALL OF THAPSUS.

Then came the advance wall, much lower than the wall proper, and in front of this the second ditch; possibly there was an outer defence of palisades, itself protected by a third ditch. The traces of exactly such a system of fortification are to be found at Thapsus. Within the casemates of the main wall there was room for three hundred elephants, four thousand cavalry, and twenty thousand infantry.

The harbours were so arranged that ships had to pass through the one to reach the other. The outer harbour was meant for merchant ships, and its entrance from the sea was closed with iron chains. In the inner harbour were kept the ships of war. There was an island in it, and on this island, as well as round the sides of the harbour, were slips in which two hundred and twenty vessels could be placed. The island also contained the admiral's house. This was so high that he could get a view of all that was going on outside. Between the two harbours there was a wall so high that it was not possible to look from the outer into the inner. There was a separate entrance from the town to the outer harbour. The inner or military harbour was evidently guarded with the greatest care.

Manilius directed his attack on the landward side of the wall; Censorinus attempted a part which, being partly protected by a lagoon, was less strongly fortified than the rest. The outer fortifications were carried, but no further progress was made. Indeed the besiegers had some serious losses, as Hasdrubal, with his lieutenants, among whom a certain Himilco,

THE GREAT WALL AT THAIYSUS.

surnamed Phamæas, was conspicuously active, continually attacked any detached parties.

Things seemed more hopeful when Censorinus, having filled up part of the lagoon, brought two battering-rams to bear on the wall, one of them worked by six thousand soldiers, the other by as many sailors. The force of these brought down part of it; and the Carthaginians built up again this portion in the night. The new work was not very strong. Then the besieged made a furious sally, set some of the works on fire, and made the whole, for a time at least, unserviceable. The next day the Romans attempted an assault by a part of the breach which had not been repaired, but were repulsed with heavy loss.

Censorinus now found that his crews suffered from the climate, for it was the height of summer. Accordingly he transferred his ships from the lagoon to the open sea. The Carthaginians took every opportunity, when the wind favoured, of sending fire ships among the Roman fleet, and thus did it a great deal of damage.

The Roman commanders continued to conduct their operations, with little skill and as little success. And just at the time when they most needed his help they had the misfortune to lose their ally Masinissa. There had been a coolness between the old man and his Roman friends, he conceiving that he had been rudely put aside, and that the task of dealing with Carthage had been unfairly taken out of his hands. And now when the consuls sent to ask his help—he had promised to give it *when they asked for it*, and this they had been too proud to do—they found him dying. He had completed his ninetieth year, retaining to the last his vigour of mind and body. The other inveterate enemy of Carthage, the old Cato, had died a few months before. Scipio, who had been distinguishing himself during the siege, was entrusted with the task of dividing the old king's dominion and wealth between his three sons. One of these, Gulussa by name, became at once an active ally, and was found especially helpful in repelling the attacks of Phamæas with his light cavalry. It was not indeed long before Phamæas himself was induced by Scipio to desert his friends.

A change of commanders, Manilius and Censorinus giving place to Piso and Mancinus, did not bring a change for the better in the conduct of the siege. This, in fact, was almost given up, the new consuls busying themselves with assaults on the neighbouring towns. Calpurnius was particularly unfortunate at Hippo (now Bizerta), where all his siege works were destroyed by a sally of the townspeople.

The spirits of the Carthaginians rose in proportion to the discouragement of the Romans. Some of Gulussa's cavalry had deserted to them; and the two other sons of Masinissa, though nominally friendly to Rome, stood aloof and waited for what might happen. Envoys were sent to them and to the independent Moors, representing that if Carthage fell they would be the next to be conquered. Communications were also opened with the Macedonian pretender who was then at war with Rome. Unfortunately the Hasdrubal who commanded outside the walls coveted the position of his namesake in the city. He accused him of

PORT OF CARTHAGE (FROM SARCOPHAGI).

treachery—it was his misfortune to be closely related to Gulussa; the unhappy man, surprised by the charge, faltered in his defence, and was murdered in the Senate-house, his senators striking him down with the fragments of the benches.

At Rome every one had expected a speedy end to the siege, and there was great vexation and even alarm at these long delays. All eyes were fixed on the one man who had showed real capacity for command, and fixed the more earnestly on account of the fortunate name that he bore. It had been a Scipio who had brought the war of Hannibal to an end; it was to be a Scipio who should complete his work and destroy Carthage itself. The young soldier went to Rome to stand for the office of Ædile—not, we may guess, without some notion of what was going to happen. The people elected him to the consulship. The consul, who was presiding, protested. Scipio was thirty-seven years old, and was therefore under the legal age. The people insisted; they were the masters of the elections and could choose whom they would. The tribunes threatened to suspend the presiding consul, unless he gave away. He yielded; as did Scipio's colleague when it came to choosing the province which each consul should have. This was commonly determined by lot, but the people was resolved that Scipio should have Africa, and it was so arranged.

The new commander's first exploit was to rescue Mancinus from a dangerous position into which he had got himself. Anxious to do something before he was superseded, he led a storming party against a weak

point in the wall, and actually made his way into the
town. But he was not strong enough to advance,
and could barely maintain his hold of what he had
gained. His colleague Piso, though summoned to
help him, made no movement; but Scipio, who, on
reaching Utica, had received a despatch describing
the situation, hastened to the spot, and carried off
Mancinus and his party in safety. The two consuls
shortly afterwards returned to Rome, and Scipio set

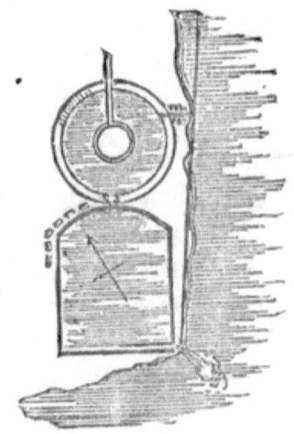

THE HARBOURS OF CARTHAGE (ACCORDING TO BEULÉ).

himself to restore the discipline and order which the
lax rule of his predecessors had suffered to decay.
He purged the Roman camp of a crowd of idlers and
plunderers which had collected there, and left nothing
but what was manageable and serviceable. His first
operation was to storm a quarter of the city which
went by the name of the Megara, and was, it would
seem the abode of the wealthier class. The assault

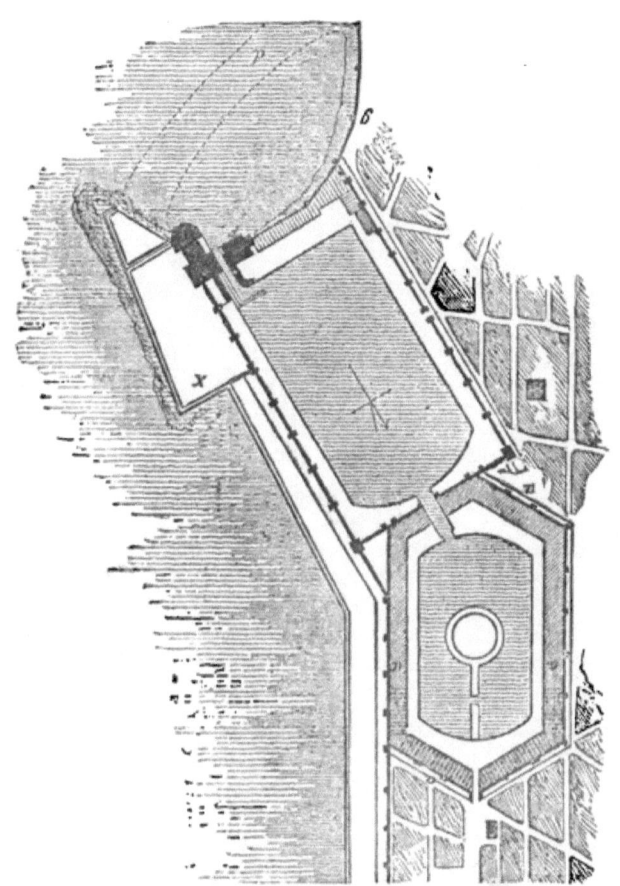

HARBOURS OF CARTHAGE (ACCORDING TO DAUX)

was made by two parties, one of them led by Scipio in person. Neither could make its way over the wall; but a tower, belonging to some private dwelling, which had been unwisely allowed to stand though it commanded the fortification, was occupied, and some

ARRANGEMENTS OF THE BERTHS (ACCORDING TO BEULÉ).

of the besiegers made their way from it on to the wall, and from the wall into the Megara. They then opened one of the gates, and Scipio with a force of four thousand men entered. He did not, however, feel it safe to remain, for the place was full of gardens, and its hedges and watercourses made it difficult ground

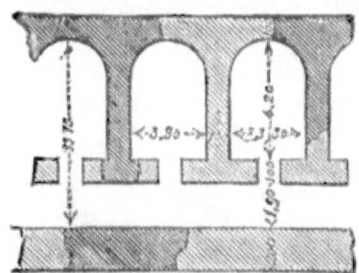

PLAN OF WALL AT BYRSA.

for the action of troops; but the operation had its results, the most important of which was that the army outside the walls, fancying that the city was taken, abandoned its camp, and retreated into the Byrsa or Upper City.

Hasdrubal, enraged at this movement, retaliated by a barbarous massacre of all the prisoners in his hands. He brought the poor wretches to the edge of the wall, subjected them to the cruellest tortures, and threw them down still alive from the height. After such an act the besieged would feel that they had no hope of mercy.

The siege now became almost a blockade. Scipio burnt the camp which the outside army had deserted in their panic, and was now master of the neck of the peninsula on which the city stood. No more food could be introduced overland, and the supplies which came by sea were small and precarious. The next step was to block up the harbour. Scipio constructed a great wall across the mouth. So huge was the work that the besieged at first believed it impossible, but when they saw it advance rapidly, the whole army labouring at it night and day, they began to be alarmed. Their own energy was not less than that of the besiegers. They dug a new channel from the harbour to the open sea, and, while this work was being carried on, they built also fifty ships of war. The besiegers knew nothing of what was being done, though they heard a continual sound of hammering. Their astonishment was very great when a fleet, of whose existence they had not an idea—for all the ships had been given up and destroyed—issued forth from a harbour mouth which had never been seen before. The Carthaginians, in great glee, manœuvred in front of the Roman fleet. If they had attacked it promptly, they might have done it irreparable damage, for the ships had been left almost entirely without protection. As it was, they contented themselves with a demonstration, and then returned to the harbour. It was an opportunity which never returned. It was fated, says the historian, that Carthage should be taken. Two days afterwards the two fleets fought; but by this time the Romans were prepared, and the battle was drawn. The next day it was renewed, and then the Carthaginians were decidedly worsted.

A determined effort was now made on the harbour side of the city. The rams were brought to bear upon the walls, and brought down a considerable part of it. But the Carthaginians made a furious sally. They plunged naked into the lagoon, carrying unlighted torches. Some waded through the shallows; others swam. Reaching the land, they lighted their torches and rushed fiercely on the siege works. Many were killed, for they had neither shields nor armour; but nothing could resist their charge. The Romans gave way in confusion, and the siege works were burnt. Even Scipio, though he ordered the flying soldiers to be cut down, could not check the panic. The day ended in a great success for the besieged.

When the winter with its cooler weather drew on, Scipio turned his attention to the region from which Carthage drew what supplies it could still obtain. His lieutenant Lælius, in concert with King Gulussa, attacked and defeated with enormous loss (though it is difficult to credit the figures of seventy thousand slain and ten thousand prisoners) an army of native allies. The food supply of the besieged city was now almost cut off, but Hasdrubal had still enough to support his garrison. The rest of the population were left to starve.

With the beginning of 146 Scipio prepared for an attack on the Upper City and the Harbour of the War-ships, or Cothon, as it was called. The Harbour was taken first, the resistance of the besieged being feeble and desultory. From the Harbour Scipio made his way into the neighbouring market-place. Even he could not check his troops in the plunder of the rich temple of Apollo. They are said to have stripped from the statue and shrine as much as a thousand talents of gold.

The next thing to be done was the attack on the Upper City. Three streets led up to it from the market-place, each of six-storied houses, from which the garrison and many of the citizen population kept up an incessant fight with the besiegers. House after house was stormed, the defenders being gradually forced back by superior strength and discipline. Another conflict was going on meanwhile in the streets, the Romans struggling up each of the three roads till they gained the Upper City. When that was accomplished, Scipio ordered the streets to be set on fire. The scene of destruction which followed was terrible. A number of non-combatants, old men, women, and children, had hidden themselves in the houses that were now blazing. Some threw themselves on to the spears and swords of the soldiers; some were burnt in their hiding places; some flung themselves from the windows into the streets. Many were buried or half-buried under the ruins, for the pioneers were busy clearing a way for the troops, and did their

FIGHTING IN THE CITY.

work careless of the living creatures that came in their way.

For six days and nights these horrors continued, described, it must be remembered, by an eye-witness, the historian Polybius; for it is from him, there is little doubt, that Appian has borrowed his vivid description of the scene. The troops worked and fought in relief parties. Scipio alone remained unceasingly at his post. He never slept, and he snatched a morsel of food as the chance came to him. On the seventh day a train of suppliants came from the temple of Æsculapius, which stood conspicuous at the summit of the citadels. They begged that the lives of such as still survived might be spared. Scipio granted the request, but excepted the deserters, and fifty thousand men and women availed themselves of his grace. The deserters shut themselves up in the temple—there were nine hundred of them, all Romans—and with them Hasdrubal and his wife and their two sons. The place was impregnable, but their position was hopeless, for there was no fighting against hunger.

Hasdrubal contrived to escape from his companions, and threw himself, humbly begging for life, at the feet of Scipio. The boon was granted, and the Roman general showed his prisoner to the deserters, who were crowded on the temple-roof. They bitterly reproached the coward who had deserted them, and then set fire to the temple. When the flames were burning fiercely, the wife of Hasdrubal came forward. She had dressed herself with all the splendour that she could command, and had her two children by her side. Turning first to Scipio, she said, "On thee, man of Rome, I call no vengeance from heaven. Thou dost but use the rights of war. But as for this Hasdrubal, this traitor to his country and his gods, to his wife and to his children, I pray that heaven, and thou as the instrument of heaven, may punish him." Then she turned to her husband. "Villain, traitor, and coward," she cried, "I and my children will find a tomb in the flames, but thou, the mighty general of Carthage, wilt adorn a Roman triumph!" She then slew her children, threw their bodies into the flames, and followed them herself.

Thus, after seven centuries of greatness, Carthage fell. The conqueror, as he looked on the awful spectacle, burst into tears, and murmured to himself, as he thought of the fate which had overtaken empire after empire, and which would one day overtake his own country, the lines of Homer, in which Hector foretells the doom of Troy.

The soldiers were permitted to plunder the city, but all the gold and silver and all the treasuries of the temples were reserved. Military decorations were liberally distributed, but none of the troops who had assisted in the spoliation of the temple of Apollo were thus distinguished. The Sicilian cities were informed that they might regain possession of the works of art which the Carthaginians had carried off during a century and a half of warfare. Agrigentum regained her famous Bull of Phalaris; Segesta her statue of Diana. The name of Scipio Africanus was long honoured by the Sicilians for this act of honesty. Before a hundred years had passed they were to lose

AFRICAN COLISEUM.

their treasures again, not by the fortune of war, but by the shameless robberies of a Roman governor.[1]

The city was razed to the ground, and a curse was pronounced on any one who should rebuild it. Notwithstanding this, some twenty years later the younger Gracchus carried a proposal for founding a colony of six thousand citizens on the site. It was never carried into execution. Neither was the similar plan which some eighty years afterwards was conceived by Julius Cæsar. Augustus, however, founded a Roman Carthage, which soon became a prosperous city. But with this my story has nothing to do. This is finished with the fall of Rome's great Phœnician rival.

[1] See the account of Verres in a classical dictionary, and in "The Story of Rome," p. 202.

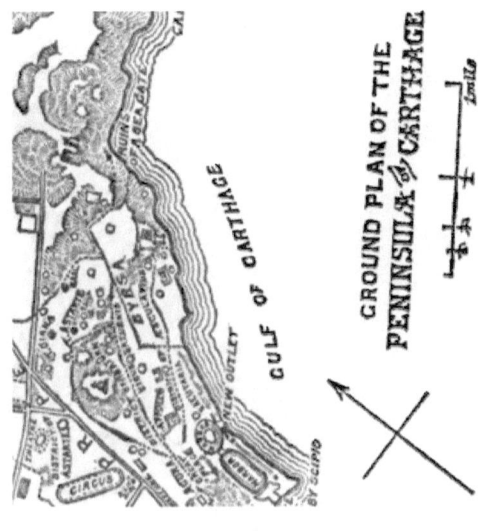

INDEX TO THE TEXT AND THE NOTES.

A

Acerbas, 3, 6
Acra, 96
Adherbal, 157
Adrumetum, 162
Ægusa, 163
Ægates Islands, battle of, 163, 164
Æschines, 122
Æsculapius, temple of, 297
Æthiopians, 97
Ætna, eruption of, 53
Ætna (town), 55
Agathocles, tyrant of Syracuse, 75; defeated at the Himera, 76; besieged in Syracuse, 77; escapes, *ib.*; lands in Africa, 80; defeats the Carthaginians, 82; takes Utica, 85; returns to Syracuse, *ib.*; comes back to Africa, 86; imprisoned by his soldiers, 88; escapes, 89
Agrigentum, 22, 27; taken by Himilco, 41, 67, 122; taken by the Romans, 132, 133; 237, 298
Alalia, battle of, 14
Aletes, 117, 180
Alexander the Great, 89
Allobroges, 188
Amber, 122
Anagnia, 234
Anio, 234
Antiochus, 254, 266, 268
Appian, 128, 279, 281, 297
Arambys, 96

Archagathus, 85-8
Archimedes, 236
Aristotle, 102-108
Armenia, 269
Artaxata, 269
Ashtaroth, 113
Athenæus, 125
Avienus, 100

B

Balearic Islands, 35, 75
Baltic Sea, 122
Beneventum, battle of, 230
Boarding apparatus, 134
Bomilcar, Suffete of Carthage, his treachery, 82; attempts a revolution and is put to death, 83
Britain, 100, 122
Bruttii, 226, 253
Byrsa, 5, 293

C

Cabala, battle of, 66
Camarina, taken by Himilco (1), 43, 158
Cambyses, king of Persia, plans the conquest of Carthage, 18
Campanian mercenaries, 37, 129
Cannæ, battle of, 218-224
Capua, joins Hannibal, 225; besieged by the Romans, 232; surrenders, 235; its severe punishment, *ib.*
Caravans, 118, 119
Carbuncle, see Carthaginian stone

304 INDEX TO THE TEXT AND THE NOTES.

Caricon, 96
Carthaginian stone, 121
Carthalo, 13
Catana, 53
Catapults, newly invented, 49
Cato, the Elder, 273, 277, 286
Catulus (Lutatius), 163
Censorinus, 277-286
Cercina, 266
Cerne, 97, 98
Chretes, 97
Chronos, see Moloch
Cineas, 89, 90
Clastidium, 200
Claudius (Appius), 131, 132
Claudius (Appius), 2, 236
Claudius (Nero) in Spain, 241; marches to join his colleague Livius, 249; defeats Hasdrubal at the Metaurus, 250-252
Claudius (Publius), 157, 158
Clubs at Carthage, 109
Clypea, 147, 152
Common meals, 106
Corinth, mother-city of Syracuse, 70
Corsica, 25, 122
Cothon, 296
Crete, 268, 269
Crimessus, battle of, 72-74.
Crispinus, 247
Crocodiles, 98
Cronium, Dionysius defeated at, 67
Crotona, 226, 253
Customs-duties, 116, 117
Cyprus, 4
Cyrene, 117

D

Dagon, 113, 114
Daphnæus, 38, 39
Deinocrates, 75
Demeter, worship of, at Carthage, 60
Dexippus, 37, 41
Dido, 3-8
Diodorus, 117
Dionysius (the Elder), attempts to relieve Gela, 43; makes peace with Carthage, 44; declares war against Carthage, 47; attacks Motya, *ib.*; takes it by storm, 50; defeated by Himilco at Catana, 53; retreats to Syracuse, 55; makes successful attack on Himilco, 57; allows Himilco to escape, 59; declares war with Carthage and defeats Mago, 64; renews the war, 66; is defeated at Cronium, 67; his death, 68
Dionysius (the Younger), tyrant of Syracuse, 70
Drepanum, battle of, 157, 158, 160, 163
Ducarius, 209
Duilius, 137

E

Ecnomus, battle of, 138-140
Egesta, 28, 298
Elba, 122
Elephants, 121. See also accounts of battles
Elissa, see Dido
Entellus, 68
Eryx, 36, 68, 159-165
Etruscans, 14, 81, 117
Eumenes, 269

F

Fabius, appointed dictator, 212; his policy of delay, 212, 213; outwitted by Hannibal, *ib.*; his unpopularity, *ib.*; recovers Tarentum, 246; crowned at Rome, 260; dies, *ib.*
Fair Promontory, 14, 15
Flaminius, defeated and killed at Trasumennus, 207-211
Flaminius (ambassador to Prussia), 270
Fregellæ, 234
Fulvius, 234, 245

G

Gades, 186
Gala, 240
Gauls, 81

INDEX TO THE TEXT AND THE NOTES. 305

Gela, taken by Himilco (1), 43; besieged by Hamilcar, 76
Gelon, of Syracuse, defeats Hamilcar (2), 26, 27
Gisco, 166-175
Gisco, father of Hannibal (1), 29
Gisco, father of Hasdrubal, 240
Gisco, 218
Gorillas, 99
Gracchus, Tib. S., 230
Gracchus (the Younger), 301
Gulussa, 286, 289, 295

H

Halycus, river, 67, 74
Hamilcar (1), son of Mago, conquers Sardinia, 17
Hamilcar (2) invades Sicily, 22-27
Hamilcar (3) commands Carthaginian army against Agathocles, 75; is victorious at Himera, 76; besieges Syracuse, 77; his death, 82
Hamilcar (4), commander at Ecnomus, 138
Hamilcar Barca (5), appointed to command fleet and army, 160; holds Hercta, ib.; holds Eryx, ib.; maintains war against Romans, 161-164; makes favourable terms of peace, 165; takes command against mercenaries, 171; breaks blockade of Carthage, 172; defeats mercenaries, ib.; attacks camp at Tunes, 176; finishes war with mercenaries, 177; crosses into Spain, 178; his conquests and death, 179
Hannibal (1) invades Sicily, 28-34; invades it again, 35; dies, 38
Hannibal (2), commander in Sicily, 132, 133, 134, 137
Hannibal (3), lieutenant in mercenary war, 176, 177
Hannibal (4) swears hatred against Rome, 181; his character, 181; campaign against Spanish tribes, 182; besieges Saguntum, ib.;

takes it, 184; in winter quarters at New Carthage, 185; crosses the Ebro, 186; his dream, ib.; crosses the Pyrenees, ib.; crosses the Rhone, 187; crosses the Alps, 189-194; descends into Italy, 194; his losses, ib.; attacks the Taurini, 195; conquers the Romans at the Ticinus, 196-199; at the Trebia, 201-205; winters in Liguria, 206; in peril of his life, ib.; crosses the marshes of the Arno, ib.; loses an eye, 207; defeats the Romans at Trasumennus, 207-209; repulsed at Spoletium, 210; rests at Hadria, 211; his policy, ib.; his campaign with Fabius, 212-216; wintering at Geronium, 217; defeats Romans at Cannæ, 222; refuses to march on Rome, 223; gains Capua, 225; sends Mago to Carthage, 227; neglected by the home government, 228; winters in Capua, ib.; besieges Nola, ib.; attempts to seize Tarentum, 229; gains Tarentum, 231; attempts to relieve Capua, 232; marches on Rome, 233; retires, 235; defeats Fulvius at Herdonia, 245; hears of Hasdrubal's death, 252; his masterly generalship in South Italy, 253; recalled home, 259; defeated at Zama, 262; advises peace, 263; in power at Carthage, 265; his reforms, ib.; flies, 266; at the court of Antiochus, 267; his answer to Antiochus, 268; possibly at Crete, 269; with Prusias of Bithynia, 269, 270; his death and character, 270, 271
Hanno (1), Suffete of Carthage, killed in battle, 82
Hanno (2), the navigator, 95-100
Hanno (3), 131
Hanno (4), 132, 133, 139, 140
Hanno (5), 163, 164

21

Hanno, the Great (6), 171–177
Hanno, leader of peace party at Carthage (7), 183, 227
Hanno (8), 187
Hanno (9), defeated at Beneventum, 230
Hanno (10), commands in Sicily, 237
Hanno (11), commands in Spain, 238
Hasdrubal (1), son of Mago, 16, 17
Hasdrubal (2), (son-in-law of Hamilcar Barca), his campaigns in Spain, 179, 180; assassinated, 180
Hasdrubal, lieutenant of Hannibal (3), 219
Hasdrubal, brother of Hannibal (4), left in command in Spain, 186; his campaigns with the Scipios, 238–241; eludes Nero, 241; defeated by Scipio Africanus, 243; crosses into Italy, 248; defeated and slain at the Metaurus, 250
Hasdrubal, son of Gisco (5), 240–289
Hasdrubal (6), commands in the last siege of Carthage, 280–300
Hebrew names, 11
Hebrews, their relations to Tyre, 10, 11
Helisyki, Volscians (?), 25
Hercta, 160
Hercules, 3, 4. See Melcarth
Hercules, Pillars of, 96, 118
Herodotus, 113, 118
Hiera, 163, 164
Hiero, 130–132, 176, 229
Hieronymus, 229, 236
Himera, first battle of, 26, 27; second battle of, 32; destroyed by Hannibal (1), 33; third battle of, 76
Himilco (1) invades Sicily, 35–45; operates against Dionysius, 48–49; returns to Carthage, 49; again appointed to command, 51; takes Massana, marches on Syracuse, besieges the city, reduced to extremities, 52–58;
escapes to Carthage, 59; commits suicide, 60
Himilco (2), discoverer, 100, 101
Himilco (3), 154
Himilco (4), 236
Hippo, 168, 286
Hippopotamus, 98
Horn, Southern, 99
Horn, Western, 99
Horace, 149, 250
Human sacrifices, 28, 33, 38, 86, 110

I

Iarbas, 6
Iberians. See Spanish troops
Iberus (Ebro), 180
Illiturgis, 239
Intibilis, 239
Iron, 122
Isére, 188
Italian mercenaries, 25, 29, 35, 37, 55, 65. See also Campanian mercenaries
Ivory, 122

J

Junius, 158

K

Kings of Carthage, 102, 103

L

Lælius, 258, 262
Lælius (the Younger), 295
Lævinus, 237
Leather money, 122, 123
Leontini, 44
Leptines (brother of Dionysius), 53, 54, 57; killed at the battle of Cronium, 67
Leptis, 115
Liby-Phœnicians, 96
Ligyes (Ligurians), 25, 206
Lilybæum, fort of, besieged by Dionysius, 68, 72; attacked by Pyrrhus, 91; besieged by Romans, 154–165
Lilybæum, promontory, 72
Lipara, 122, 134

INDEX TO THE TEXT AND THE NOTES. 307

Liris, river, 234
Livius (colleague of Nero), 248, 249
Livius (in command at Tarentum), 230, 231, 246
Livy (historian), 128, 181, 184, 193, 222, 234, 238, 253, 259, 264, 276
Lixitæ, 97, 98
Lixus, river, 97

M

Macar, river, 171
Macedonia, 272
Magnesia, battle of, 268
Mago (1), king of Carthage, 13
Mago (2), Admiral, 53
Mago (3), Carthaginian general, attacks Dionysius, 64; defeated by, *ib.*; invades Sicily, 65; is killed at Cabala, 66
Mago (4), writer on agriculture, 124
Mago (5), brother of Hannibal, 201; sent to Carthage with news of Cannæ, 227; in Spain, 240-244; goes to Liguria, *ib.*; takes Minorca, 254; recalled home, 259; dies, *ib.*
Maharbal, 210, 223
Malchus, 12, 13
Malgernus, 3
Malta, 17
Mamertines, 130, 131
Mancinus, 286, 289
Manilius, 282, 286
Manlius, 138, 142
Marcellus, appointed to command army after Cannæ, 227; relieves Nola, 228; besieges Syracuse, 236; takes it, 237; campaigns with Hannibal, 245-247; his death, 248
Marcius, 241
Massilia, 122
Masinissa defeats Syphax, 240; goes with Hasdrubal to Spain, *ib.*; with Scipio in Africa, 257; destroys the camp of Syphax, 257, 258; at variance with Carthage, 266; encroaches on Carthaginian dominions, 274; defeated by Hasdrubal, 275; is victorious, *ib.*; triumphant over Carthage, 277; dies, 286
Matho, 167-179
Megara, the, 293
Melcarth, 110-113, 186
Melita, 96
Menander, 120
Menes, 19
Messana, 44, 130-132
Metaurus, battle of, 249-252
Mines, 117
Minucius, 215, 216
Moloch, 38, 108, 109
Motya, besieged by Dionysius, 47-51; recovered by Himilco, 51
Mutines, 237
Mylæ, battle of, 137

N

Naravasus, 176
Native Carthaginian troops, 66, 72, 74, 75, 82, 85, 146, 262
Naxos (Sicily), 21
Nemausus (Nismes), 186
New Carthage, 180; captured by Scipio, 242
Nola, 228, 260

O

Olympias, 89

P

Pachynus, 158
Panormus (Palermo), 25, 67, 153, 160
Paullus (Æmilius) appointed Consul, 217; slain at Cannæ, 222
Pelorum, 52
Pentarchies, 105
Pergamus, 269
Periplus of Hanno, 95-100
Persephone, worship of, at Carthage, 60
Pestilence, 38, 44, 56, 67, 236
Phalaris, 298
Phamæas (Himilco), 286
Phidias, 120

308 *INDEX TO THE TEXT AND THE NOTES.*

Philip, king of Macedon, **229**, 254
Phœnicians, **10, 11, 18**
Phocæans, see Alalia
Pillars of Hercules, **96, 118**
Placentia, **199, 202**
Plutarch, **109, 218**
Politics, the. See Aristotle
Polybius, **128, 146, 153, 222, 258**, 262, 279, 281, 297
Prusias, 269
Pyrrhus, **89-91**

R

Regulus, commands fleet at Ecnomus, **138**; lands in Africa, **140**; vanquishes Hasdrubal, **143**; occupies Tunes, **144**; demands impossible terms of peace, *ib.*; conquered by Xantippus and taken prisoner, **147**; sent as envoy to Rome, **148**; his counsel, **149** *seq.*; his death, **151**
Rhodes, fleet of, **268**
Rhone, passage of, **187, 188**
Rome, early treaties with, **14-16**

S

Saguntum, **180**; besieged by Hannibal, **182**; taken, **184**
Sahara, **121**
Samnites, **226**
Sardinia, **invaded by Malchus**, **13**; belongs to Carthage, **17**; supplies provisions to Carthage, **63, 65**; lost by Carthage, **177**
Saturn, **see Moloch**
Scipio, **Cnæus**, sent into Spain, **189**; defeats Hasdrubal, **238**; defeats the fleet, *ib.*; joined by Publius, *ib.* (see Scipio Publius); his death, **241**
Scipio (Publius), sent to the mouth of the Rhone, **186**; misses Hannibal, **189**; returns to Italy, *ib.*; marches against Hannibal, **195**; defeated and wounded at the Ticinus, **199**; moves to the Trebia, *ib.*; returns to Spain, **258**; his campaigns in that country, **239-240**; his death, **240**
Scipio, Africanus Major, saves his father's life at the Ticinus, **199**; appointed to the command in Spain, **242**; takes Carthage, *ib.*; defeats Hasdrubal (Barca), **243**; comes into Africa, *ib.*; returns to Spain and completes conquest, **244**; comes again to Africa, **254**; besieges Utica, **257**; burns the camp of Syphax, **258**; vanquishes Syphax and Hasdrubal, **259**; defeats Hannibal at Zama, **261**, **262**; makes peace with Carthage, **263**
Scipio, Africanus Minor, his descent, **275**; arbitrates between Massinissa and Carthage, **276**; distinguishes himself in the siege, **286**; administers the effects of Masinissa, *ib.*; appointed to the command at Carthage, **289**; rescues Mancinus, **290**; restores order to the camp, *ib.*; storms the Megara, **293**; institutes a blockade, **294**; attacks the Upper City and captures it, **297**; his reflections, **298**; his disposal of the spoil, *ib.*
Scipio, Nasica, **273**
Seleucus, **267**
Selinus, **26, 27**; at war with Egesta, **28**; taken by Hannibal (1), **48, 67, 68**
Sempronius, **200**; defeated at Trebia, **201-205**
Senate of Carthage, **104, 105**
Servilius, **211, 213**
Ships built by Rome, **134, 162**
Shophetim, **103**
Sikel tribes, **44, 47, 59, 65**
Smuggling, **117**
Soloeis, **96**
Sophonisba, **244**
Spanish troops of Carthage, **25**, 29, 33, 35, **59**, **185, 186, 202**, 205, 219
Spendius, **167-179**

INDEX TO THE TEXT AND THE NOTES.

Spoletium, 210
Suffetes, 103
Syphax, 239, 243, 257-259
Syracuse, ruled by Gelon, 26; by Dionysius, 42 *et seq.*; besieged by Himilco, 53-58
Syrtis, 115

T

Tanit, 113, 114
Tarentum, 229, 230, 246
Taurini, 195
Tauromenium, 64
Terence, 120
Thebes, 119
Thermopylæ, 267
Theron, 26, 38
Thymiaterium, 96
Ticinus, battle of, 196
Tifata, Mount, 233
Timoleon, sails to Syracuse, 71; declares war against Carthage, *ib.*; defeats Carthaginians at the Crimessus, 72-74; his death, 75

Trasumennus, battle of, 207-211
Tribute, 115, 116
Triton, 113
Troglodytæ, 97
Tunes (Tunis), 12, 60, 144, 168, 172, 176
Tusculum, 234
Tyre, 3, 10, 11, 266

U

Utica, 5, 12, 168, 176, 257, 277, 290

V

Varro, 217, 221, 222, 226
Venus. See Ashtaroth
Venusia, 247
Virgil, his legend of Dido, 7-9, 121

X

Xantippus, 145, 146

Z

Zama, battle of, 260-262

UNWIN BROTHERS,
THE GRESHAM PRESS,
CHILWORTH AND LONDON.

Mr. UNWIN has pleasure in sending herewith his Catalogue of Select Books.

Book Buyers are requested to order any Books they may require from their local Bookseller.

Catalogue of Select Books in Belles Lettres, History, Biography, Theology, Travel, General Literature, and Books for Children.

Belles Lettres.

Euphorion: Studies of the Antique and the Mediæval in the Renaissance. By VERNON LEE. Cheap Edition in one volume. Demy 8vo., cloth, 7s. 6d.

"It is the fruit, as every page testifies, of singularly wide reading and independent thought, and the style combines with much picturesqueness a certain largeness of volume, that reminds us more of our earlier writers than those of our own time." —*Contemporary Review.*

Studies of the Eighteenth Century in Italy. By VERNON LEE. Demy 8vo., cloth, 7s. 6d.

"These studies show a wide range of knowledge of the subject, precise investigation, abundant power of illustration, and hearty enthusiasm. . . . The style of writing is cultivated, neatly adjusted, and markedly clever."—*Saturday Review.*

Belcaro: Being Essays on Sundry Æsthetical Questions. By VERNON LEE, Author of "Euphorion," "Baldwin," &c. Crown 8vo., cloth, 5s.

"This way of conveying ideas is very fascinating, and has an effect of creating activity in the reader's mind which no other mode can equal. From first to last there is a continuous and delightful stimulation of thought."—*Academy.*

Juvenilia: A Second Series of Essays on Sunday Æsthetical Questions. By VERNON LEE. Two vols. Small crown 8vo., cloth, 12s.

"To discuss it properly would require more space than a single number of 'The Academy' could afford."—*Academy.*

"Est agréable à lire et fait penser."—*Revue des deux Mondes.*

Belles Lettres.

Baldwin: Dialogues on Views and Aspirations. By VERNON LEE. Demy 8vo., cloth, 12s.

"The dialogues are written with . . . an intellectual courage which shrinks from no logical conclusion."—*Scotsman.*

Arcady: For Better, For Worse. By AUGUSTUS JESSOPP, D.D., Author of "One Generation of a Norfolk House." Portrait. Popular edition. Crown 8vo., cloth, 3s. 6d.

"A volume which is, to our minds, one of the most delightful ever published in English."—*Spectator.*

"A capital book, abounding in true wisdom and humour. . . . Excellent and amusing."—*Melbourne Argus.*

The Fleet: Its River, Prison, and Marriages. By JOHN ASHTON, Author of "Social Life in the Reign of Queen Anne," &c. With 70 Drawings by the Author from Original Pictures. Demy 8vo., cloth elegant, 21s.

Romances of Chivalry: Told and Illustrated in Fac-simile by JOHN ASHTON. Forty-six Illustrations. Demy 8vo., cloth elegant, gilt tops, 18s.

"The result (of the reproduction of the wood blocks) is as creditable to his artistic, as the text is to his literary, ability."—*Guardian.*

The Dawn of the Nineteenth Century in England: A Social Sketch of the Times. By JOHN ASHTON. Cheaper edition, in one vol. Illustrated. Large crown 8vo., 10s. 6d.

"The book is one continued source of pleasure and interest, and opens up a wide field for speculation and comment, and many of us will look upon it as an important contribution to contemporary history, not easily available to others than close students."—*Antiquary.*

The Legendary History of the Cross: A Series of Sixty-four Woodcuts, from a Dutch book published by VELDENER, A.D. 1483. With an Introduction Written and Illustrated by JOHN ASHTON, and a Preface by the Rev. S. BARING-GOULD, M.A. Square 8vo., bound in Parchment, old style, brass clasps, 10s. 6d.

"The book thus constituted will be a favourite with antiquaries and students of primitive art."—*Notes and Queries.*

Legends and Popular Tales of the Basque

People. By MARIANA MONTEIRO. With Full-page Illustrations in Photogravure by HAROLD COPPING. Fcap. 4to., cloth, 10s. 6d. Popular Edition, crown 8vo., cloth, gilt edges, 6s.

"In every respect this comely volume is a notable addition to the shelf devoted to folk-lore . . . . and the pictures in photogravure nobly interpret the text."—*Critic.*

Heroic Tales.

Retold from Firdusi the Persian. By HELEN ZIMMERN. With Etchings by L. ALMA TADEMA. Popular edition. Crown 8vo., cloth extra, 5s.

"Charming from beginning to end. . . . Miss Zimmern deserves all credit for her courage in attempting the task, and for her marvellous success in carrying it out."—*Saturday Review.*

Woodland Tales.

By JULIUS STINDE, Author of "The Buchholz Family." Translated by E. WRIGHT. Crown 8vo., cloth, 3s. 6d.

"They are pervaded by a quiet yet moving charm which depends, not on fine writing, but on true perception of character, simple but firm and clear delineation, and honest natural feeling."—*Scotsman.*

Pilgrim Sorrow.

By CARMEN SYLVA (The Queen of Roumania). Translated by HELEN ZIMMERN. Portrait-etching by LALAUZE. Square crown 8vo., cloth extra, 5s.

"A strain of sadness runs through the delicate thought and fancy of the Queen of Roumania. Her popularity as an author is already great in Germany, and this little work will win her a place in many English hearts."—*Standard.*

A Crystal Age.

Crown 8vo., cloth, 4s. 6d.

"The creation of a clever and poetical fancy. . . We have read it with growing pleasure."—*Saturday Review.*

"It is individual in virtue of its fine and delicate feeling for natural beauty."

St. James's Gazette.

The Poison Tree:

A Tale of Hindu Life in Bengal. By B. CHANDRA CHATTERJEE. Introduction by Sir EDWIN ARNOLD, M.A., K.C.S.I.

"This is a work of real genius. . . . As a picture of the social life of the Hindus it cannot but be regarded as masterly."—*British Quarterly Review.*

The Touchstone of Peril: A Tale of the Indian Mutiny. By DUDLEY HARDRESS THOMAS. Second edition. Crown 8vo., cloth, 6s.

"The volumes abound both in brilliant descriptive passages and in clever character-sketches. A novelist of very remarkable powers."—*Daily News.*

"'The Touchstone of Peril' is the best Anglo-Indian novel that has appeared for some years."—*Times of India.*

More than He Bargained for: An Indian Novel. By J. R. HUTCHINSON. Crown 8vo., cloth, 6s.

Tarantella: A Romance. By MATHILDE BLIND, Author of "Life of George Eliot." Second edition. Crown 8vo., cloth, 6s.

"Told with great spirit and effect, and shows very considerable power."—*Pall Mall Gazette.*

The Amazon: An Art Novel. By CARL VOSMAER. Preface by Prof. GEORG EBERS, and Frontispiece specially drawn by L. ALMA TADEMA, R.A.

"It is a work full of deep, suggestive thought."—*The Academy.*

The Temple: Sacred Poems and Private Ejaculations. By Mr. GEORGE HERBERT. New and fourth edition, with Introductory Essay by J. HENRY SHORTHOUSE. Small crown, sheep, 5s.

A fac-simile reprint of the Original Edition of 1633.

"This charming reprint has a fresh value added to it by the Introductory Essay of the Author of 'John Inglesant.'"—*Academy.*

Songs, Ballads, and A Garden Play. By A. MARY F. ROBINSON, Author of "An Italian Garden." With Frontispiece of Dürer's "Melancholia." Small crown 8vo., half bound, vellum, 5s.

Contents.—Songs of the Inner Life—II. Romantic Ballads—III. A Garden Play.

An Italian Garden: A Book of Songs. By A. MARY F. ROBINSON. Fcap. 8vo., parchment, 3s. 6d.

"They are most of them exquisite in form."—*Pall Mall Gazette.*
"Full of elegance and even tenderness."—*Spectator.*

The Sentence: A Drama. By AUGUSTA WEBSTER, Author of "In a Day," &c. Small crown 8vo., cloth, 4s. 6d.

Belles Lettres.

The Lazy Minstrel. By J. ASHBY-STERRY, Author of "Boudoir Ballads." Fourth and Popular Edition. Frontispiece by E. A. ABBEY. Fcap. 8vo., cloth, 2s. 6d.

"One of the lightest and brightest writers of vers de société."
St. James's Gazette.

The New Purgatory, and other Poems. By ELIZABETH RACHEL CHAPMAN, Author of "A Comtist Lover," &c. Square imperial 16mo., cloth, 4s. 6d.

Introductory Studies in Greek Art. Delivered in the British Museum by JANE E. HARRISON. With Illustrations. Square imperial 16mo., 7s. 6d.

"The best work of its kind in English."—*Oxford Magazine.*
"The volume is in itself a work of art."—*Contemporary Review.*

Great Minds in Art. With a Chapter on Art and Artists. By WILLIAM TIREBUCK. With many Portraits, and Frontispiece. Crown 8vo., cloth, 5s.

The Paradox Club. By EDWARD GARNETT. With Portrait of Nina Lindon. Crown 8vo., cloth, 6s.

Contents.—I. "The Windsor Castle"—II. In Defence of Woman—III. Which Leads to Socialism—IV. On London Bridge—V. On Being Anticipated—VI. The Mile End Road.

"An agreeable little book distinguished by a good deal of poetical feeling."
Spectator.

Jewish Portraits. By LADY MAGNUS. With Illustration by HARRY FURNISS. Small crown 8vo., cloth, 5s.

Gladys Fane. By T. WEMYSS REID. Fifth edition. (Unwin's Novel Series.) Small crown 8vo., 2s.

Mrs. Keith's Crime. By Mrs. W. KINGDON CLIFFORD. (Unwin's Novel Series.) Small crown 8vo., 2s.

History.

The Federalist: A Commentary, in the form of Essays, on the Constitution of the United States of 1787. Reprinted from the Original Text of Alexander Hamilton, Jay, and Madison. Edited by HENRY CABOT LODGE. Demy 8vo., half Roxburgh, 10s. 6d.

The Government Year Book: A Record of the Forms and Methods of Government in Great Britain, her Colonies, and Foreign Countries, 1888. With an Introduction on the Diffusion of Popular Government over the Surface of the Globe, and on the Nature and Extent of International Jurisdictions. To which is added a Review of the Chief Occurrences affecting National and International Government. Edited by LEWIS SERGEANT, Author of "New Greece," "England's Policy: its Traditions and Problems," &c. Large crown 8vo., cloth, 6s.

"Mr. Lewis Sergeant has most admirably performed his task."—*Athenæum.*
"The book fills a gap which has been frequently noticed by every politician, journalist, and economist."—*Journal des Débats.*

The Making of the Great West, 1512-1853. By SAMUEL ADAMS DRAKE. One hundred and forty-five Illustrations. Large crown 8vo., 9s. (After discussing in detail the Original Explorations of the Spaniards, the French, and the English, he traces the development of America as a nation by conquest, annexation, and by exploration.)

The Making of New England, 1580-1643. By SAMUEL ADAMS DRAKE. Illustrated. Crown 8vo., cloth, 5s.

"It is clearly and pleasantly written, and copiously illustrated."
—*Pall Mall Budget.*
"It is very compact, clear, and reliable."—*Nonconformist.*

History. 9

The Story of the Nations.

Crown 8vo., Illustrated, and furnished with Maps and Indexes, each 5s.

L'interessante serie l'Histoire des Nations formera . . . un cours d'histoire universelle d'une très grande valeur.—*Journal des Débats.*
The remarkable series.—*New York Critic.*
That useful series.—*The Times.*
An admirable series.—*Spectator.*
That excellent series.—*Guardian.*
The series is likely to be found indispensable in every school library.
This valuable series.—*Nonconformist.* [*Pall Mall Gazette*
Admirable series of historical monographs.—*Echo.*
An excellent series.—*Times of Morocco.*
This admirable series.—*Evangelical Review.*
The excellent series.—*Literary World.*
The Story of the Nations series is excellent.—*Literary Churchman.*

Rome. By ARTHUR GILMAN, M.A., Author of "A History of the American People," &c. Third edition.

"The author succeeds admirably in reproducing the 'Grandeur that was Rome.'"—*Sydney Morning Herald.*

The Jews. In Ancient, Mediæval, and Modern Times. By Prof. J. K. HOSMER. Second edition.

"The book possesses much of the interest, the suggestiveness, and the charm of romance."—*Saturday Review.*

Germany. By Rev. S. BARING-GOULD, Author of "Curious Myths of the Middle Ages," &c. Second edition.

"Mr. Baring-Gould tells his stirring tale with knowledge and perspicuity. He is a thorough master of his subject."—*Globe.*
"A decided success."—*Athenæum.*

Carthage. By Prof. ALFRED J. CHURCH, Author of "Stories from the Classics," &c. Second edition.

"Told with admirable lucidity."—*Observer.*
"A masterly outline with vigorous touches in detail here and there."—*Guardian.*

Alexander's Empire. By Prof. J. P. MAHAFFY, Author of "Social Life in Greece." Second edition.

"An admirable epitome."—*Melbourne Argus.*
"A wonderful success."—*Spectator.*

The Moors in Spain. By STANLEY LANE POOLE, Author of "Studies in a Mosque." Second edition.

"Is much the best on the subject that we have in English."—*Athenæum.*
"Well worth reading."—*Times of Morocco.*
"The best, the fullest, the most accurate, and most readable history of the Moors in Spain for general readers."—*St. James's Gazette.*

History.

Ancient Egypt. By Prof. Geo. Rawlinson, Author of "The Five Great Monarchies of the World." Second edition.

"The story is told of the land, people and rulers, with vivid colouring and consummate literary skill,"—*New York Critic.*

Hungary. By Prof. Arminius Vambéry, Author of "Travels in Central Asia." Second edition.

"The volume which he has contributed to 'The Story of the Nations' will be generally considered one of the most interesting and picturesque of that useful series."—*Times.*

"This eminently satisfactory book."—*St. James's Gazette.*

The Saracens: From the Earliest Times to the Fall of Bagdad. By Arthur Gilman, M.A., Author of "Rome, &c."

"Le livre de M. Gilman est destiné à être lu avidement par un grand nombre de gens pour lesquels l'étude des nombreux ouvrages déjà parus serait impossible."
Journal des Débats.

Ireland. By the Hon. Emily Lawless, Author of "Hurrish." Second Edition.

"We owe thanks to Miss Emily for this admirable volume, in some respects the very best of 'The Story of the Nations' series as yet published."—*Nonconformist.*

Chaldea. By Z. A. Ragozin, Author of "Assyria," &c.

"One of the most interesting numbers of the series in which it appears."
Scotsman.

The Goths. By Henry Bradley.

"Seems to us to be as accurate as it is undoubtedly clear, strong, and simple, and it will give to the reader an excellent idea of the varied fortunes of the two great branches of the Gothic nation."—Thomas Hodgkin in *The Academy.*

Assyria: From the Rise of the Empire to the Fall of Nineveh. By Zénaïde A. Ragozin, Author of "Chaldea," &c.

"Madame Ragozin has performed her task in it as admirably as she has done in her earlier volume on Chaldea. She has spared no pains in collecting the latest and best information on the subject."—*Extract from Letter from* Prof. Sayce.

Turkey. By Stanley Lane Poole. (Now ready.)

Holland. By Professor Thorold Rogers.   [In September.

France. By Gustav Masson.   [October.

Biography.

Anne Gilchrist: Her Life and Writings. Edited by HERBERT HARLAKENDEN GILCHRIST. Prefatory Notice by WILLIAM MICHAEL ROSSETTI. Second edition. Twelve Illustrations. Demy 8vo., cloth, 16s.

"Here we find a kind, friendly, and humorous, if splenetic Carlyle; a helpful and merry Mrs. Carlyle; and a friendly and unaffected Dante Gabriel Rossetti. These characteristics, so unlike the Carlyle of the too copious memoirs, so unlike the Mrs. Carlyle, the *femme incomprise*, so unlike the Rossetti of myth, are extremely welcome."—*Daily News*, Leader.

"A book of great worth and interest."—*Scotsman*.

Charles Dickens as I knew Him: The Story of the Reading Tours in Great Britain and America (1866-1870). By GEORGE DOLBY. New and cheaper edition. Crown 8vo., 3s. 6d.

"A book which gives us many pleasant pictures of one of the most interesting figures in modern literature."—*Saturday Review*.

"It will be welcome to all lovers of Dickens for Dickens' own sake."—*Athenæum*.

Charles Whitehead: A Critical Monograph. By H. T. MACKENZIE BELL. Cheap and Popular edition. Crown 8vo., cloth, 5s.

"Mr. Mackenzie Bell has done a good service in introducing to us a man of true genius, whose works have sunk into mysteriously swift and complete oblivion."—*Contemporary Review*.

Ole Bull: A Memoir. By SARA C. BULL. With Ole Bull's "Violin Notes" and Dr. A. B. Crosby's "Anatomy of the Violinist." Portraits. Second edition. Crown 8vo., cloth, 7s. 6d.

"Full of good stories. It is difficult to know where to choose."

"A fresh, delightful, and charming book."—*Graphic*.   [*Saturday Review*.

Johannes Brahms: A Biographical Sketch. By Dr. HERMAN DEITERS. Translated, with additions, by ROSA NEWMARCH. Edited, with a Preface, by J. A. FULLER MAITLAND. Portrait. Small crown 8vo., cloth, 6s.

The Lives of Robert and Mary Moffat.

By their Son, JOHN SMITH MOFFAT. Portraits, Illustrations, and Maps. Sixth edition. Crown 8vo., cloth, 7s. 6d. Presentation edition, full gilt elegant, bevelled boards, gilt edges, in box, 10s. 6d.

"An inspiring record of calm, brave, wise work, and will find a place of value on the honoured shelf of missionary biography. The biographer has done his work with reverent care, and in a straightforward, unaffected style."
Contemporary Review.

Two Royal Lives.

Gleanings from Berlin. By DOROTHEA ROBERTS. Fifth edition. Eight Portraits and Six Illustrations. Crown 8vo., cloth elegant, 7s. 6d.

"This deeply interesting work."—*Morning Post.*

The German Emperor and Empress:

The Late Frederick III. and Victoria. The Story of their Lives. Being the Sixth and Popular Edition of "Two Royal Lives." By DOROTHEA ROBERTS. Portraits. Crown 8vo., cloth, 2s. 6d.

"A book sure to be popular in domestic circles.'—*The Graphic.*

The Life and Times of W. Lloyd Garrison,

1805-1840: The Story of his Life told by his Children. In two volumes, with upwards of Twenty Portraits and Illustrations. Demy 8vo., cloth, £1 10s.

Arminius Vambéry:

His Life and Adventures. Written by Himself. With Portrait and Fourteen Illustrations. Fifth and Popular edition. Square Imperial 16mo., cloth extra, 6s.

"A most fascinating work, full of interesting and curious experiences."
Contemporary Review.
"The work is written in a most captivating manner."—*Novoe Vremya, Moscow.*

Henry Irving:

In England and America, 1838-1884. By FREDERIC DALY. Vignette Portrait by AD. LALAUZE. Second thousand. Crown 8vo., cloth extra, 5s.

"A very interesting account of the career of the great actor."
British Quarterly Review.

Theology and Philosophy.

"**Expositions.**" By Dr. Samuel Cox. First Series. Third Thousand. Demy 8vo., cloth, 7s. 6d.

"We have said enough to show our high opinion of Dr. Cox's volume. It is indeed full of suggestion. . . . A valuable volume."—*The Spectator.*

"**Expositions.**" By the same Author. Second Series. Second Thousand. Demy 8vo., cloth, 7s. 6d.

"Here too we have the clear exegetical insight, the lucid expository style, the chastened but effective eloquence, the high ethical standpoint, which secured for the earlier series a well-nigh unanimous award of commendation."—*Academy.*

"**Expositions.**" By the same Author. Third Series. Second edition. Demy 8vo., cloth, 7s. 6d.

"When we say that the volume possesses all the intellectual, moral, and spiritual characteristics which have won for its author so distinguished a place among the religious teachers of our time . . . what further recommendation can be necessary?"—*Nonconformist.*

"**Expositions.**" By the same Author. Fourth Series (completing the Set). Demy 8vo., cloth, 7s. 6d.

"The volume is one of the most interesting and valuable that we have received from Dr. Cox. It contains some of the strongest analytical character-sketching he has ever produced."—*Glasgow Mail.*

Theology and Philosophy

The Risen Christ: The King of Men. By the late Rev. J. BALDWIN BROWN, M.A., Author of "The Home Life," &c. Crown 8vo., cloth, 7s. 6d.

Contents.—Immortality Veiled—The Primary Lesson—Foreshadowings—Resurrection, the Key to the Life of Christ—The Witness to the Disciples—The Testimony of St. Paul—The Universal Acceptance—The Resurrection of Christ—The Risen Christ the King of Men—The Founding of the Kingdom—The Administration—The Ruling Power—The Free Citizenship—The New Humanity.

Christian Facts and Forces. By the Rev. NEWMAN SMYTH, Author of "The Reality of Faith." New Edition. Crown 8vo., cloth, 4s. 6d.

"An able and suggestive series of discourses."—*Nonconformist.*

"These sermons abound in noble and beautiful teaching clearly and eloquently expressed."—*Christian.*

Inspiration and the Bible: An Inquiry. By ROBERT HORTON, M.A., formerly Fellow of New College, Oxford. Crown 8vo., cloth, 6s.

"The work displays much earnest thought, and a sincere belief in, and love of the Bible."—*Morning Post.*

"It will be found to be a good summary, written in no iconoclastic spirit, but with perfect candour and fairness, of some of the more important results of recent Biblical criticism."—*Scotsman.*

Faint, yet Pursuing. By the Rev. E. J. HARDY, Author of "How to be Happy though Married." Sq. imp. 16mo., cloth, 6s.

"One of the most practical and readable volumes of sermons ever published. They must have been eminently hearable."—*British Weekly.*

The Meditations and Maxims of Koheleth. A Practical Exposition of the Book of Ecclesiastes. By Rev. T. CAMPBELL FINLAYSON. Crown 8vo., 6s.

"A thoughtful and practical commentary on a book of Holy Scripture which needs much spiritual wisdom for its exposition. . . . Sound and judicious handling."—*Rock.*

The Pharaohs of the Bondage and the Exodus. Lectures by CHARLES S. ROBINSON, D.D., LL.D. Second edition. Large crown 8vo., cloth, 5s.

"Both lectures are conceived in a very earnest spirit, and are developed with much dignity and force. We have the greatest satisfaction in commending it to the attention of Biblical students and Christian ministers."—*Literary World.*

Theology and Philosophy.

A Short Introduction to the History of
Ancient Israel. By the Rev. A. W. OXFORD, M.A., Vicar of St. Luke's, Berwick Street, Soho, Editor of "The Berwick Hymnal," &c. Crown 8vo., cloth, 3s. 6d.

"We can testify to the great amount of labour it represents."—*Literary World.*

The Reality of Religion.
By HENRY J. VAN DYKE, Junr., D.D., of the Brick Church, N.Y. Second edition. Crown 8vo., cloth, 4s. 6d.

"An able and eloquent review of the considerations on which the writer rests his belief in Christianity, and an impassioned statement of the strength of this belief."—*Scotsman.*

The Reality of Faith.
By the Rev. NEWMAN SMYTH, D.D., Author of "Old Faiths in New Light." Fourth and Cheaper Edition. Crown 8vo., cloth, 4s. 6d.

"They are fresh and beautiful expositions of those deep things, those foundation truths, which underlie Christian faith and spiritual life in their varied manifestations."—*Christian Age.*

A Layman's Study of the English Bible
Considered in its Literary and Secular Aspects. By FRANCIS BOWEN, LL.D. Crown 8vo., cloth, 4s. 6d.

"Most heartily do we recommend this little volume to the careful study, not only of those whose faith is not yet fixed and settled, but of those whose love for it and reliance on it grows with their growing years."—*Nonconformist.*

The Parousia.
A Critical Inquiry into the New Testament Doctrine of Our Lord's Second Coming. By the Rev. J. S. RUSSELL, M.A. New and cheaper edition. Demy 8vo., cloth, 7s. 6d.

"Critical, in the best sense of the word. Unlike many treatises on the subject, this is a sober and reverent investigation, and abounds in a careful and instructive exegesis of every passage bearing upon it."—*Nonconformist.*

The Bible and the Age;
or, An Elucidation of the Principles of a Consistent and Verifiable Interpretation of Scripture. By CUTHBERT COLLINGWOOD, M.A. and B.M. Oxon. Demy 8vo., cloth, 10s. 6d.

"We heartily congratulate the Church on so valuable an addition to its literature."—*The New Church Magazine.*

Theology and Philosophy

The Ethic of Freethought: a Selection of Essays and Lectures. By KARL PEARSON, M.A., formerly Fellow of King's College, Cambridge. Demy 8vo., cloth, 12s.

"Are characterised by much learning, much keen and forcible thinking, and a fearlessness of denunciation and exposition."—*Scotsman.*

Descartes and His School. By KUNO FISCHER. Translated from the Third and Revised German Edition by J. P. GORDY, Ph.D. Edited by NOAH PORTER, D.D., LL.D. Demy 8vo., cloth, 16s.

"A valuable addition to the literature of Philosophy."—*Scotsman.*

"No greater service could be done to English and American students than to give them a trustworthy rendering of Kuno Fischer's brilliant expositions."—*Mind.*

Socrates: A Translation of the Apology, Crito, and Parts of the Phædo of Plato. 12mo., cloth, 3s. 6d.

"The translation is clear and elegant."—*Morning Post.*

A Day in Athens with Socrates: Translations from the Protagoras and the Republic of Plato. 12mo., cloth, 3s. 6d.

"We can commend these volumes to the English reader, as giving him what he wants—the Socratic ... philosophy at first hand, with a sufficiency of explanatory and illustrative comment."—*Pall Mall Gazette.*

Talks with Socrates about Life: Translations from the Gorgias and the Republic of Plato. 12mo., cloth, 3s. 6d.

"A real service is rendered to the general reader who has no Greek, and to whom the two ancient philosophers are only names, by the publication of these three inviting little volumes.... Every young man who is forming a library ought to add them to his collection."—*Christian Leader.*

Natural Causation. An Essay in Four Parts. By C. E. PLUMPTRE, Author of "General Sketch of the History of Pantheism," &c. Demy 8vo. cloth, 7s. 6d.

"While many will find in this volume much from which they will dissent, there is in it a great deal that is deserving of careful consideration, and a great deal that is calculated to stimulate thought."—*Scotsman.*

Travel.

Guatemala: The Land of the Quetzal. By WILLIAM T. BRIGHAM. Twenty-six full-page and Seventy-nine smaller Illustrations. Five Maps. Demy 8vo., cloth, £1 1s. (Mr. Brigham brought back from Guatemala several hundred photographs from which the Illustrations have been made.)

A Summer's Cruise in the Waters of Greece, Turkey, and Russia.
By ALFRED COLBECK. Frontispiece. Crown 8vo., cloth, 10s. 6d.

The Decline of British Prestige in the East.
By SELIM FARIS, Editor of the Arabic "El-Jawaïb" of Constantinople. Crown 8vo., cloth, 5s.

Contents.—The Egyptian Question, and the English Rule in Egypt—Bismarck's Policy in the Egyptian Question—The Rivalry between England and Russia for Prestige in the East—The Haj, or Pilgrimage to Mecca; its Political and Social Object—The Egyptian Convention, and Cause of its failure.

Daily Life in India.
By the Rev. W. J. WILKINS. Illustrated. Crown 8vo., cloth, 5s.

Contents.—Calcutta—Calcutta, the Oxford of India—The People: Europeans in India—The People Generally—A Talk about Insects, Reptiles, &c.—A Chapter about the Gods—Hindu Temples—Holy Places and Pilgrims—Religious Festivals—Gurus, or Religious Teachers and their Disciples—Hindu Saints—Burning Ghats and Treatment of the Dying—Bazaar Preaching—Life on the River—Life in Tent—All about Tigers—School Work—Work amongst the Hindu Girls and Women—Bengali Christians—India's Need.

Modern Hinduism:
An Account of the Religion and Life of the Hindus in Northern India. By Rev. W. J. WILKINS. Demy 8vo., cloth, 16s.

"A solid addition to our literature."—*Westminster Review.*
"A valuable contribution to knowledge."—*Scotsman.*
"A valuable contribution to the study of a very difficult subject."—*Madras Mail.*

Central Asian Questions: Essays on Afghanistan, China, and Central Asia. By DEMETRIUS C. BOULGER. With Portrait and Three Maps. Demy 8vo., cloth, 18s.

"A mine of valuable information."—*Times.* [*Mail.*
"A mine of information on all 'Central Asian Questions.'"—*Allen's Indian*
"A very valuable contribution to our literature on subjects of vast and increasing interest."—*Collum's United Service Magazine.*

The Balkan Peninsula. By EMILE DE LAVELEYE. Translated by Mrs. THORPE. Edited and Revised for the English Public by the Author. Map. Demy 8vo., cloth, 16s.

"A lucid and impartial view of the situation in the East."—*St. James's Gazette.*
"Likely to be very useful at the present time, as it is one of the best books on the subject.—*Saturday Review.*

Tuscan Studies and Sketches. By LEADER SCOTT, Author of "A Nook in the Apennines," "Messer Agnolo's Household," &c. Many Full-page and smaller Illustrations. Sq. imp. 16mo., cloth, 10s. 6d.

Contents.—Part I. STUDIES:—The Giants at the Gate—David, Hercules Neptune—A Library of Codices—Old Organs and their Builders—Florentine Mosaics—The Bride's Room—A Recovered Fresco—A Museum of Pictorial Tapestry. Part II. SKETCHES: A Vintage Party—The Festival of the Dead—At the Baths—The Giostra—The Mushroom Merchant in the Apennines—A Mountain Funeral—A Florentine Market—The Castle of Belcaro—Volterra and the Borax Springs—A City of Frescoes—St. Gemignano.

Letters from Italy. By EMILE DE LAVELEYE. Translated by Mrs. THORPE. Revised by the Author. Portrait of the Author. Crown 8vo., 6s.

"A most delightful volume."—*Nonconformist.*
"Every page is pleasantly and brightly written."—*Times.*

Miscellaneous.

The Theory of Law and Civil Society. By Augustus Pulszky (Dr. Juris), Professor of Law at Budapest. Demy 8vo., cloth, 18s.

Contents.—Science and its Classification—Method—The Science of the Philosophy of Law and Civil Society—Division of the Philosophy of Law and Civil Society—Society and its Organization—The Mutual Relations of the Societies—The Societies in History—The State and its Constituent Elements—Origin of the State—The Aim, their Sphere of Action, and the Ideal of the State—The Notions of Law and Right—The Fundamental Principle of Law and Right—The Sources and Forms of Law.

Labour, Land, and Law: A Search for the Missing Wealth of the Working Poor. By William A. Phillips. Demy 8vo., cloth, 9s.

"He is evidently a man of considerable ability, and a student of social and economical problems. . . . There is a great deal of statistical information to be found in 'Labour, Land, and Law.'"—*St. James's Gazette.*

United States Notes: A History of the various Issues of Paper Money by the Government of the United States. By John J. Knox. With Photo-Lithographic Specimens. Demy 8vo., cloth, 12s.

"A very minute historical sketch of the treasury and other notes issued by the Government. . . . The book should be carefully studied by those who would understand the subject."—*New York Herald.*

Representative British Orations. With Introductions, &c., by Chas. K. Adams. 16mo., Roxburgh, gilt tops, 3 vols., in cloth box, 15s. The Volumes may also be had without box, 13s. 6d.

"The notes are extremely useful, and contribute largely to making the work one of value to students of political history."—*Pall Mall Gazette.*
"They are well chosen. . . . The paper and type are *de luxe.*"—*Economist.*

Miscellaneous.

Jottings from Jail. Notes and Papers on Prison Matters. By the Rev. J. W. HORSLEY, M.A. Oxon., late (and last) Chaplain of H.M. Prison, Clerkenwell. Second edition. Crown 8vo., cloth, 3s. 6d.

"The jottings are full of vivacity and shrewd common sense, and their author, amid uncongenial surroundings, has preserved a keen sense of humour."—*Echo.*

Literary Landmarks of London. By LAURENCE HUTTON. Third edition. Crown 8vo., 7s. 6d.

"He has worked out a felicitous idea with industry, skill, and success."—*Standard.*

Literary Landmarks of London. By LAURENCE HUTTON. Fourth, Revised, and Cheaper Edition. Crown 8vo., Illustrated cover, 2s. 6d.

"He has made himself an invaluable *valet de place* to the lover of literary London."—*Atlantic Monthly.*

About the Theatre: Essays and Studies. By WILLIAM ARCHER. Crown 8vo., cloth, bevelled edges, 7s. 6d.

"Theatrical subjects, from the Censorship of the Stage to the most recent phenomena of first nights, have thoroughly able and informed discussion in Mr. Archer's handsome book."—*Contemporary Review.*

How to be Happy though Married. Small crown 8vo., cloth, 3s. 6d. Bridal Gift Edition, white vellum cloth, extra gilt, bevelled boards, gilt edges, in box, 7s. 6d.

"We strongly recommend this book as one of the best of wedding presents. It is a complete handbook to an earthly Paradise, and its author may be regarded as the Murray of Matrimony and the Baedeker of Bliss."—*Pall Mall Gazette.*

"Manners Makyth Man." By the Author of "How to be Happy though Married." Popular Edition, small crown 8vo., cloth, 3s. 6d.; imp. 16mo., cloth, 6s. Presentation edition, imp. 16mo., cloth, bevelled edges, in box, 7s. 6d.

"Good-natured, wholesome, and straightforward."—*Saturday Review.*

English as She is Taught. Genuine Answers to Examination Questions in our Public Schools. Collected by CAROLINE B. LE ROW. With a Commentary thereon by MARK TWAIN. Demy 16mo., cloth, 2s.

MARK TWAIN says: "A darling literary curiosity. . . . This little book ought to set forty millions of people to thinking."

Books for Children.

The Brownies: Their Book. With all the Original Pictures and Poems by PALMER COX, as published in *St. Nicholas*, and with many new Pictures. Medium 4to., cloth, 6s.

Some of the Contents.—In the **Toy** Shop—The Singing **School**—Their Friendly **Turn**—Canoeing—The Brownies and the Bees—The **Fourth** of July —Fishing—At Archery.

New Fairy Tales from Brentano. Told in English by KATE FREILIGRATH KROEKER, and Pictured by F. CARRUTHERS GOULD. Eight Full-page Coloured Illustrations. Square 8vo., illustrated, paper boards, cloth back, 5s.; cloth, gilt edges, 6s.

Contents.—The Story of Gockel, Hinkel, and Gackeleia—**The Story of** Frisky Wisky—The Story of the Myrtle Maiden—The Story of **Brokerina**— The Story of Old Father Rhine and the Miller.

Fairy Tales from Brentano. Told in English by KATE FREILIGRATH KROEKER. Illustrated by F. CARRUTHERS GOULD. Popular edition. Sq. imp. 16mo., 3s. 6d.

"The extravagance of invention displayed in **his tales will render them welcome** in the nursery. The translation—not an easy **task—has been very cleverly** accomplished."—*The Academy.*

"An admirable translator in Madame Kroeker, and an inimitable illustrator in Mr. Carruthers Gould."—*Truth.*

Books for Children.

Tom's Adventures in Search of Shadowland:
A Fairy Tale. By HERBERT S. SWEETLAND. Thirteen Full-page Illustrations by W. H. OVEREND and GEO. HONIÈRE. Small crown 8vo., cloth, 3s. 6d.

In the Time of Roses:
A Tale of Two Summers. Told and Illustrated by FLORENCE and EDITH SCANNELL, Author and Artist of "Sylvia's Daughters." Thirty-two Full-page and other Illustrations. Sq. imp. 16mo., cloth, 5s.

"A very charming story."—*Scotsman.*
"A delightful story."—*Punch.*
"A very delightful story."—*Academy.*

Prince Peerless:
A Fairy-Folk Story-Book. By the Hon. MARGARET COLLIER (Madame Galletti di Cadilhac), Author of "Our Home by the Adriatic." Illustrated by the Hon. JOHN COLLIER. Sq. imp. 16mo., cloth, 5s.

"Delightful in style and fancy."—*Scotsman.*
"A volume of charming stories."—*Saturday Review.*

When I was a Child;
or, Left Behind. By LINDA VILLARI, Author of "On Tuscan Hills," &c. Illustrated. Square 8vo., cloth, gilt edges, 3s. 6d.

"It is fresh and bright from the first chapter to the last."—*Morning Post.*
"A very clever, vivid, and realistic story."—*Truth.*
"A finer girl's book could not be had."—*Scotsman.*

The Prince of the Hundred Soups:
A Puppet Show in Narrative. Edited, with a Preface, by VERNON LEE. Illustrated. Cheaper edition. Square 8vo., cloth, 3s. 6d.

"There is more humour in the volume than in half-a-dozen ordinary pantomimes."—*Spectator.*

Ottilie:
An Eighteenth Century Idyl. Square 8vo., cloth extra, 3s. 6d.

"A graceful little sketch. . . . Drawn with full insight into the period described."—*Spectator.*
"Pleasantly and carefully written. . . . The author lets the reader have a glimpse of Germany in the 'Sturm und Drang' period."—*Athenæum.*
"A graceful little picture. . . . Charming all through."—*Academy.*

Books for Children.

The Bird's Nest, and other Sermons for Children of all Ages. By the Rev. SAMUEL COX, D.D., Author of "Expositions," &c. Second edition. Imp. 16mo., cloth, 6s.

"These beautiful discourses were addressed to children of all ages, and must have found an echo in the hearts of many youthful listeners."—*St. James's Gazette.*

"Dr. Samuel Cox has opened up a comparatively new vein."
Nineteenth Century.

Birdsnesting and Bird-Stuffing. A Complete Description of the Nests and Eggs of Birds which Breed in Britain. By EDWARD NEWMAN. Revised and Re-written, with Directions for their Collection and Preservation; and with a Chapter on Bird-Stuffing, by MILLER CHRISTY. Crown 8vo., 1s.

Spring Blossoms and Summer Fruit; or, Sunday Talks for the Children. By the Rev. JOHN BYLES, of Ealing. Crown 8vo., cloth, 2s. 6d.

"They are of simple and instructive character."—*Dundee Advertiser.*

Arminius Vambéry: His Life and Adventures. Written by Himself. With Introductory Chapter dedicated to the Boys of England. Portrait and Seventeen Illustrations. Crown 8vo., 5s.

"We welcome it as one of the best books of travel that our boys could have possibly placed in their hands."—*Schoolmaster.*

Boys' Own Stories. By ASCOTT R. HOPE, Author of "Stories of Young Adventurers," "Stories out of School Time," &c. Eight Illustrations. Crown 8vo., cloth, 5s.

"This is a really admirable selection of genuine narrative and history, treated with discretion and skill by the author. Mr. Hope has not gathered his stores from the highway, but has explored far afield in less-beaten tracts, as may be seen in his 'Adventures of a Ship-boy' and 'A Smith among Savages.'"—*Saturday Review.*

The Adventures of Robinson Crusoe. Newly Edited after the Original Editions. Nineteen Illustrations. Large crown 8vo., cloth extra, 5s.

The Century Magazine

The chief papers of interest in THE CENTURY for 1888 are those dealing with Travel and Adventure. Mr. KENNAN describes his Adventures, Exile Life, and the People he met with in a journey of fifteen thousand miles through Russia and Siberia. Mr. ROOSEVELT treats of the Wild Industries and scarcely Wilder Sports of the great lonely plains of the Far West; while Mr. DE KAY contributes a series of studies on the Ethnology, Landscape, Literature, and Arts of Ireland.

Price 1s. 4d. Monthly. Post free, 19s. a Year.

St. Nicholas
Conducted by Mary Mapes Dodge

For 1888, contains a large number of Tales by many well-known Authors, among whom are Miss ALCOTT, Mrs. FRANCES HODGSON BURNETT, FRANK R. STOCKTON, JOEL CHANDLER HARRIS, AMELIA B. BARR, H. H. BOYESEN, Miss F. C. BAYLOR, and PALMER COX.

Price 1s. Monthly. Post free, 14s. a Year.

London:
T. FISHER UNWIN, 26, PATERNOSTER SQUARE.